digital age

Technology-Based K-12 Lesson Plans for Social Studies

 **NCSS**
Bulletin 105

**Edited by
Linda Bennett and
Michael J. Berson**

National Council for the Social Studies

8555 Sixteenth Street • Suite 500 • Silver Spring, Maryland 20910

www.**socialstudies**.org

Editorial staff on this publication: Michael Simpson, Chi Yang
Design/Production: Cowan Creative | www.cowancreative.com

Library of Congress Control Number: 2007923833
ISBN: 978-0-87986-099-8

Printed in the United States of America

5 4 3 2 1

Contents

Note: The NCSS Standards references are to the ten themes of the NCSS Standards; for convenience, they are listed in Appendix 1 and on the inside flap of the back cover.

Introduction

LINDA BENNETT AND MICHAEL BERSON

FROM THE NOVICE TO THE MASTER TEACHER, technology infusion into social studies is essential for instruction in the 21st century. Elementary through high school students use cell phones, the Internet, electronic games, and many other forms of technology in their daily lives. To maintain relevance to the lives of children and youth today, classroom instruction needs to include skills such as online banking, global information systems, and electronic voting. The exemplary social studies lessons included in this volume are designed to guide K-12 teachers in using technology in their classrooms by linking to and building upon the national social studies and technology standards.

We recommend that teachers begin by understanding and synthesizing core elements of the National Council for the Social Studies (NCSS) Standards and the National Educational Technology Standards for Students (NETS-S) (see Appendices 1 and 2). They will also benefit from the recent NCSS Technology Position Statement and Guidelines (Appendix 3). Internalizing the social studies and technology standards will help teachers to determine the technology skills that are appropriate and applicable for his or her social studies curriculum.

The primary focus of this NCSS Bulletin is on social studies lesson plans that infuse technology. When the editors published a call for exemplary social studies lessons that infuse technology, the response was astounding. After a review of about 50 technology-based social studies lessons during the last two years, 30 exemplary social studies lessons emerged. The majority of the lessons have at least one classroom teacher as an author, and we strived to select lessons that have been implemented by the authors. Educators who are specialists in the implementation of technology in K-12 social studies graciously shared their expertise. The lessons represent the work of over 60 educators from Florida to Oregon and Virginia to New Mexico. It is our pleasure to share these social studies lessons with our readers.

The lessons are divided into elementary, middle and high school sections. Each lesson plan is built on a template, which includes the grade level, the history or social science discipline, related NCSS strands, related NETS-S standards, lesson objectives, instructional directions, assessment, extensions, and resources. The NCSS strands and NETS-S should help the classroom teacher determine if the lesson is appropriate for her or his classroom. We attempted to select lessons that incorporated diverse technologies, and the lessons may need to be altered to fit the technology that is available in a specific classroom. We encouraged teachers to write the directions for lessons in a manner that would reflect their teaching style and the specific lesson plan. We wanted their teaching expertise to shine, so if part of a lesson did not fit a "pigeon hole or box," the author could adapt the format of the lesson. We suggest that teachers who use these lessons do the same so that the lesson meets the needs of the students and the social studies curriculum. The social studies content focus or the technology of a number of lessons can be altered. A review of the resources for each lesson would be helpful to the novice or master teacher in their effort to infuse technology into social studies.

Part 4 has tools and techniques for technology use. The five tools or techniques that we explored are management, internet safety, software, images, and podcasting. Part 4 is not exhaustive because we wanted the focus of the bulletin to be on the exemplary social studies lessons. To successfully integrate technology, teachers should select additional materials to expand their knowledge and skills to infuse technology into social studies.

The internet and information posted on it are constantly changing. As time passes, it is inevitable that some of the internet addresses listed in this Bulletin will change. We have, however, made every effort to provide accurate and current internet information as of the date of publication of the Bulletin.

It would be worthwhile for readers to review all lessons in this book because the strategies for teaching the use of technology apply to multiple grade levels and several social studies content areas. It was our pleasure to work with so many social studies educators of the highest quality as we edited this bulletin. We now put their work into your hands so K-12 students can be enriched by exemplary social studies lessons that infuse technology into classroom teaching. 🔲

part 1
For
Elementary
Schools

What Does Family Mean to You? Constructing an Electronic Big Book

1

Nancy P. Gallavan and Casey Juliano

Kindergarten and First Grade: Sociology, Psychology, Geography, and Economics

NCSS Thematic Strands

I CULTURE
IV INDIVIDUAL DEVELOPMENT AND IDENTITY
V INDIVIDUALS, GROUPS, AND INSTITUTIONS
IX GLOBAL CONNECTIONS

NCSS Performance Expectations

I CULTURE

a. Explore and describe similarities and differences in the ways groups, societies, and cultures address similar human needs and concerns.

b. Give examples of how experiences may be interpreted differently by people from diverse cultural perspectives and frames of reference.

d. Compare ways in which people from different cultures think about and deal with their physical environments and social conditions.

IV INDIVIDUAL DEVELOPMENT AND IDENTITY

c. Describe the unique features of one's nuclear and extended families.

V INDIVIDUALS, GROUPS, AND INSTITUTIONS

a. Identify roles as learned behavior patterns in group situations, such as student, family member, peer play group member, or club member.

g. Show how groups and institutions work to meet individual needs and promote the common good, and identify examples of where they fail to do so.

IX GLOBAL CONNECTIONS

a. Explore ways that language, art, music, belief systems, and other cultural elements may facilitate global understanding or lead to misunderstanding.

b. Give examples of conflict, cooperation, and interdependence among individuals, groups, and nations.

NETS-S National Educational Technology Standards for Students

3. Technology Productivity Tools
4. Technology Communications Tools

NETS-S Performance Expectations

3. Technology Productivity Tools

- Students use technology tools to enhance learning, increase productivity, and promote creativity.
- Students use productivity tools to collaborate in constructing technology-enhanced models, prepare publications, and produce other creative works.

4. Technology Communications Tools

- Students use telecommunications to collaborate, publish, and interact with peers, experts, and other audiences.
- Students use a variety of media and formats to communicate information and ideas effectively to multiple audiences.

Introduction

This intriguing learning experience provides teachers with the content, standards, processes and assessments for constructing Big Books with their students so students can study themselves as individuals, and as members of diverse families to learn more about families in society. This lesson features "self in the family" and "many kinds of families," academic expectations of kindergarten and first grade that offer rich and diverse vocabulary and concepts. Young learners need to increase their awareness and understanding of their own families in order to develop an understanding of other families like and unlike their own families.

The various technological tools both introduce and reinforce the students' prior knowledge and experiences with technology. Although most kindergarteners and first graders work as one large whole group, students may work independently or in small groups. Most young learners are familiar with Big Books and like to engage in conversations about their families.

This personalized learning experience integrates the cultural study of families and multiple uses of technology in ways that are developmentally appropriate for young learners.

Objective(s)

The student will be able to:

1. Generate and discuss vocabulary and concepts used to describe all kinds of families;
2. Take, bring, and/or draw a picture of his or her own family;
3. Select specific vocabulary and concepts to describe his or her own family;
4. Participate in the co-construction of an electronic Big Book by helping to add individual pictures and captions; and
5. Show the completed electronic Big Book to parents and family members at back-to-school night, open house, curriculum fairs, parent-teacher-student conferences, or at individual homes.

Time

We recommend that this learning experience is facilitated in five 30-minute sessions, with one session conducted each day throughout one week, as detailed here.

Instructional Steps

This lesson is fast and easy, with many opportunities to individualize and extend the lesson to meet various learning needs and interests. The teacher can readily modify the Instructional Steps for each specific group of students.

DAY 1. The teacher introduces the lesson by asking students to listen for vocabulary words describing families while viewing selected videos shown either on the VCR or through video streaming on the computer. Suggested videos are listed below. We recommend that teachers show approximately 10 minutes of video. If teachers want to show more videos, we recommend that the teacher interrupts the video every 10 minutes or so to generate a portion of the word wall.

Still on Day 1 and working as a whole group, students generate an electronic word wall with vocabulary words recorded together on the computer, overhead transparency, white board, black board, and/or non-electronically, using markers to record words on large sheets of paper. Each student should be expected to contribute at least one word gained from the video or inspired by the video. The first instructional step of this lesson closes with each student selecting one word as a favorite new word and using it in a sentence that is stated orally for the teacher or teaching assistant to hear and check for clarity of application.

Vocabulary could include (in alphabetical order by column):

adult	eat	holidays	pet	time
apartment	family	home	play	together
aunt	few	house	read	togetherness
baby	fish	hug	relative	toys
big	fun	husband	short	traditions
boy	gifts	large	sister	trips
brother	grandfather	laugh	small	truck
car	grandpa	little	smile	van
cat	grandma	man	special	wife
celebrations	grandmother	many	step-brother	woman
children	half-brother	meals	step-father	uncle
chores	half-father	mom/mother	step-mother	vacation
cousin	half-mother	nice	step-sister	work
customs	half-sister	older	tall	younger
dad/father	hamster	party	teenager	
dog	happy	people	television	

Day 2. The teacher says each word on the word wall aloud and students repeat the words. Then each student selects five words to describe his or her individual family in order to build vocabulary, establish schema, and personalize connections. Each student is given a sheet of paper (8½" x 11") on which to print the five words. Printing can be conducted with colorful markers or crayons, or electronically using the computer keyboard. With one or two partners, students engage in conversations to describe their families using their five words. Conversations are recorded on a tape recorder.

To close Day 2, each student takes home a letter from the teacher stating that the student needs to ask a family member to take a photograph of the family using a digital camera and send the photograph electronically to the teacher via email or, alternatively, to bring a photograph to the teacher, who will scan it into the electronic Big Book. The bottom portion of the teacher's letter has a response space for parents to let the teacher know if a photograph will be provided by the family. Students who do not provide photographs from their homes will draw pictures of their individual families using Kid Pix.

Day 3. Each student reads his or her five selected words aloud to the class. Then each student writes a two-sentence caption to accompany his or her photograph or picture. The electronic Big Book will be constructed on PowerPoint with a one-page picture with caption dedicated to each student.

For a Kindergarten/Emergent caption, students will use the electronic word wall to complete a structured writing sentence, such as:

"My family is _____."
"My family has _____."
"My family likes to _____."

For a First Grade caption, students will use the electronic word wall to self-create one or two sentences about their families.

To close Day 3, each student will read his or her completed sentences aloud to the class.

Day 4. The teacher and students will add the captions to the pictures, make hard copies of the pages, and assemble the Big Book. The teacher may want to organize this activity into small groups while other students are engaged in a different activity. The different activity certainly can be related to the word wall or families. When the book is completed, the teacher will share the Big Book with the whole class and ask each student to read his or her page aloud as that page is turned.

To close Day 4, each student will select the name of another student and either a new word selected by the student or a new word from the word wall that describes the student. The student will use the word in a sentence that describes something learned, and state it for the whole class, e.g., "Jake's family likes to play games." "Kendall's family has one boy and two girls." "Riley's family takes trips to see cousins." This process empowers students to use vocabulary words from the videos, word walls, and their own schemas appropriately, to broaden their understanding and application of concepts as well as to develop respect for and appreciation of diverse families.

Day 5. The students will share their Big Book with another class at school in the same manner as practiced on Day 4. Then students will be instructed to share their Big Book with families through the school email system. All parents in the class should have provided specific permission for the sharing of children's electronic images via email. For families with no electronic access, the Big Book will be on display at the Back-to-School Night to be held the following week. To close Day 5, each student will select three new words from the word wall that describe what they learned about themselves, one another, and families near and far. Once the PowerPoint is viewed electronically, it can be printed and posted to make a wonderful bulletin board, and later taken down and bound into a Big Book that can be read throughout the year.

Student Enrichment

Day 1
+ Contribute more than one word to the word wall
+ Write a new favorite word

Day 2
+ Expand the word wall by thinking about more families near and far, like and unlike their own
+ Select more than five words to describe one's own family

Day 3
+ Write more than one or two sentences
+ Write or dictate several paragraphs in response to various prompts related to families

Day 4
+ Read the entire book to a student from another class
+ Generate more words for the word wall

Day 5
+ Either take another photograph with one's family reviewing the Big Book or draw a picture of something important to the family

- Write a response or description with one's family to share in class

Additional Ideas
- Interview a student in a different class or school
- Construct a Big Book as Pen Pals with another class in another state or country

Teaching Tips

An electronic Big Book is more effective as teachers and students can share with a variety of audiences more easily, especially in front of a large class and at Back-to-School Nights. This learning experience captures students' attention and combines literacy with social studies and technology in ways that both build upon their technological knowledge and experiences and demonstrate important technological tools for their future learning and living.

For language arts, we suggest that teachers share a variety of text and children's literature (fiction and non-fiction; books, newspapers, video, etc.) to see and read about families in various contexts and cultures. Students can generate additional word walls based on a variety of categories and cultural universals such as food, homes, clothing, routine, and so forth. Students can write words or sentences bridging the categories and their own lives.

For math, students can create charts and graphs identifying various characteristics describing their family routines, e.g., eating at a table or eating at a counter; driving a car or a truck or a van; going on week-long vacations or taking weekend trips; stating who helps the student get ready for school every morning.

For science, students can describe their families' meals, the types of heating and cooking fuel that they use, recycling systems, forms of transportation, pets, yard care, and so forth.

For fine arts, teachers can ask students to bring in family photo albums or videos of their families, and invite family members to share their stories.

We suggest that teachers collect the materials a week before using them. View the pictures and videos in advance for appropriateness. Organize and test all of the equipment. If possible, ask a teaching assistant, university intern, or a parent volunteer (particularly one familiar with the technology) to be in the classroom at the time you intend to teach this lesson.

Technology Resources

Technology includes viewing videos via VCR, video streamed via computers, or LCD projectors; recording vocabulary via word processing or overheads; taking digital pictures or drawing pictures via Kid Pix; sending pictures via email; scanning pictures; writing captions via word processing; and constructing a Big Book via PowerPoint. Students will operate various forms of technology to help construct all parts of the book and share the outcomes.

HARDWARE
- Computer w/ internet capability
- Video streaming equipment or LCD projector
- Printer (color preferably)
- Digital camera
- Scanner
- Overhead projector
- Television & VCR

SOFTWARE
- Microsoft Word (or comparable)
- Microsoft PowerPoint (or comparable)
- Digital camera's software (if applicable)
- Kid Pix, picture viewing/editing software

Resources

INTERNET
- E-mail addresses of students' parents
- Internet search for examples of families from other cultures

PRINT
- Samples of Big Books

VIDEOS
- *Connie the Cow: Families are Special.* 2004. Our Time Publisher.
- *Barney's Families are Special.* 1995. PBS Kids.
- *Families of the World.* 1995-2004. Master Communication Inc.; 17 videos with teaching guides about Families of the World.
- *Globe Trekker.* 1995-2004. Pilot Productions. Teachers will need to preview and select developmentally appropriate portions of videos. Teachers may want to turn off the sound and show pictures only.

Other Materials Needed

If generating a word wall non-electronically, get large sheets of butcher paper, perhaps of various colors, and masking tape.

Assessment

DAY	EXPECTATION Each student will...	3 (Above average)	2 (Average)	1 (Below average)
1	Contribute words heard in the video or inspired by the video to the word wall	2 or more words	1 word	0 words
1	Use new favorite words correctly and orally in a sentence	2 or more words	1 words	0 words
2	Select words from the word wall and write them on a sheet of paper	6-10 words	5 words	0-4 words
2	Describe his or her family to a partner using the new words with descriptions recorded on a tape recorder	6-10 words	5 words	0-4 words
3	Read the selected words aloud	6-10 words	5 words	0-4 words
3	Complete or write sentences	Sentences with 6-10 words	Sentences with 5 words	Sentences with 0-4 words
3	Read the completed sentences aloud	Sentences with 6-10 words	Sentences with 5 words	Sentences with 0-4 words
4	Assist in the construction of the Big Book	Assistance is exceptional	Assistance is satisfactory	Assistance is not present or satisfactory
4	Read his or her page aloud as the teacher turns the pages	Reads exceptionally	Reads satisfactorily	Reads less than satisfactorily
4	Select another student and new words to use in a sentence to describe something learned about the other student	2-3 words	1 word	0 words
5	Read his or her page aloud to share the Big Book with peers	Reads exceptionally	Reads satisfactorily	Reads less than satisfactorily
5	Read the entire book to his or her family after the Big Book has been sent home electronically or when it is displayed at the upcoming Back-to-School Night at school; feedback provided by family	Reads exceptionally	Reads satisfactorily	Reads less than satisfactorily

Theodore Roosevelt: Promoting the Common Good in Mind and Action

Carolyn O'Mahony and Donna Shaba

Second Grade: American History, Civics, and Geography

NCSS Thematic Strands
- Ⓘ TIME, CONTINUITY, AND CHANGE
- Ⓧ CIVIC IDEALS AND PRACTICES
- Ⓘ PEOPLE, PLACES, AND ENVIRONMENTS
- Ⓥ POWER, AUTHORITY AND GOVERNANCE

NCSS Performance Expectations
Ⓘ TIME, CONTINUITY, AND CHANGE
b. Demonstrate an ability to use correctly vocabulary associated with time, such as past, present, future, and long ago; read and construct simple timelines; identify examples of change; and recognize examples of cause and effect relationships.

Ⓧ CIVIC IDEALS AND PRACTICES
j. Recognize and interpret how the "common good" can be strengthened through various forms of citizen action.

Ⓘ PEOPLE, PLACES, AND ENVIRONMENTS
b. Interpret, use, and distinguish various representations of the earth, such as maps, globes, and photographs.

Ⓥ POWER, AUTHORITY, AND GOVERNANCE
c. Give examples of how government does or does not provide for needs and wants of people.

NETS-S National Educational Technology Standards for Students
1. Basic Operations and Concepts
3. Technology Productivity Tools
4. Technology Communications Tools

NETS-S Performance Expectations
1. Basic Operations and Concepts
3. Technology Productivity Tools
+ Use a variety of media and technology resources for directed and independent learning activities.

4. Technology Communications Tools
+ Gather information and communicate with others using telecommunications, with support from teachers, family members, or student partners.

Introduction
Around Presidents' Day in February, many young students read biographies of Abraham Lincoln and George Washington. However, studies of presidents can be expanded beyond these two notable figures. In this lesson Theodore Roosevelt is acknowledged as a leader who is also worthy of respect and remembrance. His support of the protection of millions of acres of public land as parks, forests and game and bird preserves is an example of acting for the common good by making laws that shape land use for the benefit of all. Parks, teddy bears, and animal protection are meaningful for children. The history of Theodore Roosevelt touches on all of these.

Roosevelt's biography as a conservationist can lead young students into investigating the location and role of national parks, forests, preserves and sanctuaries. It can help them understand how they benefit from laws written decades ago that have protected the natural environment. It can lead into investigations of laws and rules that shape their local physical environment and protect animals and their habitats. It can help them think about how, as individuals, they contribute to the common good in their classroom and school community. It can help them realize that, as citizens in a democratic society, they can share their ideas and suggestions with lawmakers.

Objectives
Students will:
1. Construct new knowledge about Theodore Roosevelt, including:
   He was a U.S. president.
   Teddy bears are named after him.
   His likeness is found on Mount Rushmore.
   He supported the establishment of the national forest service.

2. Recall occasions when they have used public parks and spaces.
3. Make connections between public spaces, laws that create them, and acting for the common good.
4. Identify how, as individuals, they can contribute to the common good.
5. Suggest new rules and laws that can support the common good into the future.

Time
Two forty-minute sessions

Instructional Steps
DAY 1

1. Use a picture of Mount Rushmore to introduce some of the U.S. presidents to students. A clear one is available at http://bensguide.gpo.gov/3-5/symbols/mountrushmore. html.
2. Give a PowerPoint presentation of a timeline that highlights when Theodore Roosevelt supported laws to protect large acreages of land and established the National Forest System. Use information from http://www. theodoreroosevelt.org/life/conservation.htm to create the timeline.
3. Discuss the students' use of parks. Show students a map of national parks and identify major ones (e.g., Yellowstone, Yosemite). Find this at http://www.lib.utexas. edu/maps/national_parks/nps_map99.pdf
4. Emphasize how Teddy Roosevelt's support of laws to protect land from development was an example of law making for the common good (explain "common good").
5. Read *The Legend of the Teddy Bear.*
6. Show the political cartoon by Berryman. It can be accessed at http://www.theodore-roosevelt.com/ berrymanframes.html.
7. Students share how they can contribute to the common good, in the classroom, school, or in the local community. Provide them with paper in teddy bear shapes onto which they can write their ideas.
8. Display the bears.
9. Home/School Connection: Students retell the legend of the teddy bear at home and explain how decisions Teddy Roosevelt made nearly 100 years ago gave us the national parks and forests to use today.

DAY 2

1. Review students' ideas for contributing individually to the common good, e.g., cleaning up, being nice to other people, etc.
2. Revisit maps of park locations and remind students of how laws protect that land and how politicians and Teddy Roosevelt instituted those laws a long time ago.
3. Compile a list of rules or laws that the students know. Explain that laws and rules shape the decisions that people make (e.g., what people do in public places such as parks; how people drive their cars).
4. Explain that lawmakers listen to ideas from many people with different opinions when they are trying to make laws that will benefit the majority of people. Discuss the students' ideas for new rules or laws that would benefit everyone.
5. Students write their ideas for new school or classroom rules or broader reaching laws for the community, e.g., suggesting guidelines for recycling or new recreational areas onto an electronic postcard. They send the postcards to their teacher, principal, or local lawmaker. Use the resources found at http://www.blackhillsbadlands. com/go.asp?ID=86.
6. Home/School Connection: Students take home a hard copy of the electronic postcard (right-click mouse on postcard image to print it) and return to school with an idea for a new rule or law that they have discussed with a family member.

Assessment
Students will:
a. Identify images of Roosevelt as a U.S. president.
b. Explain his role in establishing national parks and bird sanctuaries as an example of acting for the common good.
c. Tell how the teddy bear got its name.
d. Relate the concept of common good to their own actions in writing.
e. Relate the concept of common good to laws or rules they compose and share with policymakers.

Student Enrichment
+ Students explore individual park websites or web-cams. They use the pictures and information on the websites to determine what is still special about these places. They paint picture postcards to illustrate the natural or

man-made features of the environment. They write to a friend about their impressions of the park.

- ◆ Students tell families about their virtual visits to national parks. They ask for details about family trips to national, state, or municipal parks.
- ◆ Students play an interactive trivia game "Dynamite Presidents" on Mount Rushmore from http://www.americaslibrary.gov/aa/game/rushmore_game.html
- ◆ Organize a picnic "at" Yellowstone National Park. Children bring bag lunches into a room with internet access. Lay out tablecloths or picnic blankets on the floor. Turn on web-cam of Old Faithful Geyser. Eat lunch on blankets, while watching the geyser at http://www.nps.gov/yell/oldfaithfulcam.htm

Technology Resources

Black Hills Badlands & Lakes Association. (n.d). Send a Postcard. Retrieved January 6, 2006, from http://www.blackhillsbadlands.com/go.asp?ID=86

Chapultepec Inc. (2004). Berryman's Teddy Bear Series. Retrieved January 6, 2006, from http://www.theodore-roosevelt.com/berrymanframes.html

Library of Congress. (2005). Meet Amazing Americans: Dynamite Presidents. Retrieved January 6, 2006, from http://americaslibrary.gov/aa/game/rushmore_game.html

National Park Service. (2005). New Old Faithful Webcam. Retrieved January 6, 2006, from http://www.nps.gov/yell/oldfaithfulcam.htm

Theodore Roosevelt Association. (2005). Conservationist: Life of Theodore Roosevelt. Retrieved January 6, 2006, from http://www.theodoreroosevelt.org/life/conservation.htm

University of Texas Libraries. (n.d). Map of National Parks System. Retrieved January 6, 2006, from http://www.lib.utexas.edu/maps/national_parks /nps_map99.pdf

U.S. Government Printing Office. (2004). Ben's Guide to U.S. Government for Kids. Mount Rushmore image retrieved January 6, 2006, from http://bensguide.gpo.gov/3-5/symbols/mountrushmore.html

Print Resources

Murphy, Frank and Gijsbert Van Frankenhuyzen. *The Legend of the Teddy Bear*. Chelsea, MI: Sleeping Bear Press, 2000.

Other Materials Needed

Teddy Bear Template: Using a photocopier, enlarge a teddy bear shape (such as a die cut or cookie cutter) to fit a 8½" x 11" piece of paper. Make tagboard stencils. Students trace outlines onto brown paper bags or construction paper and cut out their bear. 🔳

Walking Back in Time: Local History Explorations

3

Sharon A. Edwards and Robert W. Maloy

Second and Third Grades: Geography and U.S. History

NCSS Thematic Standards
Ⅱ TIME, CONTINUITY, AND CHANGE
Ⅲ PEOPLE, PLACES, AND ENVIRONMENTS

NCSS Performance Expectations
Ⅱ TIME, CONTINUITY, AND CHANGE

  b. Demonstrate an ability to use correctly vocabulary associated with time such as past, present, future and long ago; read and construct simple timelines; identify examples of change; and recognize examples of cause and effect relationships.

  d. Identify and use various sources for reconstructing the past, such as documents, letters, diaries, maps, textbooks, photos, and others.

Ⅲ PEOPLE, PLACES, AND ENVIRONMENTS

  h. Examine the interaction of human beings and their physical environment, the use of land, building of cities, and ecosystem changes in selected locales and regions.

  g. Describe how people create places that reflect ideas, personality, culture, and wants and needs as they design homes, playgrounds, classrooms and the like.

NETS-S National Educational Technology Standards for Students
3. Technology Productivity Tools
4. Technology Communications Tools

NETS-S Performance Indicators (pre K-2)
3. Technology Productivity Tools
  + Use a variety of media and technology resources for directed and independent learning activities
  + Create developmentally appropriate multimedia products with support from teachers, family members, or student partners

4. Technology Communications Tools
  + Use technology resources (e.g., puzzles, logical thinking programs, writing tools, digital cameras, drawing tools) for problem solving, communication, and illustration of thoughts, ideas and stories.
  + Gather information and communicate with others using telecommunications, with support from teachers, family members, or student partners.

Introduction

Who Came Down That Road?, a picture book by George Ella Lyon, opens an exploration of how modern life and human history are shaped by the actions of people in a place over time. As the book begins, a mother and child gaze down an old road that disappears into the woods near their Kentucky home. The child's question, "Who came down that road, mama?" opens a poetic narrative that travels back in time from present day to the beginnings of life on earth, marking the people, animals, and plants who have lived along that road.

After hearing the story, second and third graders investigate a small section of a road, river, canal, or other passageway in their community. They begin by observing the road as it currently is—who lives there, what they do, and where they have come from. Satellite photographs and online maps offer alternative visual images to what children can see by traveling the road in a car or by walking. The children take digital photographs of places along the road, compose text to accompany the photos, and post their work on a class website. Next, children use primary sources and their own imaginations to reconstruct what may have happened along the road at different times in the past. In so doing, they learn concepts, themes, and procedures for the study of history. This lesson may be used as a stand-alone activity lasting 10 to 12 class periods or as the opening experience in a longer study of local community history.

Objectives

The student will be able to:

1. Identify people who live and work along a road or river in their local community.
2. Use computers, the Internet and other technological tools in presenting the history of change in a community.
3. Construct a timeline of events, including key changes in people's lives over time.

Time

10-12 hour-long class periods

Instructional Steps

PART ONE: CHOOSING A ROAD (1 CLASS PERIOD)

Preceding a read aloud of *Who Came Down That Road?*, the teacher identifies a section of a local road, river, or other passageway with a documentary record of old photographs, maps, and written accounts that can be accessed from school or local libraries. (For example, the street in front of our school includes many family homes, the University of Massachusetts Amherst campus, and the historic village of North Amherst.) The website TerraServer USA provides satellite photographs of locations along the road, giving the children a view from space of how the road intersects the community. The teacher introduces the larger themes of the lesson: the importance of people's actions in creating places, how human beings shape the landscape, and how change happens over time, transforming people's lives in the process. Often there is change happening on the road right now (buildings going up or coming down, lakes and streams expanding or shrinking) for the class to discuss as part of both natural and human cycles.

PART TWO: THE ROAD TODAY (3-4 CLASS PERIODS)

The class examines the people who are living and the places that exist along the road today. Visible from the windows of a classroom or the parking lot of the school are examples of human activity (buildings, telecommunications equipment) and natural settings (trees, meadows). These places and spaces open discussions of how the human environment is a product of people's ongoing interactions with nature and with each other.

The class goes outdoors with digital or regular cameras to photograph places that interest students. Where a walking field trip is not possible, a class might opt for a bus trip along the road. If it is not feasible to transport the class any distance from the school, a teacher might take neighborhood photo-

graphs. Also, children might bring disposal cameras home so they and their families can take pictures along the road.

In choosing what to photograph, the "road" is viewed expansively, including sites close by, but not directly positioned on it. Our children might choose Puffer's Pond, a favorite local swimming area that was also the site of an old mill, a prominent part of the community in the 19th century. We take photos too, including locations the children might ignore such as local farms, a statue of a Native American on the University campus, and an old school building about a mile up the road from the current school.

The children write a description to accompany each picture: what it is, why they think it is an interesting place to document, and what they think happens there. In this way, there are field notes with each photograph, forming the beginning of a documentary record of places along the road. In their writing, the children focus on what they know about places today. As the lesson unfolds, they will learn about the histories of the places they chose.

PART THREE: CREATING A CLASS WEBSITE (3-4 CLASS PERIODS)

Children's photographs and written descriptions are posted on a "Who Came Down That Road" class website. Pictures are imported into PowerPoint, the text of the children's writing is added, and then each is uploaded to the website. Digital photos can be imported directly from a digital camera, while regular camera photographs need to be scanned. Online posting allows children to display their creativity as writers and their knowledge as historians, and to expand the website throughout the year in a continuous study of the community and its histories.

Students are involved in the website development, choosing which photos to post and helping create the "look" of the site. The teacher explains that writers of fiction, poetry, and historical documentaries must choose how they use words, images, and page layouts to convey ideas to readers, and this presents a way to discuss the choices children make with their writing and graphic images.

An important part of the lesson is placing children in the role of an historian. Studying the past means uncovering primary sources and historical artifacts that show how people lived, worked, thought, and acted. History is not just names, dates, and other facts in a textbook. It is people's stories to be told; it is mysteries and puzzles to be solved; it is events and decisions to be woven together into narrative tapestries of people and places.

PART FOUR: WALKING INTO HISTORY (3-4 CLASS PERIODS)

To begin the final part of the investigation, the teacher explains that photographed places have their own histories featuring the people, events, and changes that occurred there. The local library and town historical society provide primary source materials that show locations on the road 20, 50, 100 or more years ago. Teachers may also invite community members to describe what life was like on the road when they attended elementary school. Where historical photographs exist, children see that a place today looked different in the past. The children add historical information to their written descriptions on the class website, extending their role from documenters of the present to researchers of the past.

Students are often amazed to learn that their school has not always been there (for example, Mark's Meadow was constructed in 1960), and, in many cases, neither was the building where they are currently living. Their surprise inspires questions about how places change because of human and natural influences: locally, what is now a golf course was once an apple orchard, what is now a town was once a Native American homeland, what is now a valley was once buried deep beneath glaciers during the last ice age.

Illustrating a timeline, the children draw imaginative depictions of what they think life was like on the road during its earlier agricultural, colonial, and Native American eras. Historical accuracy and in-depth knowledge evolve as children do the work of historians—inquiring, investigating, documenting, illustrating and composing entries for their paper timeline and digital archive. The children can also forecast who and what they think will be coming down the road in the years ahead, linking past, present and future in a chain of historical developments.

Assessment

We assess students' historical understandings before, during, and as they finish the lesson by asking them to illustrate and write their ideas about the past. This is how historians work professionally—assessing what they think they know, researching what others have found, and then recording their own conclusions based on the evidence. The children are asked to think about what kinds of evidence they could give to support their ideas about what life was like on the road in history. Students often include errors of historical fact in their explanations of past events; for example, placing modern items in historical settings. We use these errors to launch discussions of how historians decide something is true and how they use evidence to make judgments about what life was like in earlier times. We assess student writing with a goal of improving how children communicate ideas in written language. We assist their efforts to revise their writing with word changes or phrasing that adds clarity of meaning and interest to the text and to edit the final product to include conventional spelling, punctuation, and grammar.

Student Enrichment

Take a prehistoric walk using an outline from the book *Millions of Years Ago* by David Drew. Each footstep takes students back in time billions of years to when the first living things appeared on the planet.

Virtual field trips offer a way to orient children as they walk back in time. *Opening Windows on the Past* shows how fourth and fifth graders studied the history of Amherst's historic buildings. *The Many Stories of 1704* looks at the Raid at Old Deerfield from the points of view of the English, French, Mohawk, Huron, and Wobanaki cultural groups who came into conflict as Europeans settled in western Massachusetts. *Echoes* offers historical photographs of daily community life from eastern Massachusetts during the 19th century. *History of the Connecticut River* presents the ecological and social history of the region along New England's largest river. *Big Dig Archaeology* shows what anthropologists have learned about the last 10,000 years of Boston, Massachusetts history.

Reading and discussing children's literature that focuses on people or structures along roads and rivers in the past extends our exploration of change (see print resources).

Teaching Tips

We post student photographs and writing online on the Amherst Public Schools' website, but teachers in other schools can create home grown sites using Class Homepage Builder from Scholastic.com. This format is more limited in the amount of text that can be added alongside the photographs, but the service is free and easy to use.

Technology Resources

HARDWARE
IBM or Macintosh computer with Internet access

SOFTWARE
Microsoft Office 2004

Resources

INTERNET

Biology Department, University of Massachusetts Amherst, The Connecticut River: A World Wide Web Site Containing Information about the Biology, History and Geology of New England's Largest River, n.d., http://www.bio.umass.edu/biology/conn.river (August 8, 2005).

Center for Computer-Based Instructional Technology, University of Massachusetts, Amherst, Opening Windows on the Past, 2003, http://www.arps.org/amhersthistory/ (August 8, 2005).

Northeast Massachusetts Regional Library System, Echoes: Essex County Heritage Online Exhibits, n.d., http://www.nmrls.org/enha/exhibit/images.shtml (August 8, 2005).

Pocumtuck Valley Memorial Association, Raid on Deerfield: The Many Stories of 1704, 2004 http://1704.deerfield.history.museum/ (August 8, 2005).

Science Museum of Minnesota. Mysteries of Catalhoyuk! An Archaeological Investigation, 2003 http://www.smm.org/catal/ (August 8, 2005).

TerraServer—USA, n.d., http://terraserver.microsoft.com/ (August 8, 2005).

The Museum of Science, Big Dig Archaeology, 2000, http://www.mos.org/bigdigarch/ (August 8, 2005).

PRINT

Burton, Virginia Lee. *The Little House.* Boston: Houghton Mifflin, 1942.

Cherry, Lynne. *A River Ran Wild: An Environmental History.* New York: Voyager Books, 2002.

Drew, David. *Millions of Years Ago.* Southbank, Victoria: Thomson Learning Australia, 1999.

Fleischman, Paul. *Time Train.* New York: HarperTrophy, 1994.

Lyon, George Ella. *Who Came Down That Road?* New York: Orchard Books, 2004.

McKendry, Joe. *Beneath the Streets of Boston: Building America's First Subway.* Boston: David R. Godine, 2005.

Other Materials Needed

Digital or regular cameras

Got Lemonade?
Economics in the Palm of Your Hand

Mark van 't Hooft and Kadee Anstadt

Third to Fifth Grades: Economics

NCSS Thematic Strands
Ⓥ️ **PRODUCTION, CONSUMPTION, AND DISTRIBUTION**

NCSS Performance Expectations
Ⓥ️ **PRODUCTION, CONSUMPTION, AND DISTRIBUTION**
  a. Give examples that show how scarcity and choice govern our economic decisions.
  f. Describe the influence of incentives, values, traditions, and habits on economic decisions.
  h. Describe the relationship of price to supply and demand.
  i. Use economic concepts such as supply, demand, and price to help explain events in the community and nation.
  j. Apply knowledge of economic concepts in developing a response to a current local economic issue.

NETS-S National Educational Technology Standards for Students
3. Technology Productivity Tools
4. Technology Communications Tools
5. Technology Research Tools
6. Technology Problem-solving and Decision-making Tools

NETS-S Performance Indicators (Grades 3-5)
5. Technology Research Tools
6. Technology Problem-solving and Decision-making Tools
  ♦ Use technology resources (e.g., calculators, data collection probes, videos, educational software) for problem solving, self-directed learning, and extended learning activities.

3. Technology Productivity Tools
4. Technology Communications Tools
  ♦ Use technology tools (e.g., multimedia authoring, presentation, Web tools, digital cameras, scanners) for individual and collaborative writing, communication, and publishing activities to create knowledge products for audiences inside and outside the classroom.

Introduction
Using the simulation software *Lemonade Tycoon* (see Technology Resources below), students experience what it takes to run a business. *Lemonade Tycoon* is a business simulation game that tests entrepreneurial skills to find out if people have what it takes to build a little stand into a big business. By making good business decisions and increasing cash reserves, players can move to a higher traffic location, buy a refrigerator, a faster cash register or automatic juicer to squeeze out the competition. A single license of the handheld version costs about $14.95, and can be obtained from various handheld software vendors.

Students buy supplies to stock their stands, formulate a recipe they believe consumers will like, purchase equipment if they desire, and select a location for their stand based on information they receive about weather and current events, as well as their growing experiences with consumers from previous days. The students then "experience" the day and observe as consumers accept or reject their decisions. After the day has ended, students record profit/loss data and write a reflective journal about how their businesses performed and changes they will make to do better the next business day. They also share their decisions about supplies, recipe, equipment, and location with other business owners in the "Chamber of Commerce" discussions at the end of each business week. Students learn to identify the various resources needed to produce a good and suggest the opportunity costs for those resources. A rubric assigns points for journal reflections on decisions about resources, risk-taking, problem solving, and evidence of use of the steps in the problem solving model (Identify, Gather, List Options, Consider Advantages/Disadvantages, Choose Solutions, and Judge Effectiveness).

Objectives
Students will be able to:
  1. Practice problem solving skills as they make decisions about the productive resources they need to produce lemonade.

2. Describe the relationship of price to supply and demand in their quest to attract customers.

3. Consider options for their individual business, organize their productive resources, and use economic concepts such as supply, demand, and price to help explain events related to their businesses.

4. Apply knowledge of economic concepts in developing a response to a current local economic issue, and seek to make a profit as they take the necessary risks to meet demand.

Time

Initial lesson of 30 minutes followed by 30 sessions of approximately fifteen minutes each and several 20-30 minute sessions for Chamber of Commerce meetings. "Business days" can be combined to condense the unit into two weeks by playing and responding to more than one day of play in a session.

Instructional Steps

Begin by having students talk about what they'd need to start a lemonade business. Discuss supplies, resources, and location, and probe for other factors that might determine where they should locate a lemonade stand. Elementary students will initially only think of the traditional stand in their neighborhood. Lead them into discussions of how someone might make enough money to do this for a full-time business.

Many students are familiar with game simulations, including other "Tycoon" software like *Roller Coaster* and *Mall Tycoon*. Inform students that they will be playing *Lemonade Tycoon*.

Introduce the software by walking students through all the components of the game: choosing daily supplies, setting price, determining location, purchasing capital equipment, and creating a recipe their customers will like. Discuss the fact that items like cups can be purchased in larger quantities because they can be stored, but that ice melts and needs to be purchased on a daily basis.

In *Lemonade Tycoon*, select "Challenge Mode," in which students will run their businesses over a "30-day" period.

After students have entered their names, have them make decisions about daily supplies, setting price, determining location, purchasing capital equipment, and determining a recipe. Initially, all players in "Challenge Mode" will have to play in the suburbs. After the first day, students can choose from several locations for varying rent levels.

Review the procedures for daily play so students are ready to begin playing independently each day when social studies begins:

- Get your Handheld and Keyboard and select "Lemonade Tycoon."
- Select "Play Game" and your name.
- Buy supplies, choose a location, make changes to your recipe, and buy equipment if you choose.
- Using your scratch journal paper, record the forecast and news flash.
- Begin your day.
- Record your sales, profits, and customer satisfaction on your scratch paper.
- Write your journal entry using the rubric and scratch paper notes as your guide.

After setting up the day, students are ready to play "Day 1." Be sure that before they begin they note the weather and the "News Flash" in their journals. If you are using an electronic journal, it may be handy to have scratch paper for these notes so they can go back and make the journal entry later (see the Journal Template).

Students need to watch the day's events very closely. Customers will react to their recipes by making sour or happy faces and to their prices by either a single ($) dollar sign for satisfaction, or a double ($$) dollar sign if they feel the price is too high. These are mental notes that students need to take as they watch their day.

When the day is completed, students should jot down their ending statistics on their scratch paper (cups sold, profit, spoilage, and customer satisfaction).

Next, students should record the statistical data as well as anecdotal information in their journals. Discuss and model an appropriate journal entry according to the predetermined standards (See the Journal Template). Journal entries should always include a reflection on what went well on that day, what didn't work, and what changes, if any, should be made to improve customer satisfaction. A sample journal entry and rubric for the journal entries are included in this article. At the end of five sessions, students should be placed in small groups for discussions on how their businesses are thriving. These discussions should be modeled beforehand and include information from the reflective journal entries the students have made throughout the week. Discussions of location, price determination, recipe changes, and capital purchases are also appropriate during these discussions. This exchange of information,

Lemonade Tycoon Journal Template

The weather forecast today was:

My newsflash said that…

I chose _____ for my location because …

Changes I made to my recipe include:

I purchased the following inventory:

I am selling my lemonade for $_____

_____ lemons

_____ ice

_____ sugar

_____ cups

Equipment I own or purchased today includes _____.

Journal Entry begins here (include sales and profit/loss information in your entry):

Sample Lemonade Tycoon Journal Entry

The weather forecast today was cloudy with a 50% chance of rain. The temperature range was forecasted for 85-90 degrees.

My newsflash said that there was a volleyball tournament at the beach.

I chose the beach because of the volleyball tournament. I figured with the hot day, many people might want to buy lemonade.

I added more ice to my recipe today because it's supposed to be hot.

I am selling my lemonade for $1.25/cup. I hope I can pay for my beach rent by charging more.

I purchased the following inventory:
10 lemons
3 ice
2 sugar
75 cups

Equipment I own or purchased today includes:
NONE.

Journal Entry begins here (include sales and profit/loss information in your entry):

Going to the beach turned out to be a good idea. Yesterday I was in the park and had a terrible day because of the rain. Even though it was supposed to rain today, it didn't. I sold 70 cups—that's the most ever. My profit was $38. Demand was so great because of the temperature and the volleyball tournament, I think. I was glad I bought 3 bags of ice because I used a lot of ice in my new recipe. My supplies held out, but I will need to buy more cups tomorrow. Even though my expenses are higher at the beach, I am glad I chose it. If I have a few more days like this I could make a capital purchase of equipment like a juicer or something. I'll wait to see what the forecast is tomorrow before I decide if I will keep my price the same.

also called "Chamber of Commerce Meeting," is a very important part of the unit. Students need time to reflect aloud on the decisions they've made and the impact those decisions have had on their businesses. By collaborating with other business owners, students begin to review other ideas and consider risks they may wish to take in their own businesses. Open these discussions up to whole class discussions so that groups can hear about others' experiences.

Next, have students trade journals. Using the rubric supplied or one you've designed, have students assess each others' work. Before beginning, show several examples of journal entries (exemplary, proficient, and not-yet) so students can see what a good journal entry looks like.

Assessment

A rubric for the journal writing is used (see rubric). Note that students should not be graded on the performance of their business, but on how they use information to make business decisions.

Student Enrichment

+ Plotting daily profit or sales on a graph.
+ Have students work in "Chamber of Commerce" groupings to complete the entire unit—modeling what larger corporations do with regard to team-decision making.
+ Analyzing the sales data to find relationships (e.g., between temperature and profit margin).

Teaching Tips

+ Use large chart paper to list daily procedures so students can work independently as soon as you are ready to begin.
+ Be sure students name and number their journal entries to match the day they are playing. This makes the journals much easier for you to find and grade, especially if students are beaming their journals to your handheld computer.

Lemonade Tycoon Writing Rubric		
AN EXEMPLARY JOURNAL ENTRY INCLUDES:	Possible Points	Total Points
+ Weather and the news flash + Location and recipe were discussed (not just mentioned)	15 Points	
OBSERVATIONS ABOUT THE DAY AND ABOUT + Waiting time + Recipe + Location + Supply/demand + Other possible effects the news flash or weather may have had on my day.	15 Points	
ECONOMICS VOCABULARY: (one or more of the following) + Resources + Consumers/Producers + Supply/demand + Inventory + Profit/loss + Good/services + Scarcity + Opportunity costs + Factors of production	10 Points	
SPELLING	5 Points	
COMPLETE SENTENCES; GRAMMAR & PUNCTUATION	5 Points	
TOTAL	/50	/50

Technology Resources

HARDWARE

Handheld computers with keyboards (one per student is best). At least one desktop to back up handheld data is recommended, but not essential. An LCD projector for whole group sharing (optional)

SOFTWARE

Lemonade Tycoon. Made by Jamdat (now EAMobile), this simulation is available for Palm OS. http://handheld.softpedia.com/get/Games/Strategy/Lemonade-Tycoon-for-Palm-OS-1135.shtml

Resources

INTERNET

None needed.

PRINT

Journal template (both large chart and student sheets)

OTHER MATERIALS NEEDED

Scrap journal template paper for each student every day, large chart paper with journal template to post in the room.

Student Voices

"You tricked us, I thought we were having fun playing with the Handhelds and you taught us stuff."

"Oh, this is economics. I thought it was going to be hard."

Westward, Ho!

Lori Mathys

5

Fourth Grade: U.S. History, Geography, and Economics

NCSS Thematic Strands
Ⅱ **TIME, CONTINUITY, AND CHANGE**
Ⅲ **PEOPLE, PLACES, AND ENVIRONMENTS**

NCSS Performance Expectations
Ⅱ **TIME, CONTINUITY, AND CHANGE**

c. Identify and describe selected historical periods and patterns of change within and across cultures, such as the rise of civilizations, the development of transportation systems, the growth and breakdown of colonial systems, and others.

d. Identify and use processes important to reconstructing and reinterpreting the past, such as using a variety of sources, providing, validating, and weighing evidence for claims, checking credibility of sources, and searching for causality.

e. Develop critical sensitivities such as empathy and skepticism regarding attitudes, values, and behaviors of people in different historical contexts.

f. Use knowledge of facts and concepts drawn from history, along with methods of historical inquiry, to inform decision making about and action-taking on public issues.

Ⅲ PEOPLE, PLACES, AND ENVIRONMENTS

h. Examine, interpret, and analyze physical and cultural patterns and their interactions, such as land use, settlement patterns, cultural transmission of customs and ideas, and ecosystem changes.

i. Describe ways that historical events have been influenced by, and have influenced, physical and human geographic factors in local, regional, national, and global settings.

NETS-S National Educational Technology Standards for Students
3. Technology Productivity Tools
4. Technology Communications Tools
6. Technology Problem-solving and Decision-making Tools

NETS-S Performance Indicators (Grades 3-5)
3. Technology Productivity Tools

♦ Use technology tools for individual and collaborative writing, communication, and publishing activities to create knowledge products for audiences inside and outside the classroom.

4. Technology Communications Tools

♦ Use telecommunications and online resources to participate in collaborative problem-solving activities for the purpose of developing solutions or products for audiences inside and outside the classroom.

6. Technology Problem-solving and Decision-making Tools

♦ Use technology resources for problem solving, self-directed learning, and extended learning activities.

Introduction
Integrating technology into the social studies classroom expands the learning for students, making it meaningful and connected to the real world. In this lesson, students become members of "Pioneer families" comprising 4-5 students and become engaged in an online project to travel the Oregon Trail in the 1800s. Not only are students responsible for creating their "identities" based upon primary-source historical documents, but they also must pack their wagons using an Excel Spreadsheet, and take a virtual journey, facing life-and-death decisions daily. Every decision has a consequence for the Pioneer student families, reflected in the students' journals. Students are also involved in online discussion lists and weekly chat features with students all across the United States taking the same virtual journey. To see a glimpse of this project in my classroom, watch the *Westward Ho!* video online:

http://www.emints.org/about/video/index.shtml#westward

Objectives

The student will be able to:

1. Summarize the events in Westward Expansion, including people's motivation and their hardships.
2. Identify Missouri as a jumping-off point to the West and explain how the state was impacted by the Oregon Trail and the Westward Movement of goods and people.
3. Compare how people's needs have been met in different ways in different cultures at various times.
4. Evaluate the impact of Westward Expansion on Native Americans in Missouri.
5. Describe how people are affected by, depend on, adapt to, and change their environments.
6. Identify, use, and create primary and secondary sources.
7. Identify and use library and media resources.

Time

This unit lasts 5 weeks – 50 minutes per day.

Instructional Steps

1. This unit is developed to engage the students in the *Westward Ho!* online project: http://www.cyberbee.com/wwho/. This project runs from mid-January through mid-February each year, with hundreds of classrooms involved.

The week the project begins, students are organized into family groups of 4-5 students. Researching on the Internet, students read primary source diaries from Pioneers from the 1800s to create a virtual identity, including a name, occupation, family history, hopes and dreams, and reasons for traveling to Oregon. Guidelines for students are that family groups should

be related and must have at least one adult. Students may not be younger than 10 years old in their virtual families. (Note: In their research for reasons Pioneers traveled to Oregon, students will discover that a married husband and wife would receive more land than a single male, and unmarried women would not receive any land in the Homestead Acts—this encourages the students to become families like those who traveled the Oregon Trail in the 1800s.)

Links to Research Pioneer Families

Authentic Pioneer Diaries: http://heritage.uen.org/

Pioneer names: http://lib-operations.sonoma.edu/fin/aaa-0709.html

Pioneer multimedia: http://heritage.uen.org/resources/multimedia.html

Homestead Act of 1852: http://www.pbs.org/weta/thewest/resources/archives/five/homestd.htm

A collection of links to support this unit: http://teachers.emints.org/mathysl/missouri.html#Westward%20Expansion

2. Students create a way to describe their Pioneer families to their classmates. Ideas include a poster, a skit or speech, or a PowerPoint presentation. The sharing of the family biographies is important to create the setting for the project and encourages dialogue between families later. It also provides time to share learning about the Pioneers so far. Family introductions should include a description of each family member, reasons for going West on the Oregon Trail, hopes for their future in Oregon, and other pertinent information the students want to share about their Pioneer families.

The Oregon Trail: http://www.isu.edu/%7Etrinmich/Oregontrail.html

If You Traveled West in a Pioneer Wagon: http://skenoyer.org/west.html

Westward Movement: http://www.deweybrowse.org/westward.htm

3. As a class, create K-W-L charts for the Pioneers. The questions on the "What I Want to Know" chart and "What I think I Know" chart will help to determine what knowledge students have and need to acquire throughout the unit. Post the charts for reference throughout the unit, and frequently set aside time to refer to the students' questions and knowledge.

4. On the bulletin board on the Online Project site http://www.cyberbee.com/wwho/ students write a few sentences to introduce their Pioneer families. On the first scheduled chat for the Online Project, students will also be introducing their families and describing why they are planning to travel to Oregon. The bulletin board and chat features of the Online Project contribute to the interactivity of the experience for the students. Since students all across America are traveling the Oregon Trail using the same project, the audience for the students is larger than just within the classroom.

5. After creating their Pioneer families, the students then pack their wagons. They must decide not only the type of wagon and animals to take, but also supplies and luxury items. The students use an Excel Spreadsheet to pack their wagons. The Spreadsheet will also be used to track income and expenses throughout the project. Students must research the supplies that Pioneers would have taken on the journey in the 1800s, being careful not to over pack their wagons; and keeping in mind that they won't be able to replenish supplies until they come to a trading post or buy them from a fellow traveler with extra supplies.

Excel Spreadsheet: http://teachers.emints.org/mathysl/supplies.xls

Links to research supplies for the trail: http://teachers.emints.org/mathysl/missouri.html#Westward%20Expansion

6. Students use an outline of the United States to draw a map of the Oregon Trail and major landmarks along the journey. During the journey, students will be tracking their travels on the maps. They will also be able to see the historic sites by viewing them on the Internet. This adds to the travel experience.

Route of the Oregon Trail: http://www.endoftheoregontrail.org/maplibrary/oregontrail.html

Historic Sites Along the Trail: http://www.isu.edu/~trinmich/Sites.html

Landmarks on the Oregon Trail: http://www.beavton.k12.or.us/greenway/leahy/ot/landmarks.htm

7. During the weeks of the Online Project, students are given

daily tasks, in which they must make decisions such as how to cross various rivers, how to cure a snakebite, and what to do when encountering Indians. The daily tasks are accessible to the teacher, after signing up for the Online Project. After students make decisions with their families, the teacher reads their fates aloud. Some of the consequences are good and some are bad: The students may gain or lose supplies, need to make wagon repairs, or ask for help from fellow travelers. The students keep track of supplies on their Excel Spreadsheets. The Internet is used for research to see how the real Pioneers handled the same problems. The discussion board on the Online Project is used to share general information and to buy and sell supplies. Weekly Friday chats are held for the students to discuss various Pioneer scenarios with others participating across the United States.

Links for students to use to research to make decisions for the daily tasks: http://teachers.emints.org/mathysl/missouri.html#Westward%20Expansion

8. During the project, the students keep a journal written from their first person point of view about their travels along the Oregon Trail. This journal can be written on paper, kept online in a blog format, or created as a series of slides in a PowerPoint presentation.

9. The project ends when the students arrive in Oregon City.

Assessment

The students' journal entries provide feedback to the teacher. The Excel Spreadsheet provides evidence of understanding the Pioneer time period. Teacher observation and questioning can be used as the students work to form solutions to each of the daily fates. A checklist of computer skills can be used to evaluate students as they research and create presentation projects utilizing the technology.

Student Enrichment

EXTENSIONS

After traveling the Oregon Trail for 2–3 weeks, students should dress as Pioneers for a school day. The students pose for "Family Portraits" using the sepia setting of a digital camera to appear as "Old Fashioned Pictures." While dressed as Pioneers, the students should go on a mile long walk in the school neighborhood. Have the students watch for Landmarks or objects to represent the Oregon Trail landmarks; and talk as Pioneers while on the journey. For lunch, the students should sit around a "campfire" and tell tall tales while eating authentic pioneer foods.

>Pioneer student family photos: http://teachers.emints.org/
>mathysl/Pioneers/PioneerFamilies2004.html
>http://teachers.emints.org/mathysl/Pioneers2005/PioneerFamilies2005.
>html

Teaching Tips

Providing a daily essential question for your students as they progress along the trail helps to focus their thinking. For example, "How will you decide which supplies to leave behind as your wagon becomes too heavy for the oxen?" "What inventions or innovations would have helped to make the lives of the Pioneers easier on the trail?" "Thinking as your Pioneer character, how have your hopes and dreams for Oregon changed as you have traveled on this journey?" I taught about Pioneers and Westward Expansion for years doing the typical activities—making butter, drawing the trails on maps, and making quilt squares, but it wasn't until I engaged my students in this *Westward Ho!* online project that I saw their learning soar to new heights! The authentic learning and quality of the task carries over into all subject areas. My students are having fun, but they are making connections and acquiring knowledge in the process. This is one project that my students talk about for months, and former students still reflect about their time on the Oregon Trail… no textbook can do that!

Technology Resources
HARDWARE
Internet connectivity

SOFTWARE
Microsoft Excel; PowerPoint and Word can be utilized

Resources
INTERNET

Cyberbee, "*Westward Ho!* Online Project," Leni Donlan, http://www.cyberbee.com/wwho/

eMINTS National Center, "*Westward Ho!* Digital Story," Lori Mathys, http://www.emints.org/about/video/index.shtml#westward

Mrs. Mathys' Magnificent Fourth Grade Class Website, Lori Mathys, http://teachers.emints.org/mathysl/missouri.html#Westward%20Expansion

http://teachers.emints.org/mathysl/Pioneers2005/PioneerFamilies2005.html

http://teachers.emints.org/mathysl/Pioneers/PioneerFamilies2004.html

Heritage Gateways, Utah State Office of Education, http://heritage.uen.org/

Memoirs of Travel, Newton G. Finley, http://lib-operations.sonoma.edu/fin/aaa-0709.html

PBS, Homestead Act of 1852, http://www.pbs.org/weta/thewest/resources/archives/five/homestd.htm

The Oregon Trail, Mike Trinklein and Steve Boettcher, http://www.isu.edu/%7Etrinmich/Oregontrail.html

If You Traveled West in a Pioneer Wagon, Kenoyer's Classy Kids, http://skenoyer.org/west.html

Westward Movement, Gail Shea Grainger, http://www.deweybrowse.org/westward.htm

Route of the Oregon Trail, End of the Oregon Trail, http://www.endoftheoregontrail.org/maplibrary/oregontrail.html

Landmarks on the Oregon Trail, Mr. Leahy's Class, http://www.beavton.k12.or.us/greenway/leahy/ot/landmarks.htm

A Printable Pioneer Town, Herbert Hoover Presidential Library and Museum, http://www.hoover.archives.gov/LIW/pioneertown/activities_pioneertown.html

PRINT
None

OTHER MATERIALS NEEDED
None

Student Voices (Student Journal Entries)

JESSICA GAMMON: Sept. 4, 1845, mile 1217 "Today we found out that Indians attack commonly where we are. It's the Sioux. We hope they don't attack, but if they do we will fight back." Sept. 8, 1845, mile 1250 "Pa decided he would be a sacrifice even though we tried to tell him not to. I think he has gone off his rocker. The Sioux Indians are attacking at this very moment. Pa just left the wagon. I ran to the back where I could not see through the cloth. I heard screams of pain and then nothing. Ma started crying at the front of the wagon. I hope Pa is OK."

ALAYNA YORK: May 5-7, 1845, mile 54, Wakarusa River "We made it across the river. The Ferry did not make it. The mud was too gushy. A Shawnee Indian who helped us across impressed me and my friends. We were soaking wet. I was so cold I felt like a frozen caveman just being discovered."

AUDREY IMHOFF: May 30, 1845, mile 319, Fort Kearney: "We have reached Fort Kearney. Yes! But there were also some problems. Most of the soldiers were drunk so we headed out earlier. We also bought some beans, bacon, flour, and traded an oxen." June 10, 1845, mile 383, Midway Station, Nebraska: "I have waited so long to just stop and rest. My children are collecting buffalo chips. We are also going to play ball with a skull we found on the side of the road."

Chuck Wagons, Cowboys, and Cattle Drives

Judith A. Hakes, Marilyn Eisenwine and Sandra Pedersen

Fourth Grade: American History and Geography

NCSS Thematic Strands
⊕ TIME, CONTINUITY, AND CHANGE
Social studies programs should include experiences that provide for the study of the ways human beings view themselves in and over time.

NCSS Performance Expectations
⊕ TIME, CONTINUITY, AND CHANGE

   c. Compare and contrast different stories or accounts about past events, people, places, or situations, identifying how they contribute to our understanding of the past;

   d. Identify and use various sources for reconstructing the past, such as documents, letters, diaries, maps, textbooks, and others;

   e. Demonstrate an understanding that people in different times and places view the world differently.

NETS-S National Educational Technology Standards for Students
3. Technology Productivity Tools
5. Technology Research Tools

NETS-S Performance Expectations
3. Technology Productivity Tools

- Students use technology tools to enhance learning, increase productivity, and promote creativity.
- Students use productivity tools to collaborate in constructing technology-enhanced models, prepare publications, and produce other creative works.

5. Technology Research Tools

- Students use technology to locate, evaluate, and collect information from a variety of sources.

Introduction
Prior to the student production and presentation of an electronic Student Exploration Trip (SET), groups of students/individuals research using online and/or print resources to collect information concerning the late 1800s era of the cowboy and cattle drives from Texas to the railheads in Kansas. Students may obtain additional data through online interviews and/or guest speakers. One of the most exciting sources for first hand interaction includes a modern day reenactment with an authentic chuck wagon to demonstrate how to cook a cowboy meal for the students. Laptops, digital photography, and Personal Digital Assistants (PDAs) facilitate the students' recording of this memorable event. During classroom lessons, students organize their findings for the creation of an electronic field trip, or Student Exploration Trip (SET) into the past. Students structure the information to build the SET in an electronic format of their choice that they may present later to classmates, other classes, and/or parents.

Objectives
The student will be able to…

- Research historical information concerning the cowboy era of the late 1800s using print resources, the Internet, and online interviews.
- Collect firsthand information using technology during guest speaker visits and an authentic chuck wagon cooking presentation.
- Design a multimedia project to showcase information collected.

Time
Approximate times for three phases are as follows:

- Research – 2-3 hours
- Planning – 1-2 hours
- Building and Sharing – 3-4 hours

   A shorter version of the entire project might be done in groups over two or three class periods.

Instructional Steps
The teacher may organize this lesson series into the following three phases to expedite student completion of activities:

- ◆ Research
- ◆ Planning the Student Exploration Trip (SET)
- ◆ Building and Sharing the SETs

Research Phase

Individuals or groups of students collect print, graphic, and statistical data on the American cowboy and western cattle drive era of the late 1800s. A variety of sources including books, websites, and resource people contribute to the knowledge base, as students take notes, collect pictures, and locate maps using the Internet, PDAs, digital and video cameras, as available.

Planning the Student Exploration Trip (SET)

In this important phase of the lesson series, students need ample time to organize research data into a workable plan for the SET, in order to transport them and others back to the cowboy era through electronic field trips into the past. They may select from a variety of SET formats for showcasing the information as follows:

- ◆ PowerPoint presentation: may include sound, graphics, photos, and animations; also available through Documents to Go for PDAs

- ◆ Video production: video clips titled, organized, and edited
- ◆ Claymation creation: using clay figures posed in different positions; animation may be done in PowerPoint or Moviemaker
- ◆ Website design: sharing of factual information through graphic design
- ◆ Animated timeline: rudimentary animation to illustrate a timeline incorporating still photographs projected in a short time sequence
- ◆ Hyperlinked map: locations on map are hyperlinked out to pages of information on that place (as illustrated in the Texas Beyond History website listed in the resources)

To complete this phase, students must script the production to fit the format selected. Techniques like "storyboarding" or software including Kidspiration or Inspiration facilitate this process. Also, drawing or sketching on an electronic graphics tablet, using PDAs, or sequencing photographs and video clips might prove helpful. Some may simply choose to write a narrative script through a word processing document.

Building and Sharing the SET

This final phase not only contains the transformation of the proposed SET into electronic reality, it also ensures that students share the SET with others. Time, technology assistance, and encouragement are all vital parts of this phase. Students may share their SET with other classrooms, parents, schools, and even larger audiences through e-mail contacts.

Assessment

Assessment occurs through both process and product while students engage in the ownership of social studies and technology excellence. Teachers may design rubrics for all three phases including data gathered, script created, and multimedia product, thereby tailoring the rubric to individualize assessment for each classroom. For example, point values, check marks, and/or informative notes may be incorporated as follows:

SET Scoring Rubric

	Needs Improvement	Acceptable	Exemplary
Process			
Phase I – Research			
1. Note-taking			
2. Sources (variety/quality)			
3. Technology use			
Phase II – Planning			
1. Selection of format			
2. Scripting of SET			
Product			
Phase III – Building SET			
1. Technology proficiency			
2. Data conversion/format			

Student Enrichment

+ Additional topics for study might be horses, brands, ranching, barbed wire, and cultural diversity of the cowboys
+ E-trail project with electronic sharing of SETs
+ CD compilation of all students' SETS
+ Displays at conferences, such as a Young Scholars' Conference
+ Study of the music/art/literature resulting from the cowboy era
+ Dramatic presentation of cowboy skits or stories

Teaching Tips

+ Locate and incorporate community resources such as museums, libraries, and resource people to expedite the gathering of information.
+ Seek technology assistance from parents, older students, district technology personnel, or others as needed in the production of an electronic SET.
+ Develop calendar/schedule with students to keep them focused on the task.
+ Schedule "buddy classes" with older or younger ages for technology assistants, planning and research, and/or audience participation.
+ Contact volunteers including senior citizens, parents, and/or college students specifically to individualize the projects.

Technology Resources

HARDWARE

Digital cameras and video, Internet, telecollaboration, laptop and classroom computers, PDAs, Scanner, electronic drawing tablets

SOFTWARE

Kidspiration/Inspiration, Documents to Go for PDAs including Microsoft Word, PowerPoint, and Excel, Adobe Photoshop, Windows Moviemaker

Resources

INTERNET

Chuck Wagon Central: history and information about chuck wagons. http://lonehand.com/chuckwagon_central.htm

Cowboy Clipart: Free downloads of graphics, animation, backgrounds. http://www.cowboyclipart.net/

Cowboy Photograph Collection – Erwin Smith. http://www.cartermuseum.org/collections/smith

History of Cattle Brands. http://barbwiremuseum.com/cattlebrandhistory.htm

Kansas Heritage Center: information on Cattle Drives. http://www.readinks.info/khc/

Ken's Country and Western Clipart: Free downloads. http://www.btinternet.com/~western.clipart/

Inspiration and Kidspiration: software for brainstorming. http://www.inspiration.com

Microsoft Office: PowerPoint, Excel, and Word. http://www.microsoft.com

Montana Kids' Site: information about Cattle Drives. http://montanakids.com/db_engine/presentations/presentation.asp?pid=53&sub=Cattle+Drives

National Cowgirl Museum and Hall of Fame. http://www.cowgirl.net/

National Historic Site: with a traveling trunk. http://www.nps.gov/grko/education.htm

Grant-Kohrs Ranch NHS including lesson plans. http://www.nps.gov/grko/lessonfrontpage.htm

Texas Beyond History: The Virtual Museum of Texas' Cultural Heritage. http://www.texasbeyondhistory.net

Texas Cattle Drives: excellent information from PBS. http://www.pbs.org/weta/thewest/places/trails_ter/cattle.htm

Trail Drives of the Old West: by Randy Leonard, good graphics, with information about the Goodnight-Loving Trail. http://www.net.westhost.com/loving.shtml

Trails West Website: by Elizabeth Larson, includes many links. http://www.over-land.com/trwestsouth.html

Print Resources

CHILDREN'S LITERATURE

Ann Herbert Scott. *Cowboy Country.* New York: Clarion, 1993.

Gail Gibbons. *Yippee-yay!: A Book about Cowboys and Cowgirls.* Boston: Little, Brown, 1998.

Joan Anderson. *Cowboys: Roundup on an American Ranch.* New York: Scholastic Inc., 1996.

Robert Klausmeier. *Cowboy.* Minneapolis, Minn.: Lerner Publications Company, 1990.

Russell Freedman. *In the Days of the Vaqueros: America's First True Cowboys.* New York: Clarion Books, 2001.

Ubet Tomb. *Cowboys.* Santa Barbara, Calif.: Bellerophon Books, 1997.

Ubet Tomb. *Cowgirls.* Santa Barbara, Calif.: Bellerophon Books, 1997.

FICTIONAL COWBOYS

Scott Emerson and Howard Post. *The Magic Boots.* Salt Lake City: Gibbs-Smith Publisher, 1994.

Brian Gleeson. *Pecos Bill.* Rowayton, Conn.: Abdo Publishing Company, 2005.

Tony Johnston and Warren Ludwig. *The Cowboy and the Black-Eyed Pea.* New York: Putnam and Grosset Group, 1996.

Steven Kellogg. *Pecos Bill.* New York: Scholastic, 1986.

Susan Lowell. *Little Red Cowboy Hat.* New York: Henry Holt and Company, 1997.

Susan Lowell. *Cindy Ellen: A Wild Western Cinderella.* New York: Harper Collins, 2000.

FOR ADULTS

Duncan Emrich. *The Cowboy's Own Brand Book.* New York: Dover Publications, Inc., 1995.

Glenn Varnum. *Man on Horseback: The Story of the Mounted Man from Scythians to the American Cowboy.* Lincoln: University of Nebraska, 1972.

Jo Mora. *Californios.* Ketchum, Idaho: Stoecklein, 1994.

Jo Mora. *Trail Dust and Saddle Leather.* New York: Charles Scribner's Sons, 1946.

Other Materials Needed

Video tapes, CDs, memory sticks

Student Voices

In a field trial of the SET last spring, the students below reported on planning, using technology, and sharing presentations.

"That we got to do so many different things. And whenever I took the pictures, it was real cool; 'cause then, like if you wanted to see something again, all you had to do was look at the pictures." *Nate*

"The best part was making memories, and it's so cool to share it with other people!" *Austin*

The classroom teacher had the following to say about the SET experience:

"Some children struggle with reading and math, but in this project, they had the chance to really shine through technology and sharing with others." *Mrs. Pedersen*

Mr. Money and Money Matters

PATRICIA A. PALMER AND ANNE JESCHKE

7

FOURTH AND FIFTH GRADES: ECONOMICS AND AMERICAN HISTORY

NCSS Thematic Strands
- Ⓘ TIME, CONTINUITY, AND CHANGE
- Ⓥ PRODUCTION, DISTRIBUTION, AND CONSUMPTION
- Ⓥ SCIENCE, TECHNOLOGY, AND SOCIETY

NCSS Performance Expectations
Ⓘ TIME, CONTINUITY, AND CHANGE
b. Demonstrate an ability to use correctly vocabulary associated with time such as past, present, future, and long ago; read and construct simple timelines; identify examples of change; and recognize examples of cause and effect relationships.

Ⓥ PRODUCTION, DISTRIBUTION, AND CONSUMPTION
g. Explain and demonstrate the role of money in everyday life.

Ⓥ SCIENCE, TECHNOLOGY, AND SOCIETY
a. Identify and describe examples in which science and technology have changed the lives of people, such as in homemaking, childcare, work, transportation, and communication.

NETS-S National Educational Technology Standards for Students
3. Technology Productivity Tools
5. Technology Research Tools

NETS-S Performance Expectatations
3. Technology Productivity Tools
- Students use technology tools to enhance learning, increase productivity, and promote creativity.
- Students use productivity tools to collaborate in constructing technology-enhanced models, prepare publications, and produce other creative works.

5. Technology Research Tools
- Students use technology to locate, evaluate, and collect information from a variety of sources.
- Students use technology tools to process data and report results.
- Students evaluate and select new information resources and technological innovations based on the appropriateness for specific tasks.

Introduction
This personal finance lesson asks the student to research trade from barter through the ages to our current banking system, obtain information on the banking practices that consumers used historically, identify how those practices have changed and what are still in place today, and finally predict how the banking industry will evolve for future generations. Students will construct a timeline of the major changes in banking practices and how those changes have impacted the lives of consumers as they participate in the marketplace. The main focus of the lesson is the need for trade to satisfy our wants and how the way we accomplish that has changed, evolved, expanded and lastly, how those changes affect the consumer.

Objectives
The student will be able to...
1. Analyze how the evolution of trade from barter to banking has impacted the role of the trade partners and created a need for a banking system.
2. Recognize the role banks play in the economic system for the consumer.
3. Analyze current banking practices and how these practices relate to the daily activities in the life of a consumer.
4. Formulate banking services for the future based on consumer wants and technological advances.
5. Evaluate (using Cost/Benefit Analysis) the technological changes in banking services over time and the overall effect on the consumer.
6. Determine technology to use for best means of communicating student work.

Time
Approximately 4 class sessions over a period of several weeks; 45 minute sessions with outside class assignment for initial research.

Continued on page 43

Yesterday's Money

Mr. Money and his son, Summy, had stopped at the ATM on the way to school this morning. Summy needed money for his school field trip. Mr. Money wanted to explain to Summy that paying for things we want, such as going on a field trip, was not always so easy... shhh... let's listen in again...

Summy, do you think people have always used money?

How else would we get what we want?

"I am glad you asked!" Mr. Money said. "Let me just give you a few facts and then you can check it out for yourself on your computer after your snack."

- Many thousands of years ago, people used *barter* to trade for the goods they wanted.
- Cattle and grain were used to trade instead of money as we know it today.
- For the trade to take place, there had to be a coincidence of wants. In other words, I want what you have to trade and you want what I have to trade.
- Think about using barter to trade today. What would you use to trade and what would you expect to get in return? "In my day, Summy, we traded baseball cards!"
- *Find out more about barter.*

After Barter, Then What?

Dad, I think I am getting the idea... but when did we change to using paper money? I can't imagine trading for these skates!

"You are so right, Summy," said Mr. Money. "That would have probably been a difficult trade."

- The barter system is still in use at times in our society but it is not convenient.
- Wampum became a means of trade in the 1600's when the value of fur pelts was discovered.
- From the *Native Tech* website **"The use of wampum as money, even among the English, continued until the American Revolution. Important matters such as treaty agreements were likely to be marked by an exchange of Wampum belts, with designs in two colors, which thereafter served as visual reminders of the event itself, and to call to memory the arrangements agreed on" (Russel 1980: 185).**

"Summy, do you think you could have traded wampum for your skates?"

Barter, Wampum...
What Was Next?

 The earliest form of *banking* probably took place in temples where precious metals for trading were stored. Greece even had evidence that loans were made! Check out the *History of Banking* . Paper money came about because of a scarcity of coins dating back to China in the 600s. There is so much to know about money and early banking...

Were there *always* banks?

"Summy, you ask great questions!" said Mr. Money. "I was reading about banks just the other day and what the word *bank* first meant. Here is what I found out:

The earliest record of banking is in the year 1587, in Venice Italy. The word banking comes from the *Italian* word banco, which means *bench*. Early Italian bankers used to do their business on the street at a bench. Slowly, banking activity began to spread throughout Europe. In the 1600's in England, goldsmiths made things out of gold and silver and they kept their metals in strong vaults. People began to bring their money to the goldsmiths to be stored in their vaults for safety. The goldsmiths gave receipts to the people for their putting their money in the vaults. These receipts were easier to carry than coins, so the people began to use them as money. The goldsmiths gradually became bankers."

Money…what is it really?

"Good question, Summy. Money is whatever we use to *exchange* for goods and services; it has taken many forms over the centuries. What really *matters* is that it meets these three important characteristics:

- Medium of Exchange—each party agrees that this is a standard that is acceptable to all for payment of a debt. It is easy to trade and transport.
- Unit of Account—it can easily be divided for payment unlike a cow or other items used long ago; a way of measuring what we owe that is understandable to all.
- Store of Value—the item, money, will be good for future trade and not perishable such as food items."

You can see examples of *Money Through the Ages*. Take a virtual tour of the Money Museum at the Federal Reserve Bank of Richmond and see everything from the Cowrie shells of Indochina to coins and currency we have used in this country.

Mr. Money "Sums" It Up…

Dad, hold on, you are going so fast! There is so much to know! I am making notes about this *virtual* field trip…it would not cost my class anything…I need to tell my teacher tomorrow so we can plan this tour!

Well, Summy, our family has always talked about Money! My dad always told me it was a name no one would forget! There is a lot to learn about Money Matters…now we are ready to talk about Money Today…

Today's Money

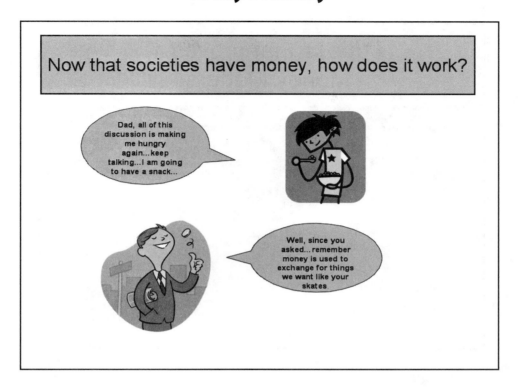

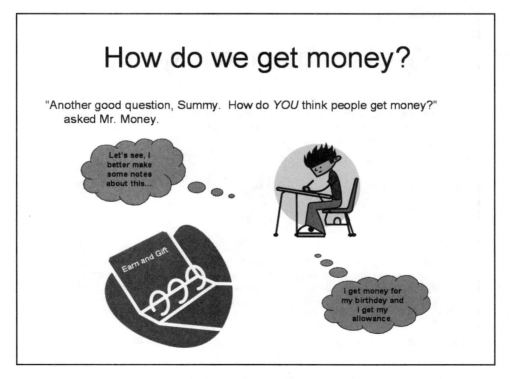

I guess that proves it, Money Matters!

"What do you mean, Money Matters, dad?" asked Summy. "Well, we have to <u>earn</u> the money to buy the goods and services we want. So, doesn't Money Matter?" responded Mr. Money. "Gift money is great but we can't count on it. We have to plan ahead how to use the money we <u>earn</u>."

What to do with our Money…

"Dad, what do **you** do with the money you earn?" asked Summy. "That's a slam dunk, Summy!" "Thanks, dad!" exclaimed Summy. "Well, I really meant deciding what to do with my money is a 'slam dunk,' Summy, but good move on the court too, son."

"The first thing that I do with my money is deposit it in the bank. I want to know it is safe and that it will be there when I need it. Like this morning to pay for your field trip. Banks are a great service. They help us to be able to buy the goods and services we want," stated Mr. Money.

Bank Services Today

"Summy, banks today are not what they were when I was your age or when your grandfather was your age. You should ask him sometime what it was like when he went to the bank. I know *his* dad, your great-grandfather, did not stop at the ATM on the way to school!"

 # I'm getting there!

"Banking services today include the following:
- $ Checking Accounts
- $ *Savings Accounts*
- $ Safe Deposit Boxes
- $ Loans
- $ Investment Services
- $ And lots more…let's just go to your computer and log on to see what else they offer! *Bank Jr.* brings us up-to-date!

"Banking" Long Ago... The Way It Used To Be...

The ATM told Mr. Money that the Money Family should learn about the way people long ago used to barter for the things they wanted.

Help the Money Family research the way people traded before there was paper money. Then make a timeline of the changes in trade including when money was first in use.

Progress to the current day noting the technology that helped improve banking services.

On your timeline, mark the dates and the big changes that have taken place. Use the timeline maker your teacher will show you or ask your teacher for posterboard or butcher paper to make your timeline.

The Money Family wants to learn about how banking has changed. They really need your help!

Student and Teacher Name Here

History of Banking

Add a title for your timeline here

Insert Picture Insert Picture Insert Picture Insert Picture Insert Picture Insert Picture Insert Picture Insert Picture Insert Picture Insert Picture

Event 1 Event 2 Event 3 Event 4 Event 5 Event 6 Event 7 Event 8 Event 9 Event 10

| 1st Date | 2nd Date | 3rd Date | 4th Date | 5th Date | 6th Date | 7th Date | 8th Date | 9th Date | 10th Date |

Description of Event (×10)

How Money and Banking Services Have Changed Over Time

Directions

- Meet with your assigned group to plan your writing project
- Together with your group members, one report will be written
- Use the timelines for the changes in money and banking services to make an outline for your report
- Decide which details from each of your timelines to include
- Review the interviews to determine which examples would add to your report; be sure to tell who is being quoted in the report

- Assign roles to everyone in your group such as: composer, word processor, copy editor, illustrator, oral reporter
- Complete the written report and include video clips or PowerPoint presentation for your oral report to your classmates
- Evaluate the information from your report and determine the costs and benefits of the means of trade and banking services during the time period (past, present or future) your report reflects

Planning Guide

List the members of your group:

Composer _____   Word Processor _____

Copy Editor _____   Illustrator _____

Oral Reporter _____

Your group assignment (past, present or future) _____

From your individual timelines, make a final list of the means of trade used through your assigned time period. As you make your list, be sure to include dates (years) and decide on which ones to name in your report. Give the name of the goods used in trade or the name of the currency used. Include at least 6 in your report.

Means of Trade (commodity goods or money)   Date

_____   _____

_____   _____

_____   _____

_____   _____

_____   _____

_____   _____

From your individual interviews, make a list of the names of the person interviewed and list the person in your group who has the exact quote.

Person Interviewed   **Group Member**

_____   _____

_____   _____

_____   _____

_____   _____

_____   _____

_____   _____

List the Costs and Benefits of Trade during the time period assigned to your group.

Costs	**Benefits**

Instructional Steps
Procedure: Teacher Input

Whole Group Activities for Instructional Purposes: Use the PowerPoint presentation "Mr. Money and Money Matters," or print out transparencies to trace the history of trade from barter to banking. Be sure to ask probing questions of the students to make them think about how money helps us trade and how our banking system has evolved.

Class Discussion: use online blogs (high tech), small group discussions (no tech) about how banks have provided essential services for consumers historically, do so today, and will continue to do in the future. *High Tech:* View blogs on Smart Board and discuss or *No Tech:* Reporter from each group summarizes student responses to questions. Sample questions might include:

> *Identify how banks first served consumers.*
>
> *How do the services banks provide today compare to those 100 years ago or longer?*
>
> *Noting how banking has changed over time, what would you predict that banking services would include 10, 25 or even 50 years from now?*

Whether online blogging or in discussion group, each student should respond to each question and comment, add information to or pose a question to one other student response.

Segue to Student Activities: Use a book, article from MoneyWise, *The Kansas City Star*, or a Federal Reserve Bank videotape such as "Once Upon A Dime" to bring closure and challenge students to learn more about the important personal finance concept of banking services. Discussion of the importance of households and individuals being responsible financial planners and of how banks assist consumers in this role would be appropriate at this point. Stress *why* being informed and proactive will enhance their financial well being.

Student Activities

Research the history of banking and develop a timeline.

High Tech: formulate information and graphics for each time period and insert information into the Excel template or use the template as a guide to create your own Excel timeline (template provided).

Optional high tech opportunities:
- Create a timeline using PowerPoint action buttons to link to different years and information.
- Create digital video using Windows Movie Maker, digital images, and a narrated audio script to showcase the timeline.

- Use the Inspiration or Smart Ideas graphic organizer software program to create a timeline using images

Low Tech: Use a word processing program to print out clip art, photos and a typed timeline to assemble and use on paper. A sample timeline which begins in the year 1600 can be seen at: http://www.pbs.org/opb/electricmoney/before_computers/timeline/page1.htm. Student research should document earlier times but this is one example to review. See Student Handout #1 for directions and scoring guide.

Interview three age groups to determine the banking services used in each generation. Examples could include a grandparent or friend of the grandparent to document how banking was in their early years; a parent or family friend the same age as the parent to document banking in their lives as a young person; and peer interviews to see how youth use banking today. Report the findings using the highest level of tech available, such as video, PowerPoint with digital images, etc. See Student Handout #2 for Directions and Scoring Guide Hint: http://www.harvestofhistory.org/ there are directions and examples for how to make a video history… see the sample of a student-made video and how it works!

Using the history research and the interviews, describe in writing how banking has changed for consumers over the past 150 years. Participate in one of three groups: prepare a report on the way banking used to be, how banking is today or what banking will look like when you are an adult or for your own children in 20-30 years. See Student Handout #3 for Directions and Scoring Guide.

Assessment

Using the history research and the interviews, describe in writing how banking has changed for consumers over the past 150 years. Participate in one of three groups: prepare a report on the way banking used to be, how banking is today or what banking will look like when you are an adult or for your own children in 20-30 years. Each group will select a reporter to give an oral presentation to the class. See Student Handout #3 for Directions and Scoring Guide.

Changes in Banking Rubric

Student Name:

Criteria	Excellent-3	Average-2	Unsatisfactory-1	Total
Writing Conventions	Report has fewer than 3 errors in mechanics or grammar	Report has between 4-6 errors in mechanics or grammar	Report has more than 6 errors in mechanics or grammar.	
Report Content	Report gives rich detail for 6 changes in banking over the last 150 years, using specific examples from either the history research or the interviews	Report gives detail of the changes in banking over the last 150 years using at least 4 examples from the history research or the interviews.	Report gives little or no detail of the changes in banking over the last 150 years or gives no examples from either the history research or the interviews.	
Group Participation	Can give a very descriptive oral or written summary of the group's activities and your part in the report.	Can give a brief oral or written summary about the group's activities and your part in the report.	Cannot give oral or written summary of the group's activities or your part in the report.	
Oral Report	Report is well organized and gives logical sequence detail. Includes the group's conclusion after weighing the costs and benefits of this time period.	Report gives overview of the time period with some details. The cost/benefit analysis is included but group opinion is not clear.	Report is given with only 2-3 details. Cost/Benefit Analysis is incomplete.	

Student Enrichment

For extending student learning, try the Time Warp at http://www.bankjr.com/pground/lookingback/ to see what a dollar was worth at different times in history.

Use http://www.bankjr.com/pground/aroundworld/egypt.jsp to identify a country around the world, see its flag, currency, history, geography, learn about its economy and much more.

Money Trivia from ThinkQuest: http://library.thinkquest.org/J003358F/trivia.html

Including children's literature enriches any lesson. Here are three suggestions:

Tom Birdseye, *Tarantula Shoes*. New York: Holiday House, 1995.

Andrew Clements, *Lunch Money*. New York: Simon & Schuster Children's Publishing, 2005.

Neale S. Godfrey, *Neale S. Godfrey's Ultimate Kid's Money Book*. New York: Simon and Schuster, 1998.

Teaching Tips

See "History of Wampum" at http://www.wampumworks.com/history2.html. This site includes a timeline at the bottom of the page. Use this timeline to help the students understand the role wampum has played throughout history.

At http://www.pbs.org/opb/electricmoney/before_computers/what/page1.htm you will find a good overview of the definition of money. Be sure to click on the "Historical Monetary Units" icon on the bottom of the page. A smaller window will open to show examples of currency through the ages, including a Euro.

Technology Resources

HARDWARE
Computer, Video Camera (optional), Digital Camera, LCD projector

SOFTWARE
Microsoft Office, PowerPoint, Excel

Resources

Internet

http://www.econedlink.net

http://www.bankjr.com/pground/moneytech/ This site offers information on historical and current banking.

http://www.bankjr.com/classroom/eDoc.jsp?doc=atmsAndDebitCards.html This site offers information about ATM machines.

http://www.bankjr.com/classroom/eDoc.jsp?doc=howBanksWork.html This site explains how banks work.

http://www.pbs.org/opb/electricmoney/before_computers/what/page1.htm Addresses the question: what is money?

http://www.pbs.org/opb/electricmoney/teaching_guide/eMoney_Lesson_one.pdf Deals with "plastic" money (credit and debit cards).

Other Materials Needed

Poster paper or butcher paper for no-tech timelines
Expansion card for digital camera ▨

Littlest Laborers: One Hundred Years of Child Labor

8

Paula S. Marron and Diane Provvido

Fourth to Sixth Grades: U.S. History, Civics, and Global Studies

NCSS Thematic Strands
Ⓧ **CIVIC IDEALS AND PRACTICES**
Ⓧ **GLOBAL CONNECTIONS**

NCSS Performance Expectations
Ⓧ **CIVIC IDEALS AND PRACTICES**

    a. Examine the origins and continuing influence of key ideals of the democratic republican form of government, such as individual human dignity, liberty, justice, equality, and the rule of law.

    c. Locate, access, analyze, organize, and apply information about selected public issues—recognizing and explaining multiple points of view.

Ⓧ **GLOBAL CONNECTIONS**

    f. Demonstrate understanding of concerns, standards, issues, and conflicts related to universal human rights.

NETS-S National Educational Technology Standards for Students
4. Technology Communications Tools
5. Technology Research Tools

NETS-S Performance Indicators (Grades 6 – 8)
4. Technology Communications Tools
5. Technology Research Tools

    ✦ Design, develop, publish, and present products (e.g., web pages, videotapes) using technology resources that demonstrate and communicate curriculum concepts to audiences inside and outside the classroom.

Introduction

Participation in democracy requires an educated citizenry, and in today's world, with the onslaught of information that comes at citizens, it is essential to teach students to think critically and constructively about their world. If the aim is to develop active meaning-making citizens, then involving students in "doing social studies"[1] will support genuine interest as it promotes at-tention to societal aims. This unit outlines particular lessons that provide upper elementary grade students with technology research and communication tools. The unit intends to help students learn to access and process information resources and to communicate new ideas effectively with multiple audiences.

The twelve-session unit is divided into three sections: research and idea development; change over time for child labor practices; and presentation and communication through the use of technology. During the first segment, students construct theories about child labor during the early 1900s as they read and summarize important concepts from different types of documents and source materials. In the course of the second segment, students independently access reliable documents and sources from Internet sites as they investigate multiple accounts of child labor in today's world. Students grow ideas as they collaboratively summarize important concepts from the documents, drawing conclusions about how child labor practices changed over time. Finally, in the quest to communicate new understanding to audiences inside and outside the classroom, students use technology to design pertinent presentations to share new ways of thinking about their changing worldviews.

Objectives
The student will be able to:

1. Locate, gather, and evaluate primary and secondary source documents from a variety of research sources.
2. Accurately summarize important concepts, draw conclusions and construct interpretations by reading multiple accounts of the same event.
3. Use online research sources to design and create technological publications (using Windows Movie Maker or Microsoft PowerPoint), that provide a forum for them to communicate new ways of thinking for a variety of audiences.

Time
The twelve-session unit is divided into three sections: research and idea development; change over time for child labor

practices; and presentation and communication through the use of technology. Four forty-five minute sessions for the three consecutive weeks accommodate the unit.

There are many configurations for the timing of this unit. For upper grade classes using block scheduling, three ninety minute sessions (one for each segment) represent one possibility. Focusing the research by limiting the technology resources and product requirements may be one way for teachers to use this unit as a three day lesson. In some cases, teachers may choose to use two ninety minute class sessions in conjunction with one homework assignment. Given previous instruction at other times in the school year, any of the three stages may serve as homework. Again depending on students' prior knowledge, another variation may be to focus on just one of the three segments, e.g. research and idea development in two sixty minute sessions.

One caveat to consider: One major goal for this unit is to teach students how to learn. That said, repeated two-day assignments throughout the year using this structure might be one way to foster increasing independence.

Instructional Steps

The Industrial Revolution in America is the sixth unit in the fourth grade social studies curriculum, the last of the school year. At this time of the school year, students understand that research can be enormously thought-provoking. They have learned that "instead of just telling all they know, they can puzzle over questions that intrigue them" as they investigate "the surprise, the perplexity, the mystery…by integrating new information with old, book information with life experience, the ideas of others with their own ideas, abstract notions with concrete facts."[2] Although students understand that essential questions (big ideas) frame each unit, they also understand that focusing the inquiry allows them to develop ideas and grow significance. Given these assumptions, this unit begins with a sweeping understanding of what Joy Hakim calls the *Age of Extremes*,[3] and narrows into an exploration of the changes in the face of child labor during that last one hundred years.

The next section details the instructional steps for each of three stages in this unit. Generally, each begins with an overview lesson that immerses the students in the subject matter. Next, there are descriptions of specific lessons that aim to support students as they manipulate technology in a way that allows them to construct new theories. Each segment concludes with a lesson that shows how students use technology to record and/or communicate new thinking.

Segment #1: Research and Idea Development
(Week # 1 – four sessions)

BACKGROUND: Each workshop lasts 45 minutes, with 15 minutes for lesson, modeling, and student "try it," and 30 minutes for children's "doing history" (often collaboratively in small groups or in partnership).

DAY 1

Introduce the Industrial Revolution. Provide background historical context framed in the essential question: Why was industrialization a major turning point in our nation's history?

Read the preface of Joy Hakim's *A History of US: Age of Extremes*.[4] Teach students to build an interpretation by paying close attention to the exact words of the text. Summarize Hakim's ideas, using content details from her text and begin to build interpretations. Teach students that one way to build interpretations is by talking back to the text, first agreeing and then disagreeing with it. (15 minutes)

Students collaboratively examine key ideas from Lewis Hine's photographs, building interpretations. Expectations for guided note-taking include: key vocabulary, historical context, and cited sources. Provide students with handouts from *The History Place: Child Labor in America 1908-1912*.[5] Students may use Inspiration as an organizing tool for notes. Students share tentative interpretations, reflecting on them in a short free write. (30 minutes).

DAYS 2 / 3

Teach students how to develop clear, focused positions on child labor, integrating multiple sources. Using two different resources, the teacher models double entry notes that incorporate content details and reflections. Provide students with Bruce VanSledright's *Questions Historical Detectives Ask*[6] as one way to help them layer their thinking. (See Appendix A) (15 minutes)

Students locate and evaluate reliable documents, summarizing each of them as they refine initial interpretations. (Internet resources attached.) Students add details to original Inspiration web. (30 minutes).

Day 4

After presenting students with a visual model, ask students to collaboratively design, construct, and present Microsoft PowerPoint or Windows Movie Maker projects sharing one interpretation of America's child labor movement in the early 1900s. Given time constraints, limit the video to eight frames: three primary source documents (e.g. photographs) and three quotes, plus title page and credits (including cited sources).

Segment # 2: Change Over Time for Child Labor Practices

(Week # 2 — four sessions)

BACKGROUND: During the second phase of this unit, students repeat many of the steps from the first segment independently. Although teachers guide the process, the students will be expected to collaboratively explore reliable Internet sources, develop a position on early 21st century child labor, and communicate their interpretation via Microsoft PowerPoint or Windows Movie Maker.

Days 1-3

Introduce "Child Labor: the Situation," providing documentation and data from Free the Children.[7] Provide a list of acceptable resource sites. Students should create multiple folders in Microsoft Word that will hold the documents they collect. Remind students to: (1) cite sources; (2) summarize, using key vocabulary and historical context; and, (3) develop clear, focused positions on child labor, integrating these multiple sources.

Day 4

Students collaboratively design, construct, and make Microsoft PowerPoint or Windows Movie Maker presentations sharing one interpretation of child labor today. Given time constraints, limit the video to eight frames: three primary source documents (e.g. photographs) and three quotes, plus title page and credits (including cited sources).

Segment # 3: Presentation and Communication Through the Use of Technology

(Week# 3 — four sessions)

BACKGROUND: The final segment gives students an opportunity to explore their ideas about how the face of child labor changed over one hundred years. It also provides them with an opportunity to think globally and act responsibly.

Day 1

First, whole class discussion centers on student plans for designing and developing technological representations of their new thinking about the universal human rights issue of child labor. In small groups, students plan for publication, conveying revised ideas through the creation of a final publication using Microsoft PowerPoint or Windows Movie Maker. Finally, students investigate avenues of publication, such as Youth in Action Projects.[8]

Day 2-3

These sessions are marked by implementation and revision. Students design storyboards using photos/data gathered in previous segments, creating the desired timeline. Students edit clips, add transitions and effects, and import audio. Students write collaboratively to communicate their final narration, emphasizing the parallels between the graphic and textual representations of these two time periods.

Day 4

Publish new understandings communicating to audiences inside and outside the classroom. Based on previous rubrics, attach a self-assessment and reflection to the project.

Assessment

Teacher and students create a rubric that delineates the number and kind of documents, the number and kind of cited sources, and the visual graphic requirements. The rubric may be given at the end of each segment, with a self-assessment added to the final stage. An example of one possible rubric is attached. (See Appendix B)

Student Enrichment

Teachers may choose to have students investigate different aspects of America's Industrialization. Diana Cohn's children's book, *Si, Se Puede! Yes, We Can! Janitor's Strike in L.A.*[9] offers insights into issues of unions uniting for fair working conditions in 2001. Another avenue for enrichment is the addition of a component that addresses how the issues of child labor were resolved in America and why it is a predominantly global issue today.

Teaching Tips

1. Tutorials for Windows Movie Maker or any other appropriate tool can be found on different Internet sites. One possibility: http://www.microsoft.com/windowsxp/using/moviemaker/videos/create.mspx

2. The Toshiba document camera enlarges original document sources from the Internet or from trade books for whole class demonstrations.

Technology Resources

HARDWARE
Microsoft Windows XP, Home Edition

SOFTWARE
Microsoft PowerPoint; Windows Movie Maker; Inspiration Software, Inc. (www.inspiration.com/home.cfm)
Alternate technology production tool: Microsoft Publisher

Resources

INTERNET
Global March Against Child Labour http://globalmarch.org/index.php. The site documents the international protest march and provides information about the lives of child laborers, girl workers, education and child soldiers.
International Child Labor Program http://www.dol.gov/ILAB/media/reports/iclp/main.htm This group, created by Congressional mandate, has prepared several informative, downloadable reports.

PRINT
Russell Freedman, *Kids at Work: Lewis Hine and the Crusade against Child Labor*. New York: Clarion, 1994. 🔳

Appendix A: Bruce VanSledright's Questions Historical Detectives Ask

Questions Historical Detectives Ask To Solve the Mysteries of the Past

What happened here? How do I find out?

What evidence will tell me what happened?

DIG UP EVIDENCE

Where does the evidence come from?

How do I know where the evidence comes from?

CHECK SOURCES

How do I decide how trustworthy and reliable a piece of evidence is?

CHECK THE RELIABILITY OF THE SOURCES

How do I decide how important a piece of evidence is?

JUDGE THE IMPORTANCE OF EACH PIECE OF EVIDENCE

How do I use all the evidence to build an idea in my head about what happened?

BUILD AN IDEA OF WHAT HAPPENED

How do I use the evidence and this idea in my head to make a case for describing what happened?

MAKE AN ARGUMENT FOR WHAT HAPPENED

Littlest Laborers : One Hundred Years of Child Labor

Teacher Name: _____

Student Name: _____

CATEGORY	4	3	2	1
Organization	Content is well organized, using storyboards and timelines to support final production.	Uses storyboard and timelines to organize, but the overall organization of topics appears flawed.	Content is logically organized for the most part.	There was no clear or logical organizational structure, just lots of facts.
Content	Covers topic in-depth with details and examples. All content is accurate and uses appropriate primary and secondary sources. Purposeful use of key vocabulary is evident.	Includes essential knowledge about the topic. Most content is accurate. Key vocabulary is evident.	Includes essential information about the topic but there are 1-2 factual errors. Some use of key vocabulary.	Content is minimal OR there are several factual errors.
Use of Graphics / Audio Imports	All graphics and audio imports support theme/content. Font formats (e.g., color, bold, italic) have been carefully planned to enhance readability and content.	Graphics and audio imports generally support theme/content. Font formats have been carefully planned to enhance readability.	Graphics are attractive, but do not seem to support the theme/content. Font formatting may be a little hard to read.	Several graphics detract from the content. Font formatting makes it very difficult to read the material.
Integration of Technology	Technology enhances project as a research tool, a publishing tool, and a communication device.	Use of technology somewhat enhances project as research tool, publishing tool, and a communication device. Use of technology tools is uneven.	Technology is limited to using the computer as a research tool, a publishing tool, or a communication device.	No relationship between the use of technology and student learning is exhibited in the project.
Cooperation	Group delegates responsibility. The workload is divided and shared equally by all team members.	The workload is divided and shared fairly by all team members, though workloads may vary from person to person.	The workload was divided, but one person in the group is viewed as not doing his/her fair share of the work.	The workload was not divided OR several people in the group are viewed as not doing their fair share of the work.

Child Labor Then and Now

ALEXANDRA AVYAS

JUNE, 2005

"51 inches high… 48 cents a day"[10]   **"3 years old… 75 cents a day"** [11]

Notes

1. *Middle School* (Mahwah, NJ: Lawrence Erlbaum Associates, Publishers, 2001).

2. Lucy McCormick Calkins, *The Art of Teaching Writing* (Portsmouth, NH: Heinemann, 1994), 438.

3. Joy Hakim, *A History of US: An Age of Extremes* (New York: Oxford University Press, 1994).

4. Ibid., 9-12.

5. History Place: Child Labor in America 1908 – 1912, "The Photographs of Lewis W. Hine" (1998), www.historyplace.com/unitedstates/childlabor.

6. Bruce VanSledright, *In Search of America's Past: Learning to Read History in Elementary School* (New York: Teachers College Press, 2002), 40.

7. Kids Can Free the Children, "Child Labor: The Situation"(2005), www.freethechildren.org.

8. Ibid., "Youth in Action."

9. Diana Cohn, *Si, Se Puede! Yes, We Can! Janitor's Strike in L.A.* (El Paso, Texas, Cinco Puntas Press, 2002).

10. History Place: Child Labor in America 1908 – 1912, "The Photographs of Lewis W. Hine" (1998), www.historyplace.com/unitedstates/childlabor

11. Sydney H. Schanberg, "On the Playgrounds of America, Every Kid's Every Kid's Goal is to Score: In Pakistan Where Children Stitch Soccer Balls for Six Cents an Hour, the Goal is to Survive." *Life* (June 1996): 41.

Standard of Living Around the World: From Analysis to Action

ANDREA S. LIBRESCO AND KAREN PHUA

FIFTH AND SIXTH GRADES: ECONOMICS AND CIVICS

"To know is to care; to care is to act; to act is to make a difference." — Harry Chapin

NCSS Thematic Strands
Ⓧ GLOBAL CONNECTIONS
Ⓧ CIVIC IDEALS AND PRACTICES

NCSS Performance Expectations
Ⓧ GLOBAL CONNECTIONS

d. Explore the causes, consequences, and possible solutions to persistent, contemporary, and emerging global issues, such as health, security, resource allocation, economic development, and environmental quality.

Ⓧ CIVIC IDEALS AND PRACTICES

j. Examine strategies designed to strengthen the "common good," which consider a range of options for citizen action.

NETS-S National Educational Technology Standards for Students

4. Technology Communication Tools
5. Technology Research Tools

NETS-S Performance Indicators (Grades 6-8)

4. Technology Communication Tools
5. Technology Research Tools
+ Design, develop, publish, and present products (e.g., Web pages, videotapes) using technology resources that demonstrate and communicate curriculum concepts to audiences inside and outside the classroom.
+ Collaborate with peers, experts, and others using telecommunications and collaborative tools to investigate curriculum-related problems, issues, and information, and to develop solutions or products for audiences inside and outside the classroom.

Introduction

The lesson comes near the beginning of the year in grades 5 and 6, where students look at the geography, political systems, economics, technology and culture of the Western and Eastern Hemispheres. The essential questions guiding this opening unit are: What are the important geographic, political, economic, technological and social-cultural issues affecting the hemisphere today? How well are these issues being addressed? This lesson begins by asking students what factors would be most important in deciding where to live. From this discussion, students derive many of the categories that make up a standard of living. Students then use a variety of websites and children's books to compare and contrast different indices of standards of living among a variety of countries. Groups of students pick different statistics and use the spreadsheet and graphing interactive tools on the websites to organize and display their information. Students analyze their findings, discovering which countries have the highest and lowest standards of living and explain how they arrived at these judgments. Discussion of what the students, themselves, can do to improve the lives of people, especially children, in countries with low standards of living follows, based on research on the Internet and other print sources. The class selects one or more action projects where students work on the issues, perhaps with the organizations they have researched.

Objectives
Students will be able to:
1. Define, identify and describe factors that measure standard of living.
2. Analyze, graph, and evaluate standard of living data for different countries from varied research sources.
3. Locate, gather, and evaluate data on the actions by different people and organizations to raise the standard of living for the world's children.

4. Discuss strategies for and take action on raising the standard of living for the world's children.

Time

2 weeks of 40 minute class periods.

Instructional Steps

1. Ask students what factors they would consider important when choosing a country in which to live. Students should be able to derive most of the ideas, if not the terms, on the standard of living vocabulary sheet. Then pass out the vocabulary sheet and elicit formal definitions. Students may also create a symbol for each term; e.g., an open book to represent the literacy rate. Terms on the sheet may include but are not limited to: population density, life expectancy, literacy, GDP, school enrollment, population living below the poverty line, infant mortality, access to clean water, and/or population under age 15. (1 class period)

2. The teacher should introduce students to the UN Cyberschoolbus web site[1] to model how to locate, research and graph data on the standard of living of different countries. The site is set up so that students can select up to six countries, and six different statistics (statistics are grouped into five categories for easy reference—population, economy, technology, health, and environment). Students should be given time to explore the site, its statistics, and its graphing opportunities, and then make recommendations as to which statistics should be compared. Ultimately, the teachers should select the six countries that students will research. It is recommended that teachers select countries across the economic and geographic spectrum. In addition, there is a logic in selecting a country that has a higher standard of living than the United States to give students perspective. It also makes sense to select at least one country in the news. (2 class periods)

3. Pairs or groups of students (depending on access to technology) will then be given different statistics to gather and compare data for the six countries selected. Students will share their findings with the class, analyzing and evaluating the countries' standard of living based on their particular statistics. Students' statistical findings may be collected in a class spreadsheet so that students can evaluate and rank the countries' standards of living based on all of the groups' data. (2 class periods)

4. After students have been exposed to the low standard of living of some of the countries in the world, students can explore what they can do to make a difference. The teacher can share a list of web sites with students, including UNICEF,[2] Heifer International,[3] Oxfam International,[4] and Free the Children.[5] Students can explore the mission and programs of these organizations, and then decide what projects to undertake. The project will be the assessment for the lesson. (2 periods)

Assessment

Groups of students will design a fund-raising project for the organization that they think best addresses the standard of living issues they have researched. The project will include the creation of:

+ Easy-to-understand data sheets about the standard of living that will explain to those whom they solicit the nature of the low standard of living of some countries in the world.
+ Handouts about the organization to which they are donating.
+ Fact sheets about how the money they raise will be spent.
+ A poster or PowerPoint presentation with pictures, statistics and language, illustrating the connection between raising money and raising the standard of living.

The fundraising project will be judged by the quality of students':

+ Explanations of their selection of statistics to illustrate the standard of living.
+ Data on the organization they are supporting.
+ Ability to establish a clear connection between fundraising for this organization and raising the standard of living.
+ Passionate persuasion evident in their projects.

Student Enrichment

RESEARCHING OTHER STATISTICS

1. Students who wish to do further research may revisit the standard of living statistics, breaking them down and graphing them by gender. One resource is the GenderStats[6] web site.

2. Students may wish to supplement statistics on the Cyberschoolbus site with data from other sources. The Human Development Report put out by the UN Development Programme[7] is an excellent web site for this purpose, as is the UNICEF Information by Country[8] site.

Student Voices

Which country has the higher standard of living – Japan or Sweden?

Country	Population Density	Literacy Rate	Per Capita GDP	% Population Under 15	Life Expectancy
Japan	873	99%	$28,200	14%	81
Sweden	52	99%	$26,800	18%	80

Michelle: I think it's Japan because the average person has more money to spend each year and they live longer. Both [countries] have good literacy rates.

Ben: Yeah but it's so crowded there. That's not good.

Michelle: How do you know that 873 people per square mile is crowded? Maybe that's not so bad. Look at the numbers for Bangladesh. 2542 people per square mile—that seems a lot more crowded to me.

Maria: Maybe we can compare it to the United States to see if the population density seems high. We know what the United States feels like. In the US, it's 79 people per square mile and we have some pretty crowded cities so that makes me think that 873 is a pretty high number. I agree with Ben, Japan seems very crowded.

Michelle: Okay but isn't the problem with too many people that you have disease? That can't be the problem here [in Japan] 'cause they're living longer. I think that's important.

Matan: But it's only one year longer. That's not much.

Ben: Yeah but maybe one year is a lot when you're old.

Maria: What about the number of kids? Japan has 'less' kids compared to the adults so they don't have to spend so much money on their children.

Michelle: Right. That's another reason why I think Japan is higher [standard of living].

Ben: But maybe you can have too little kids.

Michelle: No, no, no you always want the percent of kids to be small 'cause kids cost a lot and don't make any money for your economy.

Ben: But if it's [the percentage of the population under 15] too small, who's "gonna" make the money in the next generation?

[Silence as the group thinks about this idea.]

Maria: That makes sense. I think I agree with Ben. Sweden is better.

Matan: Me too. I think Sweden too. They live longer, it's less crowded and they have a 'good number' of kids. It's not too high, but there are kids to grow up and work in the future. Hey, can't we just look at the HDI?

[Time called. Discussion ends.]

ANALYZING STANDARD OF LIVING STATISTICS PERTAINING
TO CHILDREN WITH RESPECT TO THE CONVENTION ON THE
RIGHTS OF THE CHILD

3. Using the Cyberschoolbus and UN Development Programme data, students can separate out the standard of living statistics that pertain particularly to children and compare this data to the relevant articles in the U.N. Convention on the Rights of the Child[9] (or its summary[10]) to see the extent to which children's rights are being protected or violated.

VISUALIZING THE DATA IN HUMAN TERMS

4. *Material World: A Global Family Portrait*,[11] which looks at the material possessions of families throughout the world, may help make the statistics visual for students. The people pictured have been determined "average" for their countries and have agreed to have photographers move the contents of their houses outside in order to create visible representations of their relative standards of living. The dirt house and few possessions of Mali residents contrast with the four cars, forty-five-foot sofa, and twelve oriental carpets lined up outside the luxury home of a family from Kuwait. Each chapter includes the original spread of possessions, statistics about each family and country, as well as further pictures of daily life and some observations by the photographer.

5. *Beatrice's Goat*,[12] which tells the story of an impoverished family in Uganda that begins to flourish after receiving a special gift of a goat, may be a vehicle to get students involved on a more emotional level. The goat provides the family with sweet milk to enjoy and sell and a pair of kids that will eventually be sold as well. With the goat's bounty, the family soon has enough money to send Beatrice to school. The tale demonstrates the positive ripple effect of the efforts of one organization, Heifer International, a nonprofit group working to end global hunger by providing livestock and training to people in need.

6. Another source that connects statistics with people is *A Life Like Mine: How Children Live Around the World*.[13] This book explores what life is like for children around the world, focusing on four main topics: survival, development, protection and participation. Each topic begins with a definition of the word and basic ideas under those; e.g., the subtopics under survival are water, food, home, and health. The statistics for each subtopic are followed by the stories of real children's survival in a few different places.

USING TECHNOLOGY TO STAY CONNECTED TO DONORS

7. Students may elect to keep an email list of those who donate, and then continue to keep them apprised by sending updates of how the money they contributed was used and the difference it made.

Teaching Tips

1. The teacher may wish to introduce students to the UN Human Development Index[14] (HDI) that measures poverty, literacy, life expectancy and other factors. It is a standard means of measuring well-being, especially child welfare. More specifically, the HDI measures the average achievements in a country in three basic dimensions of human development: a long healthy life as measured by life expectancy at birth; knowledge, as measured by the adult literacy rate (with two-thirds weight) and the combined primary, secondary and tertiary gross enrollment ratio (with one-third weight); and a decent standard of living, as measured by GDP per capita.

2. If students have difficulty with the concept of percent, the book, *If the World Were a Village*[15] may prove helpful, as it compresses the 6.2 billion people in the world down to a more understandable figure, 100 persons, and offers data on such topics as nationalities, languages, ages, religions, education, and access to water and electricity, as represented in a condensed global village. Surprising statistics follow; for example, many kids in the United States take computers for granted, but only seven people in the global village own one.

Technology Resources

HARDWARE
Computer and projector, projection screen

SOFTWARE
Spreadsheet program

Internet

United Nations Cyberschoolbus, "Infonation Global Teaching and Learning Project" (NY: United Nations, 2002). http://www.un.org/Pubs/CyberSchoolBus/infonation3/menu/advanced.asp.

UNICEF, "Home" (NY: UNICEF). http://www.unicef.org/.

Heifer International (Little Rock, Arkansas: Heifer Project International). http://www.heifer.org/.

Oxfam International (New York: Oxfam International, 2005). http://www.oxfam.org/eng/.

Kids Can Free the Children (Toronto, Ontario: Free the Children, 2005). http://www.freethechildren.org/.

GenderStats Database of Gender Statistics (Washington, D.C.: The World Bank, 2002). http://devdata.worldbank.org/genderstats/.

Human Development Reports (New York: United Nations Development Programme, 2005). http://hdr.undp.org/statistics/data/.

UNICEF, "Information by Country" (NY: UNICEF). http://www.unicef.org/infobycountry/.

UNICEF, "Convention on the Rights of the Child" (NY: UNICEF). http://www.unicef.org/crc/fulltext.htm.

Children's Rights, "Convention on the Rights of the Child: Unofficial Summary of Main Provisions of the Convention" (New York: Amnesty International, 2005). http://www.amnestyusa.org/children/crn_summary.html.

Human Development Reports "FAQ on HDR Statistics" (New York: United Nations Development Programme, 2005). http://hdr.undp.org/statistics/faq/#21.

PRINT

Peter Menzel, Charles C. Mann, and Paul Kennedy, *Material World: A Global Family Portrait* (San Francisco: Sierra Club Books, 1995).

Page McBrier, *Beatrice's Goat* (New York: Atheneum, 2001).

Jemima Khan, *A Life Like Mine: How Children Live Around the World* (New York: Penguin Books Ltd., 2003).

David J. Smith, *If the World Were a Village* (Tonawanda, New York: Kids Can Press, 2002).

Part 2
For Middle
Schools

Daily Life in Ancient Rome

10

Lynne Kirby, Kati Linn and George Lipscomb

Sixth Grade: World Cultures and World History

NCSS Thematic Strands

❶ CULTURE

❿ TIME, CONTINUITY, AND CHANGE

NCSS Performance Expectations

❶ CULTURE

d. Explain why individuals and groups respond differently to their physical and social environments and/or changes to them on the basis of shared assumptions, values, and beliefs.

❿ TIME, CONTINUITY, AND CHANGE

d. Identify and use processes important to reconstructing and reinterpreting the past, such as using a variety of sources, providing, validating, and weighing evidence for claims, checking credibility of sources, and searching for causality.

f. Use knowledge of facts and concepts drawn from history, along with methods of historical inquiry, to inform decision making about and action-taking on public issues.

NETS-S National Educational Technology Standards for Students

3. Technology Productivity Tools
5. Technology Research Tools

NETS-S Performance Indicators (Grades 6-8)

3. Technology Productivity Tools
5. Technology Research Tools
   + Use content-specific tools, software, and simulations (e.g., environmental probes, graphing calculators, exploratory environments, Web tools) to support learning and research.

3. Technology Productivity Tools
   + Apply productivity/multimedia tools and peripherals to support personal productivity, group collaboration, and learning throughout the curriculum.

Introduction

In this lesson, students will gather information about life for various groups in ancient Roman society. The lesson begins with an internet scavenger hunt where students research daily activities as members of various social classes in Rome. Students will then write journal entries to describe their daily life and compile the entries into booklets. Internet research is used next as students create questions regarding Roman society. Collaborative groups will present these questions and answer them in a whole-class setting. A computer simulation culminates the lesson as students take on the role of a Roman emperor.

Objectives

The student will be able to:

+ Describe characteristics of life in ancient Rome
+ Compare and contrast living conditions among different groups in Roman society
+ Research and analyze the role of the emperor in Roman civilization

Time

Four to five 1 hour sessions

Instructional Steps

1. Students will complete an introductory activity, "If I Were a Roman..." (see activity sheet) using the following website: http://rome.mrdonn.org/empire.html. Students will choose a social class and discover various aspects of daily life in that social class. Responses are recorded on a summary sheet.

2. Students will use the "If I Were a Roman" activity sheet on page 60 to construct a journal entry chronicling the daily life of a Roman citizen. The students will be able to choose the gender, age, and social class of the citizen they write about. The entries should include the daily activities of their chosen citizen, including the activities that the citizen participates in for entertainment. Creativity is encouraged while preserving the historical accuracy of the information.

3. The students will take their research a step further by

creating "I wonder" questions for further research. Each student should list several questions that he or she would like answered about the Roman society. The student should research several of his or her "I wonder" questions. The source of the student research should be documented by the student.

4. The students will be placed in groups of three to create PowerPoint presentations of their "I wonder" questions. The teams of three will work together to select the most interesting questions and answers from each student's research. Once the group has selected the best questions, they will work together to create the PowerPoint presentation to present their research to the rest of the class. The presentations should include examples of each member's research and work. Students will be graded according to the rubric for the PowerPoint presentation (see p. 62)

5. Students will participate in a computer simulation entitled "Emperor of Rome," found at http://www.pbs.org/empires/romans/special/emperor_game.html. Working through this interactive game, students will take the role of Emperor Tiberius and make decisions regarding the progress of the empire. Students will evaluate the effectiveness of their leadership with a concluding assignment (see the activity sheet "Emperor of Rome," p. 61).

Assessment

See the rubrics on p. 62 for the historical journal entry for the PowerPoint presentation.

Student Enrichment

+ Create a comic book depicting daily life in Ancient Rome based upon new learning about Roman social classes.
+ Create a board game about the expansion of the Roman Empire using knowledge gained from lesson activities and additional student research.

Teaching Tips

+ Prior to using these lessons, provide vocabulary activities to build knowledge of Roman social class terminology.
+ Preview all websites before use to assure online connections and workability.
+ Model using the websites with the students to assist in navigating through the sites and assignments.
+ For the "I Wonder" activity, ensure that at least one group member is knowledgeable in basic PowerPoint application.

+ Select websites and print sources for students to research their "I wonder" questions, ensuring that the students find accurate information.
+ Complete assignments in pairs or individually.
+ Additional suggestions for using computer simulations in the classroom can be found in these resources:

Bennett, Linda and Jonathan Pye, "Usage of instructional technology in teaching middle school social studies," *Meridian: A Middle School Computer Technologies Journal* 6, no. 1 (2003), http://www.ncsu.edu/meridian/win2003/instruct_tech/ (12 January 2006).

Grabe, Mark and Cindy Grabe, "Categories of Instructional Software," in *Integrating Technology for Meaningful Learning* (New York: Houghton Mifflin Company, 2004), 133-146.

Resources

INTERNET

PBS, The Roman Empire in the First Century, July 2001, http://www.pbs.org/empires/romans/special/emperor_game.html (October 23, 2006).

Don Donn, "Daily Life in Ancient Rome," http://rome.mrdonn.org/empire.html (October 23, 2006).

PRINT

Activity Sheets: "If I Were a Roman..." and "Emperor of Rome"

Student Voices

Students enjoyed the activities in this lesson while increasing their knowledge on Roman social classes. Responses from students included:

"If I were a Roman..." gave me ideas about their life. It helped me picture how a child would live in ancient Rome. I think their food for breakfast was very weird — not something we would eat today!" — *Jeanne A.*

"It helped me learn about the foods that people ate and how the upper class lived. I learned that it was really hard to be an emperor of an empire." — *Matt P.*

"In the computer simulation, I learned that rulers made all the decisions and that there were positives and negatives from the decisions. Being an emperor is harder than it would seem." — *Daniel C.*

"If I Were a Roman…"

What was it like to live during the days of the ancient Romans? Would life be very different than it is now? Find out as you experience a day in the life of ancient Rome.

You may choose whom to be in Roman society. Mark your selection for A, B, and C below:

A.	_____ Patrician	*or*	_____ Plebeian
B.	_____ Male	*or*	_____ Female
C.	_____ Adult	*or*	_____ Child

Use the website given to learn about your life as a Roman. Write your findings below in complete sentences. Enjoy your day!

Breakfast:

_____

_____

Clothing:

_____

_____

Shopping (For Adult) Or Schools (For Child):

_____

_____

Roman Baths (Adult):

_____

_____

Lunch:

_____

_____

Housing:

_____

_____

Religion:

_____

_____

Toys And Pets (Child):

_____

_____

Dinner:

_____

_____

Entertainment
Colosseum:

_____

_____

Circus Maximus:

_____

_____

Field and Track:

_____

_____

"Emperor of Rome"

(PBS computer simulation; see http://www.pbs.org/empires/romans/special/emperor_game.html*)*

After completing the simulation on "Emperor of Rome," answer the following:

1. Mark the outcome of your simulation:
   - ☐ Tiberius Deified   ☐ Fate Tarnishes Tiberius
   - ☐ Tiberius Successful   ☐ Fate Finishes Tiberius
   - ☐ Mixed Blessing

2. What would your outcome mean for the Roman Empire?

3. What kind of decisions did you have to make as emperor?

4. What factors made being an emperor a difficult task?

5. How does this simulation help you better understand the role of emperors in the Roman Empire?

6. After completing the simulation, what characteristics do you think make a good leader?

Rubric 1: Historical Journal Entry Assessment

	Student Score
KNOWLEDGE AND UNDERSTANDING: The student demonstrates an understanding of the time period, uses historical terms correctly, and places the events in proper sequence.	40 points
RESEARCH: The student uses research to support the fictional entry, and the entry is historically accurate.	40 points
SKILLS: The entry is clearly organized and sequenced; it is free of grammatical and spelling errors, and is a work of high quality.	20 points
Total:	100 points

Rubric 2: PowerPoint Rubric

The project must include the following:

TITLE SLIDE (10 points)
a. Name of presentation
b. List of group members

TWO SLIDES PER STUDENT (six slides – 15 points per slide)
a. One slide states an "I Wonder" question
b. Second slide answers question (pictures may be included).
c. Factual, accurate information
d. Appropriate slide mechanics (background, transitions, animations, etc)

GROUP MEMBERS
_____
_____
_____
_____
_____

Slide Number	Type	Student responsible	Points
1	_____	_____	_____
2	_____	_____	_____
3	_____	_____	_____
4	_____	_____	_____
5	_____	_____	_____
6	_____	_____	_____
		Total	_____

Geography Sleuths: Using Primary Documents to Develop Critical Thinking Skills

Elaine M. Lawrence and Megan Tweedie

Sixth to Eighth Grades: U.S. History, Geography, and Economics

NCSS Thematic Strands
Ⅲ PEOPLE, PLACES, AND ENVIRONMENTS
Ⅶ PRODUCTION, DISTRIBUTION, AND CONSUMPTION

NCSS Performance Expectations
Ⅲ PEOPLE, PLACES, AND ENVIRONMENTS

h.   Examine, interpret, and analyze physical and cultural patterns and their interactions, such as land use, settlement patterns, cultural transmission of customs and ideas, and ecosystem changes.

k.   Propose, compare, and evaluate alternative uses of land and resources in communities, regions, nations, and the world.

Ⅶ PRODUCTION, DISTRIBUTION, AND CONSUMPTION

i.   Use economic concepts to help explain historical and current developments and issues in local, national, or global contexts.

NETS-S National Educational Technology Standards for Students
3. Technology Productivity Tools
5. Technology Research Tools

NETS-S Performance Indicators (Grades 6-8)
3. Technology Productivity Tools
5. Technology Research Tools

+   Use content-specific tools, software, and simulations (e.g., environmental probes, graphing calculators, exploratory environments, Web tools) to support learning and research.

3. Technology Productivity Tools

+   Apply productivity/multimedia tools and peripherals to support personal productivity, group collaboration, and learning throughout the curriculum.

5. Technology Research Tools

+   Select and use appropriate tools and technology resources to accomplish a variety of tasks and solve problems.

Introduction
This lesson requires students to utilize maps found in local, state, and national historical collections; their knowledge of social studies; critical thinking skills; and group collaboration to develop a solution to aid the growth and development of a region. Students will analyze regional maps of a given time period and generate a trade route and explanation of why it is the most ideal. They will use concept mapping to develop connections between: needs and resources, technology and geography, and ramifications of the project. Students will develop a written proposal for the trade route. The report will include a graphic organizer with the connections mentioned above. Students will then conduct an analysis of the growth and development of the actual route utilizing regional maps from various time periods. To culminate the lesson, students will present their proposal, economic and environmental considerations, and the growth and development analysis of the actual route. The students are to develop and include a comparison of their proposal to the actual route. This lesson is adaptable for high school grades and a variety of American and World History topics.

Objectives
The student will be able to:

1.   Analyze maps found in local, state, and national historical collections to develop a proposal for a new trade route.

2.   Analyze maps found in local, state, and national historical collections to develop hypotheses about the growth and development of a region.

3.   Predict possible economic and environmental ramifications of the proposed trade route.

4.   Assess regional growth and development by comparing maps from different time periods.

Time

Four 1-hour sessions (modified version: two or three 1-hour sessions).

Instructional Steps

SESSION 1: The instructor selects a region and initial time period (for example New York State during the late 1700s and early 1800s). Students will be divided into groups of three. Students are then presented with a challenge:

> SAMPLE CHALLENGE:
> The State of (New York) is interested in developing its economy. You have been hired by the governor to map an east-west trade route to allow for optimal flow of goods within the state. Plot what you believe to be the best course/route. Be sure to consider how this will enhance the region's growth and development.

Each group will be given access to the same map (for example, search the Library of Congress website for Emanuel Bowen's 1747 topographic map at http://memory.loc.gov/) to begin the task, and a list of websites and other resources (Table 1) will be provided to locate other maps. Each group will begin by completing a K-W-L chart describing what they know and what they want to find out about the time period and location. Groups will then divide up research tasks: needs and resources of the time, environmental issues, transportation technology of the time period. The remainder of the session will be spent researching (using the internet and/or library) the answers to the tasks listed above. Timeframe for session: 10 minutes to create groups, introduce the challenge, and distribute handouts; 10 minutes to generate K-W-L charts; 10 minutes to divide the research tasks; and 30 minutes to begin the research (timeframes can be reduced by having students do segments as homework task).

Figure 1: Sample Graphic Organizer

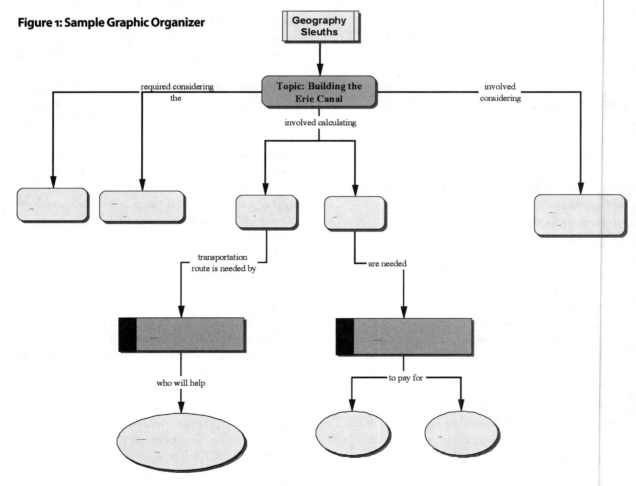

SESSION 2: This session is best conducted in a computer lab but can be adapted by using paper and pen for some aspects. Based on the research the groups will utilize Inspiration software (or drawing tools in a paint or word processing application), to generate a concept map (visual depiction) to demonstrate connections between: needs and resources, technology and geography, and possible ramifications of the project (see Figure 1 for a sample organizer). Utilizing the concept maps, students will design a route proposal on the scanned or downloaded map utilized in session 1 (the route can be created using a basic paint or draw application. If these are not available, groups could draw on a printed map.) Students will develop a written proposal for the trade route during the time period. The report will include a graphic organizer with the connections mentioned above as well as a graphic depiction of the route. The group report is to be submitted to the teacher at the end of class. Timeframe for session: 15 minutes to generate a graphic organizer; 10 minutes to draw the route on the map; 5 minutes to adapt the route if needed; 30 minutes to type up the proposal (the teacher may want to create a template to expedite this portion).

SESSION 3: During this session students will conduct an analysis of actual growth and development utilizing regional maps from various time periods. Students will need access to a library and/or computer lab to retrieve maps, census data, and/or almanacs from varying intervals of time regarding the region (teachers should prepare a list of sites to expedite this search and to reduce frustration). Students will research the impact of the actual route (locate an 1825 Erie Canal map and profile at http://www.eriecanal.org/maps.html for an example) by analyzing data from intervals of about 75 years. For this example, the intervals would coincide with the late 1800s, mid-twentieth century, and today (resources listed in Table 1 would be useful). Groups could divide the tasks by time intervals or data type (geography/environment, population, and/or industrial growth). The homework task will be for the groups to generate a presentation that includes the comparison of their proposed route versus the actual one. Timeframe for this session: 10 minutes for the group to divide up the tasks; 40 minutes to begin research; 10 minutes to divide up the group presentation tasks. The teacher may want to determine how many students have computer access at home before assigning this as homework. If many students do not have computer access, then class time can be reserved to complete the presentation.

SESSION 4: Students will conduct an oral presentation that includes their proposal, economic and environmental considerations, and the growth and development analysis of the actual route. They should include a comparison of their proposal to the actual route. Each group can conduct this individually with computerized projections, hard copy presentations, or by having stations set up around the room.

Assessment

Items to be evaluated for the route proposal portion could include: the completed K-W-L chart, the concept map, the map of the proposed route, and the written proposal (to include analysis of the needs and resources, environmental issues and the transportation technology of the time period, as well as grammar, spelling and citations). The presentation portion could include: the completed proposal, economic considerations, environmental considerations, growth and development of the actual route (including intervals), comparison of the proposed route to the actual route, citations, organization of presentation and visuals (see the rubric for basic criteria).

Student Enrichment

Students interested in an additional challenge may want to research how local history played into the scheme of the larger state history picture regarding transportation. They could include this information in their presentation by comparing the past to the present in the local community. For example, locate a photo of where the railroad station was in town and what the building has been used for over the years (maybe it no longer exists). This would also be an excellent opportunity for students to work closely with members of the community or with the local historical association. Another option for exceptional students would be to create a 3-D representation of the proposed route. This process would be very similar to what architects and designers create to explain proposals to companies or to the public. Special needs students might have a classmate designated as a resource to help with the process.

Teaching Tips

The teacher may want to: (a) prepare templates for the paper and/or presentation for students to follow; (b) familiarize herself or himself with search tools in the websites supplied to students; (c) collaborate during planning with the computer lab staff, librarian, and local historical society; (d) add time if students are not familiar with Inspiration or the graphic organizer; and (e) provide students with guided notes to assist in navigating websites and finding needed information. An extension of the project might be to display the research and

Table 1: Geography Sleuth Resources

Name/Title	Location	Use
U.S. CENSUS BUREAU	http://www.census.gov	Click on American Fact Finder and then click on Population finder for updated information per location
U.S. CENSUS BUREAU POPULATION MAPS	http://www.census.gov/dmd/www/maps1790to2000.html http://fisher.lib.virginia.edu/collections/stats/histcensus/	Maps indicate city population growth per the 10 year census data. The years begin with 1790 and go to 2000 in intervals of 10.
LIBRARY OF CONGRESS (AMERICAN MEMORY SECTION)	http://lcweb2.loc.gov/ammem Features links for maps, expansion, landscape, etc.	Type keywords into search box. For example, "New York State" and "topography" will produce maps for use in the lesson.
STATE HISTORICAL ASSOCIATION	For example, New York's website is http://www.nysha.org State historical associations can help educators locate primary documents.	Resources such as census data for the state could be available. For example, students could look at the "occupation" listing over time intervals to make hypotheses about the impact of change.
STATE MUSEUM	For example, New York's website is http://www.nysm.nysed.gov	They can help educators locate primary documents.
TERRASERVER USA	Maps available for download, print, email. www.terraserverusa.com	Click on state of interest. User can zoom in on area of interest on the state map or by completing the search boxes in left-hand column.
ERIE CANAL MAPS	http://www.eriecanal.org/maps.html http://www.nyhistory.com/links/ Erie_Canal.htm	A collection of early and more modern maps.

analysis in public areas such as hallway bulletin boards or the library. Given the tasks involved, the sessions should not necessarily be conducted within four consecutive days. The three-session version has each group generate a paper as a homework task instead of conducting a presentation. The two-session version eliminates the creation of graphic organizers by the groups, the additional research into development over time and the presentations. Instead the teacher will provide period specific map and data handouts for students. Utilizing these handouts, the teacher will initiate a class discussion that will generate route proposals, and debate the viability of the proposals, as well as consider various changes over time of the actual route. To aid students with concept connections, a graphic organizer will result (visual depiction either on the blackboard or via electronic projection should occur as ideas develop) from this discussion.

Technology Resources

HARDWARE

Computers with internet access, projection device

SOFTWARE

A word processing application, a draw or paint application, Inspiration (optional), Encarta

Resources

INTERNET

Encarta Online. Resources include an atlas; an encyclopedia can be found at the Encarta website, http://encarta.msn.com.

The Library of Congress. Resources categorized by collection topics can be found at the Library of Congress website, http://memory.loc.gov/ammem/.

Table 2: Geography Sleuths Sample Route Proposal Rubric

Proposal Rubric	3 Points Contains no errors, inconsistencies, or inaccuracies.	2 Points Contains a few errors, inconsistencies, or inaccuracies.	1 Point Numerous errors, inconsistencies, or inaccuracies. Work may be incomplete.
K-W-L Chart			
Concept Map			
Map of Proposed Route			
Needs and Resources			
Environmental Issues			
Transportation and Technology of the Time			
Spelling/Grammar			
Works Cited			
Total per Column			
27			
Final Score			

TerraServer USA. A variety of recent national demographic and topographical datasets are available on the TerraServer USA website, http://www.terraserverusa.com. Click on the map to indicate the region.

PRINT

Textbooks and reference books such as almanacs and encyclopedias. Some texts have supplemental materials, such as blank maps, for use.

OTHER MATERIALS NEEDED

Contact information for local and/or state historical association. 🖾

References

Bowen, E. 1747. *A new and accurate map of New Jersey, Pensilvania, New York and New England, with the adjacent countries. Drawn from surveys, assisted by the most approved modern maps & charts and regulated by astronomical observations.* http://memory.loc.gov/.

The Erie Canal. 2005. 1825 Erie Canal map and profile. http://www.eriecanal.org/maps.html.

Why Did They Do It? What Were the Purposes of Lewis and Clark's Corps of Discovery Expedition?

Cynthia Szymanski Sunal, Dennis W. Sunal and Melinda Odom Stubbs

Sixth to Eighth Grades: U.S. History

NCSS Thematic Strands
- **II TIME, CONTINUITY, AND CHANGE**
- **III PEOPLE, PLACES, AND ENVIRONMENTS**
- **IV INDIVIDUAL DEVELOPMENT AND IDENTITY**

NCSS Performance Expectations

II TIME, CONTINUITY, AND CHANGE
a. Demonstrate an understanding that different scholars may describe the same event or situation in different ways but must provide reasons or evidence for their views.
b. Identify and use processes important to reconstructing and reinterpreting the past, such as using a variety of sources, providing, validating, and weighing evidence for claims, checking credibility of sources, and searching for causality.

III PEOPLE, PLACES, AND ENVIRONMENTS
h. Examine, interpret, and analyze physical and cultural patterns and their interactions, such as land use, settlement patterns, cultural transmission of customs and ideas, and ecosystem changes.

IV INDIVIDUAL DEVELOPMENT AND IDENTITY
c. Describe the ways family, gender, ethnicity, nationality, and institutional affiliations contribute to personal identity.

NETS-S National Educational Technology Standards for Students
3. Technology Productivity Tools
5. Technology Research Tools

NETS-S Performance Indicators (Grades 6-8)
3. Technology Productivity Tools
5. Technology Research Tools
   + Use content-specific tools, software, and simulations to support learning and research.

3. Technology Productivity Tools
   + Collaborate with peers, experts, and others using telecommunications and collaborative tools to investigate curriculum-related problems, issues, and information, and to develop solutions or products for audiences inside and outside the classroom.

Introduction
This lesson involves students in constructing hypotheses in response to an essential question about the purpose of Lewis and Clark's Corps of Discovery expedition. Then, the lesson involves students in data collection and interpretation through which they build an evidence base that indicates whether their initial hypotheses are supported. They are encouraged to revise their hypotheses as they work with the data. The final part of the lesson involves students in determining whether their hypothesis has wider applicability in new contexts. The lesson builds inquiry skills with a focus on the analysis of evidence. It uses content that focuses students on the stated and enacted purposes of an expedition that had a major impact on U.S. history.

Objectives
1. Students will identify the stated purposes of Lewis and Clark's Corps of Discovery expedition.
2. Students will identify the enacted purposes of Lewis and Clark's Corps of Discovery expedition using evidence from a variety of sources.
3. Students will identify changes in physical and cultural

patterns in the region of the Lewis and Clark expedition's trail since the time of the expedition.

4. Students will identify the relationship of the stated and enacted purposes of Lewis and Clark's Corps of Discovery expedition to those of another expedition of discovery.

Time

Four to five one-hour sessions.

Instructional Steps

This lesson uses a three-phase constructivist learning cycle format aimed at engaging students' prior knowledge, enabling them to reconstruct existing incomplete ideas and inquiry skills, and encouraging them to apply and expand the use of their new ideas and skills.

Exploratory Introduction Phase

1. Divide students into small cooperative groups and negotiate roles: manager, recorder, discussant, and observer. Show students a clip of the end of the Lewis and Clark expedition's trail near Astoria, Oregon across the Columbia River from Washington State. Ask groups to consider and respond to the essential question: Why did some well-known Americans go on a long trip of discovery that ended here? Possible sources for views of the trail's ending point are: Ft. Clatsop National Memorial, http://www.nps.gov/lewi/ and Cape Disappointment, Washington, http://www.nps.gov/lewi/historyculture/histcult-places-caped.htm. After groups have developed a response, have them share their initial hypotheses. Then, have students examine additional sources of evidence regarding the cloud rainforest and Columbia River in Oregon and Washington where the trail ended. Use sites such as: http://www.fs.fed.us/r6/centraloregon/about/photo-19540spanish.shtml (Spanish Peak); http://www.fs.fed.us/r6/centraloregon/about/photo-08232metolius.shtml (Metolius River); http://www.fs.fed.us/r6/centraloregon/about/photo-27961east.shtml (East Lake); and http://www.fs.fed.us/r6/centraloregon/about/photo-06428broken.shtml (Broken Top). Ask student groups to list clues (evidence) which they can use to further consider their hypotheses.

2. Have groups check their lists of clues against their initial responses to the essential question, deciding which clues do or do not support their hypotheses. Encourage revision of hypotheses as appropriate. Have groups post their consensus hypothesis and supporting evidence on a discussion board for others to consider.

Lesson Development Phase

1. Ask students to read the Letter from President Thomas Jefferson at http://www.nwrel.org/teachlewisandclark/jefferson.html. Guide their reading using the following three individual tasks:

(Task A) Identify the major purpose of the Lewis and Clark mission. Ask students, what overall perspectives and attitudes are expressed by Jefferson?

(Task B) List the sub-purposes of the expedition as identified by Jefferson. Ask students, how are the perspectives and attitudes commonly expressed by citizens of the U.S.A. today similar to, or different from, those of Jefferson?

(Task C) Reflect on the overall perspectives and attitudes that Jefferson is expressing. Note, some historians tell us it is difficult to really understand the past because you need to get into the context of the times: to think as people of that time thought, to know their values and aspirations. Ask students, does the letter from Thomas Jefferson support this view or not? Give evidence to support your response from the Letter from President Thomas Jefferson.

2. Ask students to share responses to the three tasks in number 1 with their group members and arrive at a consensus response, sharing it on the discussion board. Have students read and consider others' postings.

3. Ask student groups to assign each member one of the four sets of websites and related activities that follow below. Each member visits the selected set of websites, completes the activities associated with it, and shares results with other group members. Four suggested sets are identified as follows (others may be selected): (Set 1) Sites A, B, and C, (Set 2) Sites D, E, F, and G, (Set 3) Sites H, I, and J, and (Set 4) Sites K, L, and M.

GROUP MEMBER 1 – (SET 1) SITES A, B, AND C:

A. Colorful families – A roster of the Lewis & Clark expedition, http://www.rootsweb.com/~genepool/lewiclar.htm

B. Find a Grave – Charles Floyd, http://www.findagrave.com/pictures/2346.html

C. Find a Grave – Jean Baptiste Charbonneau, http://www.findagrave.com/pictures/3553.html

First. Examine Site A. Identify the caution given about the accuracy of the "true roster" of the Lewis and Clark expedition by the authors of the roster. Make a list of the types of information shown on the roster, such as date of birth. Identify the number of expedition members, the diversity of experiences they represented, and your ideas about why they might have been selected to be members of the expedition.

Second. Examine the information about Charles Floyd on Site B. Answer the questions, what is significant about Charles Floyd? Why would there be a monument honoring him?

Third. Examine the information about Jean Baptiste Charbonneau on Site C. Answer the questions, what is significant about him? Why doesn't Charbonneau appear on the Lewis and Clark expedition roster on Site A?

Fourth. Select three other expedition members and search for them using the "Find A Grave" website. Who did you choose? What was significant about each person you chose?

Fifth. Share your findings from these four activities with your group.

GROUP MEMBER TWO – (SET 2) SITES D, E, F, AND G

D. Lewis & Clark Trail History, http://www.nps.gov/lecl/VisitorInfo/pics/maps.htm
E. Trail Sites, http://www.nps.gov/lecl/
F. The Ethnography of Lewis and Clark, map page http://www.peabody.harvard.edu/Lewis_and_Clark/map.html
G. Fort Clatsop National Memorial, http://www.nps.gov/focl/index.htm

First. Create a timeline of the Lewis and Clark expedition using the brief information given on Site D: Lewis & Clark Trail History. Using the limited information you now have, answer the question, why do you think this expedition was given the name "Corps of Discovery"?

Second. Study the general route map of the Lewis and Clark National Historic Trail (Site E). Study the map found at Site F. Find a U.S.A. map on the Internet. Compare all three maps to develop an idea of the route in terms of what the U.S.A. looks like today. Respond to these questions: which states did the route pass through? Why did they use the rivers so much? Why did the route wander in some places? How might the route be different today?

Third. Select and identify two federal trail sites, other than Fort Clatsop, and one state or local site on the Internet. Create a list of types of information found at each site. Use the information on the website to describe why this location is considered a major trail site.

Fourth. Visit Site G and describe why this is an important place.

Fifth. Share your findings from these four activities with your group.

GROUP MEMBER THREE – (SET 3) SITES H AND I, AND J

H. Journal of Meriwether Lewis, http://www.pbs.org/lewisandclark/archive/journal-results.html?offset=1&corpall=all&lewis=lewis&dateall=all&year=1804&indmonth=12&indday=25&indyear=1805&r1month=03&r1day=3&r1year=1804&r2month=09&r2day=26&r2year=1806&numpage=10&x=29&y=7
I. Sacagawea (Sakakawea), a True American Heroine, http://www.idahoptv.org/lc/sacagawea/importance2.html
J. The Importance of "Old Toby", http://idptv.state.id.us/lc/oldtoby.html

First. Read the information at Site H and write a one or two sentence description of Lewis' personal characteristics and major role in the expedition.

Second. Read the information at Site I on Sacagawea (or Sakakawea). Write a one or 2 sentence description of her personal characteristics and major role in the expedition.

Third. Read about Toby on Site J. Write a one or two sentence description of his personal characteristics and major role in the expedition.

Fourth. Use your descriptions to create a chart that lists each person along the left side and gives the two categories along the top: Major Role and Personal Characteristics.

Expedition Member	Personal Characteristics	Major Role in the Expedition
Lewis		
Sacagawea (Sakakawea)		
Old Toby		

Fifth. What does the information at Sites H, I, and J tell you about the purpose of the expedition? What evidence from Sites H, I, and J supports your conclusions?

Sixth. Share your findings from these five activities with your group.

GROUP MEMBER FOUR – (SET 4) SITES K, L, AND M

K. Lewis and Clark Brought Along High-Tech Tools of the Time, http://www.pbs.org/lewisandclark/inside/idx_equ.html
L. The Beads of Lewis and Clark, http://www.thebeadsite.com/FRO-LaC.htm (at the website, click on site search engine and type in Lewis & Clark to find the beads)

M. Logging Plans Threaten Lewis and Clark Trail, http://www.wildrockies.org/awr/news/aa_lewis_and_clark.html

First. Read the information at Site K. Create a list of "the latest in technology" brought by Lewis and Clark on the expedition.

Second. Read the information at Site L. Develop a description of the types of beads brought by the Lewis and Clark expedition, their purpose(s), and how they might be considered "technology".

Third. Read the information at site M. Respond to the question: How has current technology had an effect on the ecosystems with which Lewis and Clark's expedition interacted?

Fourth. Share your findings from the three activities above with your group members.

5. Ask all groups to post a consensus of their findings on the discussion board. Have each group read other groups' postings.

6. Ask groups to reflect on, and then describe, how their findings provide information and insights related to the essential question: Why did some well-known Americans go on a long trip of discovery that ended here?

7. Ask groups to consider three secondary questions: (1) What impact did the technology of the time have on the expedition? (2) What impact has technology today had on the ecosystems with which the Lewis and Clark expedition interacted? (3) What impacts did the expedition have on local indigenous cultures along the trail? Have groups develop a consensus and post it on the discussion board.

4. Closure: After students have read other groups' postings, have a class discussion to arrive at a class consensus responding to the key question and three secondary questions and post it for all to utilize.

Expansion Phase

1. Now that students have investigated the Lewis and Clark Corps of Discovery expedition, its purposes, experiences, and effects, have them decide how similar the purpose of another expedition of discovery was to that of the Lewis and Clark expedition. Have groups select one of the following expeditions (others can be used): the Torvey Arctic expedition, http://www.accessexcellence.org/AE/mspot/arc/ep2/; Richard E. Byrd's Antarctic expedition, http://www.south-pole.com/p0000107.htm; Richard F. Scott's Antarctic expedition, http://www.south-pole.com/p0000089.htm; Samuel Champlain's northeastern North American expeditions, http://www.enchantedlearning.com/explorers/page/c/champlain.shtml and http://www.win.tue.nl/~engels/discovery/alpha/c.html#champlain; or Louis Agassiz Fuertes and the Harriman Alaska expedition, http://rmc.library.cornell.edu/Alaska/Default.html. Have students describe, as possible, the stated and enacted purposes and the physical and cultural effects of the selected expedition.

2. Lesson summary. Ask students to identify briefly the activities of this lesson and the main idea(s) investigated.

Assessment

Ask each student to complete the following two tasks:

Task 1. Construct and complete the following chart.

Expedition Purpose and Effects	Lewis & Clark's Corps of Discovery	Another selected expedition (identify)	Commonalities between the two expeditions
Stated Purpose			
Enacted Purpose			
Long term effects on the land in the region			
Long term effects on the culture			

Task 2. The U.S. government has announced that it will send an expedition to Mars. Using information from the chart in Task 1 above, what inferences can you make about the Mars expedition of discovery's likely:

(a) Stated purpose(s)

(b) Enacted purpose(s)

(c) Physical effects and

(d) Cultural effects?

(Resources: National Aeronautics and Space Administration [NASA] *Why Explore Mars?* http://nmp.jpl.nasa.gov/ds2/mission/why.html and *Mars Team Online* http://quest.arc.nasa.gov/mars/)

Rubric

1. Task one is completed appropriately: stated and enacted purposes are identified accurately, and appropriate and relevant long term effects on land and culture in the region are identified.

All parts of task 1 are appropriately completed, relevant, and accurate. **5 points**
Most parts of task 1 are appropriately completed, relevant, and accurate **3 points**
Most parts of task 1 are not appropriately completed, relevant, or accurate **1 point**

2. Task 2 inferences are appropriate and use appropriate and accurate evidence from the chart as support.

All parts of task 2 are appropriately completed, inferences appropriate to the evidence are used, and accurate evidence is used. **5 points**
Most parts of task 2 are appropriately completed, most inferences are appropriate to the evidence used, and accurate evidence is used. **3 points**
Most parts of task 2 are not appropriately completed, most inferences are not appropriate to the evidence used, and inaccurate evidence is used. **1 point**

Student Enrichment

1. Within recent memory, there have been several expeditions to the earth's moon that are voyages of discovery, and more are planned. Have students analyze their stated and enacted purposes, and physical and cultural effects using resources such as NASA's http://spaceplace.nasa.gov/en/kids/phonedrmarc/2003_december.shtml.

2. Have student groups develop, use, and critique a role play that includes both the explorer and the indigenous people in the place explored. The role play should consider the first impressions each has of the other. It also should consider the extent of interest in sharing ideas about how some ordinary tasks are done (e.g. planting crops, hunting a small animal, preparing and storing food for future use).

3. Ask students to electronically correspond with a school in a school system along the Lewis and Clark trail, investigating what the ecology and human culture of that part of the trail were like during the years of the expedition and how they have changed today. Students could examine digital photos of today's ecology, for example, and compare them to descriptions in the journals of Lewis and Clark.

Teaching Tips

Additional websites and expeditions for this lesson's Expansion phase can be identified by students as part of their activities.

Technology Resources:

HARDWARE

This lesson requires computers with Internet capability and with discussion board capability. An inexpensive digital camera will be useful.

SOFTWARE

The discussion board can be hosted on a school system's server or through building a webpage using one of the following free or inexpensive sites: Teach-nology, http://www.teach-nology.com/; Teacher Web, http://teacherweb.com/ and http://worknotes.com/; GeoCities, http://geocities.yahoo.com; Netfirms, http://www.netfirms.com; Scholastic, www.scholastic.com; and Freewebs, http://www.freewebs.com. Two useful software programs are Web Studio http://www.webstudio.com and Print Master http://www.printmaster.com to help you set up web pages. See also Lewis and Clark Rediscovery Project (2001). Lewis and

Clark Rediscovery. CD-Rom. InfiMedia, Inc., http://www.infimedia-inc.com.

Resources

INTERNET

PBS Online (historical background, biographies, interviews) http://www.pbs.org/lewisandclark

Bitterroot Mountains (a breakdown of the expedition's tortured passage over the Bitterroot Mountains, the roughest part of the route), http://www.bitterroot.net/usdafs/lcindex.html

A play about Sacagawea, http://www.teachervision.com/lesson-plans/lesson-3843.html

Mountain Men and the fur trade from 1800 – 1850, http://www.xmission.com/~drudy/amm.html

PRINT

Torrance, H. (1999). *Lewis and Clark: Across a Vast Land, An Historical Play by Harold Torrance*. Carlisle, MA: Discovery Enterprises, Ltd., Northwest Regional Education Laboratory (Summer, 2003).

Discoveries in Learning: Lessons from Lewis & Clark. NW, 8(4). Bergon, F. (Ed.) (1995).

The Journals of Lewis & Clark. NY: Penguin Nature Classics. 🖼

Engaging the Community in Civil War Studies with Digital Video

Andrew Stotz, Savilla Banister and John Fischer

Sixth to Eighth Grades: U.S. History and Sociology

NCSS Thematic Strand
◍ TIME, CONTINUITY AND CHANGE

NCSS Performance Expectations
c. Identify and describe selected historical periods and patterns of change within and across cultures.
d. Identify and use processes important to reconstructing and reinterpreting the past, such as using a variety of sources, providing, validating, and weighing evidence for claims, checking credibility of sources and searching for causality.

NETS-S National Educational Technology Standards for Students
3. Technology Productivity Tools
5. Technology Communication Tools

NETS-S Performance Indicators (Grades 6-8)
3. Technology Productivity Tools
5. Technology Communication Tools
+ Use content-specific tools, software, and simulations (e.g., environmental probes, graphing calculators, exploratory environments, Web tools) to support learning and research.

5. Technology Communication Tools
+ Design, develop, publish, and present products (e.g., Web pages, videotapes) using technology resources that demonstrate and communicate curriculum concepts to audiences inside and outside the classroom.

Introduction
Students use text and web resources to research key elements of the Civil War with an emphasis on original sources. From this evidence, students, working in groups, develop a storyboard to support their thesis on causes, battles, slavery, and other identified themes. The storyboard is used to identify media elements (text, audio, video, images) to be used in a digital video to present the information and arguments constructed. These digital videos are based in part on the work of Joe Lambert and the Digital Storytelling workshop.[1] These movies are put on DVD to share with community and family members along with displays, reenactments and arts presentations.

Objectives
1. The student will be able to construct a digital video that illustrates significant elements and themes demonstrating key features of the Civil War.
2. The student will be able to locate reliable and appropriate information on his or her selected Civil War topic through the use of internet search protocols, as well as other resources.
3. The student will be able to collect detailed analysis of sources and data related to key aspects of the Civil War era.
4. The student will be able to construct, edit and present narratives that explain key elements of the Civil War era.

Time
Approximately 4 or 5 one-hour sessions.

Instructional Steps
Students have previously been engaged in a unit on the study of the Civil War. During the unit they hear from speakers, read texts (fiction and non-fiction), collect notes, images and data about the Civil War and work to create a data-rich environment in the classroom.

As the end of the unit approaches students are informed that the cluster/team will be hosting a "Civil War Day" for their parents, friends and community members. The day occurs on a Saturday and lasts for approximately 3 hours.

As part of the day, student projects will be created, displayed and presented. Included in the projects will be student-

made display boards on individual themes and aspects of the Civil War. Groups will be asked to perform music, stage reenactments, model costumes and engage community members in activities. As a major part of the day students and teachers will share digital videos created by students to share information and images about the various themes studied as part of the Civil War.

Assigning Themes

After introducing the culminating project, brainstorm themes related to the stories, images, data and information students have been gathering and displaying on the walls of the classroom. These themes might reflect people they are studying (e.g. Harriet Tubman, Robert E. Lee). The themes might also reflect essential questions students have been trying to answer (e.g. What was life like for slaves?). After delineating various themes, form students into groups and have them choose themes they would like to work on.

Designing Storyboards

(http://www.storycenter.org/memvoice/pages/tutorial_3.html)
Place key steps in the development process on the time line: research and data, script development, recording of script, collection of images and graphics, merging of images and script, addition of musical soundtrack.

Research and data—students gather data, historical ac-

counts and information about their theme.

Script development—students develop a storyboard with a script to be spoken as part of the soundtrack.

Recording of script—using digital video software, students record the script. Insert pauses of silence wherever music is expected to go.

Collection of images and graphics—students sort images and resize them to help illustrate script.

Merging of images and script—using digital video software students insert images and graphics over the top of the sound track. (See http://www.apple.com/support/imovie/tutorial/ and http://www.microsoft.com/windowsxp/using/moviemaker/making/default.mspx)

Addition of musical soundtrack—students load sound/music and adjust volume to allow spoken script to be heard.

Sharing Projects

Civil War Day provides one opportunity to gather an authentic audience for student projects. Various laptops might run next to student display boards in a museum type environment. Also, select projects might be projected on to large screens or walls and shared with larger groups at one time.

Assessment

Students are presented with a rubric at the beginning of the culminating project section of the Civil War Unit. The rubric

scores them on key aspects of the project including: research and data, quality of presentation constructed, and actual presentation to parents and community members. (http://www.ncrel.org/tech/nets/rubrics.htm and http://rubistar.4teachers.org/index.php)

Student Enrichment

Working with digital video provides many opportunities for student enrichment. Students can be involved in multiple areas of the digital video creation process and can become room experts at various aspects including: sound, editing, graphics, script development.

Students might also work to enhance the community day by contacting historical organizations and inviting them to share in the events.

Teaching Tips

This lesson, and the digital projects that are created as a part of it, works best when various students are responsible for small pieces of the final products.

Each student must be required to:

+ Conduct research
+ Participate in the production of a product
+ Have a role in the community day

Technology Resources

HARDWARE

Computers with internet access for research

Macintosh computers (iMovie, iDVD) or Windows (Movie Maker)

SOFTWARE

Internet browser (Internet Explorer, Safari, Mozilla FireFox, etc.)

iMovie, iPhoto, iDVD, all included in Macintosh operating system or MovieMaker for Windows operating system

Resources

INTERNET

http://americancivilwar.com/civil.html

http://www.civilwarhome.com/

http://sunsite.utk.edu/civil-war/warweb.html

http://www.cwc.lsu.edu/

Lambert, J., & Mullen, N. (2004). Center for Digital Storytelling. http://www.storycenter.org/index1.html

Notes

1. Joe Lambert, *Digital Storytelling: Capturing Lives, Creating Community* (Berkeley: Digital Diner Press, 2002).

What is the Best Way to Govern a Nation? 14

JASON ENDACOTT

SIXTH TO EIGHTH GRADES: GOVERNMENT, GLOBAL STUDIES, WORLD HISTORY AND CIVICS

NCSS Thematic Strands
ⓥ **POWER, AUTHORITY, AND GOVERNANCE**
Ⓘ **TIME, CONTINUITY, AND CHANGE**

NCSS Performance Expectations
ⓥ **POWER, AUTHORITY AND GOVERNANCE**
  b. Describe the purpose of government and how its powers are acquired, used, and justified.

Ⓘ **TIME, CONTINUITY AND CHANGE**
  c. Identify and describe selected historical periods and patterns of change within and across cultures, such as the rise of civilizations, the development of transportation systems, the growth and breakdown of colonial systems, and others.
  f. Use knowledge of facts and concepts drawn from history, along with methods of historical inquiry, to inform decision-making about and action taking on public issues.

NETS-S National Educational Technology Standards for Students
3. Technology Productivity Tools
4. Technology Communications Tools
5. Technology Research Tools

NETS-S Performance Expectations
3. Technology Productivity Tools
  ♦ Students use technology tools to enhance learning, increase productivity, and promote creativity.
  ♦ Students use productivity tools to collaborate in constructing technology-enhanced models, prepare publications, and produce other creative works.

4. Technology Communications Tools
  ♦ Students use telecommunications to collaborate, publish, and interact with peers, experts, and other audiences.

5. Technology Research Tools
  ♦ Students use technology to locate, evaluate, and collect information from a variety of sources.

Introduction
This lesson is designed to study the concept of limited and unlimited government using an overarching question that students are to keep in mind throughout the course of their work. The overarching question for this lesson is, "What is the best way to govern a nation?"

To facilitate their research, the students are given an online research track that guides them through the definitions and some historical examples of government. Using information gained from teacher selected websites, the students engage in a simulation and online discussion with the teacher and other students in which they are asked to form an opinion on how a nation should be governed while using historical evidence to defend their positions. Their final product of knowledge is a persuasive paper, speech or multimedia presentation that clearly states their position on government and utilizes examples from history to help make their case. Additionally, student experiences in the online discussion will tighten up arguments and prepare them for counterpoints that could weaken their thesis.

Objectives
The student will be able to:
1. Identify and define various forms of government.
2. Develop an understanding of how government has evolved and not evolved over time.
3. Analyze the comparative advantages and disadvantages of limited and unlimited government.
4. Evaluate and decide on the best way to govern a nation and defend that choice against possible criticisms.
5. Apply productivity/multimedia tools and peripherals to support personal productivity, group collaboration, and learning throughout the curriculum. (From NETS-S)
6. Collaborate with peers, experts, and others using telecommunications and collaborative tools to investigate curriculum-related problems, issues, and information, and to develop solutions or products for audiences inside and outside the classroom. (From NETS-S)

Time

Four 50 minute sessions

Lesson Steps:

Step One: Define and Examine Historical Examples

This lesson consists of 4 major components with each requiring about one class period of approximately 50 minutes to complete. The ultimate goal of this lesson is for the students to come to a decision that they can defend regarding the type of government they think is best for running a nation. The first step in doing so is to identify and define the various forms of government to be studied and to examine a handful of historical examples of these government types.

An online research track is an efficient method for facilitating student research. There are many ways to create an Internet based research track for students to follow. For example, some teachers prefer to create their own web page that contains all of the information that the students will need to know for their research. The ease of student research, minimal time required to locate information and opportunity for the teacher to pre-screen information for accuracy are the main advantages to this option. Another method for facilitating student research is to create a research track to link the teacher-created site to outside websites containing the information students need. Some points to keep in mind when creating an online research track are:

+ Choose web pages that help students define limited and unlimited government as well as examples of each. Examples might include monarchy, democracy, theocracy,

feudal, fascist or any other type of government that is pertinent to the lesson. In addition to the definitions for these forms of government, the research track should include historical examples of each form of government listed.

+ Websites such as TrackStar are excellent vehicles for building student research tracks. TrackStar is free to use for teachers, and multiple types of research tracks can be created for student use. One example of a research track created using TrackStar for this lesson that is available for any class to use can be found at: http://wizard.hprtec.org/builder/worksheet.php3?ID=67917

+ Include sites that introduce the terms and provide historical examples as well as links to credible outside sources that describe the governments of various civilizations past and present. The example track above includes links to websites about the Sumerians, Egyptians, Greeks, Romans, and feudal societies as well as modern day examples of autocracy in Singapore and democracy in the United States.

Example questions to be asked on the research track might include:

+ What is the difference between limited and unlimited government?
+ What are some examples of limited/unlimited government?
+ What type of government did the Sumerians (or other society) practice?
+ Who held the power in this form of government?

Figure 1

Advantages and Disadvantages of Government Types

Democracy – Limited Government	Autocracy – Unlimited Government
ADVANTAGES 1. Happier citizens 2. Increased fairness 3. Power comes from the people 4. Easier to get rid of bad leaders	ADVANTAGES 1. Faster decision making 2. Faster change
DISADVANTAGES 1. Takes time to make decisions 2. Change is slow 3. Hard to make everybody happy 4. Possibility for fraud	DISADVANTAGES 1. Easy to corrupt 2. Citizens have no voice 3. Harder to get bad leaders out of power 4. Decisions are often made to please only a few people

- Was this an example of limited or unlimited government?

Other questions might be designed to jog the memories of the students' prior studies of these societies and how their form of government affected the people who lived in them. Examples might include:

- How were the hardships that feudal peasants faced related to their type of government?
- Why did the Roman people tolerate the excesses of some Roman Emperors?
- How was democracy in Ancient Athens different from democracy in the United States today?

Have students keep the information they gathered from the online research track to use as evidence for their persuasive essay.

Step Two: Simulation

The simulation is designed to allow the students to put the information they learned into practice. A simulation of limited and unlimited government can be run in a single class period using situations that the students might face in their everyday lives. Many different scenarios could be used to run the simulation, but it is recommended that the choice of scenario be interesting to students. For this lesson, two example scenarios are used, planning a class party and ordering pizzas. It is certainly possible to use scenarios other than these two; however, be careful not to introduce too much new information that may interfere with the students' comprehension of the process used to make decisions.

DEMOCRACY: LET'S PLAN A PARTY

When planning a party we often have to choose the location, the type of food and beverage to be served, activities that will take place, who will be invited and so on. All these are questions that greatly concern students. Plan to spend about a third of the class period democratically planning a class party.

Solicit ideas and encourage students to speak up, vote and participate in every aspect of the decision. The goal is to have the students experience the benefits and drawbacks of democratic decision-making so they can record them during the debriefing. These benefits and drawbacks will become even more evident during the autocratic phase when the students lose all of their voting rights.

AUTOCRACY: PIZZA MY WAY

Ordering pizzas requires many decisions as well. Where will

the pizza come from? What type of crust will be ordered? What about toppings? How many pieces does each person get? Again, these are all questions that greatly interest students. Plan to spend the second third of the class planning a pizza party using an unlimited form of government.

Before the day of the simulation, the teacher should pull aside a student who would make a good candidate for "class dictator." During the pizza party scenario, this student will serve as totalitarian leader of the class. He or she may entertain suggestions or request input from his or her classmates, but in the end all decisions should be his/hers alone to make. Make it clear to the class dictator that in an unlimited form of government, they are above the law. Encourage the student to be creative with his/her powers.

DEBRIEFING: WHAT HAVE WE LEARNED?

At the conclusion of the simulation, debrief the students by listing the advantages and disadvantages of limited and unlimited government in a chart. Figure 1 is an example of such a chart with student answers. This listing of ideas will also prove useful in the discussion step of the lesson.

Step Three: Electronic Discussion

The popularity of online discussion boards has increased dramatically in recent years and there are many benefits to using an online discussion board with students. Discussion boards allow for multiple responses to a single query, allowing many students to respond at the same time. Also, discussions can be separated into "threads" to keep the electronic conversations on topic. Within the individual threads, participants can respond to the points of others by using the "quote" function. Quoting a previous response helps to clarify the points being addressed with either a counterpoint or further support for a previously asserted argument.

It is not difficult to find no-cost discussion boards that are remotely hosted for this purpose. A simple Internet search will turn up many options such as ezboard.com and proboards.com that take very little technical skill to use. Other options for many teachers are the various subscription websites designed for classroom use such as Blackboard that include discussion board options. Some message boards require parental permission for children less than thirteen years of age which can make the teacher subscribed boards a more convenient option.

One of the teacher's roles when using discussion boards is to moderate the discussions of the students. Remind students to stay on topic, refrain from personal attacks stemming from

Figure 2

Persuasive Essay: What is the Best Way to Govern a Nation?

Category	4: Above Standards	3: Meets Standards	2: Approaching Standards	1: Below Standards	Score
Position Statement	The position statement provides a clear, strong statement of the author's position on the topic of how to govern a nation.	The position statement provides a clear statement of the author's position on the topic of how to govern a nation.	A position statement is present, but does not make the the author's position clear.	There is no position statement.	
Support for Position	Includes 3 or more pieces of evidence that support the position statement. The writer obviously has a working knowledge of limited and unlimited government and has included at least one counterargument.	Includes 3 or more pieces of evidence (facts, statistics, examples, real-life experiences) that support the position statement. Writer clearly understands the concepts of limited and unlimited government.	Includes 2 pieces of evidence (facts, statistics, examples, real-life experiences) that support the position statement. Student has knowledge of limited and unlimited government.	Includes 1 or fewer pieces of evidence (facts, statistics, examples, real-life experiences). Student demonstrates some knowledge of limited and unlimited government.	
Evidence and Examples	All of the evidence and examples are specific and relevant, and explanations are given that show how each piece of evidence supports the author's position.	Most of the evidence and examples are specific and relevant, and explanations are given that show how each piece of evidence supports the author's position.	At least one of the pieces of evidence and examples is relevant and has an explanation that shows how that piece of evidence supports the author's position.	Evidence and examples are NOT relevant AND/OR are not explained.	
Accuracy	All supportive facts and statistics are reported accurately.	Almost all supportive facts and statistics are reported accurately.	Most supportive facts and statistics are reported accurately.	Most supportive facts and statistics were inaccurately reported.	
Grammar & Spelling	Author makes no errors in grammar or spelling that distract the reader from the content.	Author makes 1-2 errors in grammar or spelling that distract the reader from the content.	Author makes 3-4 errors in grammar or spelling that distract the reader from the content.	Author makes more than 4 errors in grammar or spelling that distract the reader from the content.	

disagreements and use examples from the research track and simulation to strengthen their arguments. The teacher's other role in this step is to begin the discussion threads for the students to use. Since discussion threads often take on a life of their own, it is best to keep these prompts simple. Example thread prompts might include:

+ What is the best way to govern a nation?
+ If you could be the leader of a limited or unlimited government, which would you choose and why?
+ Would you say that government has improved throughout history?

Once the discussions heat up, teachers might be surprised at how well some students participate. The relative anonymity of posting messages on the internet brings some of the more bashful students out of their shells and into the fray.

Step Four: Assessment

Assessment opportunities exist throughout this lesson. During the course of the lesson, the students' answers to the questions on the internet research track can be graded for accuracy. It is also possible to include a grade for participation in the online discussion based upon the students' use of the information they garnered from the research track, the simulation and their own personal ideals.

A short position paper is a perfect synthesis of student knowledge for this lesson. This paper could be a standard persuasive essay or perhaps take the form of a letter to our nation's founding fathers outlining the reasoning for a particular form of government. Student papers should address the question of, "What is the best way to govern a nation?" This overarching question can be answered using the definitions and historical examples discovered using the online research track, and the personal experiences gleaned from the simulation, as well as the points and counterpoints made during the online discussion. By this point in the lesson, the students should be able to advance a reasoned argument using supporting evidence. A rubric (Figure 2) can be used to assess the position paper. Other options for the final product of knowledge might include a persuasive speech or multimedia presentation given to the class. These options can be assessed in the same fashion, basing students' grades on the strength of their argument and support.

Assessment

See Figure 2.

Student Enrichment

+ Tie the lesson into the student government of the school by having the students draft a proposal for redrawing the framework for their school's student government according to the conclusions they drew from the lesson.
+ Have students choose a country that practices the form of government they supported in their paper and research the history of government for that nation.
+ Allow students to hold a live debate in addition to the electronic discussion.
+ Have the students research and compare the standard of living between nations that practice limited government and nations that have unlimited governments.

Teaching Tips

This lesson can be conducted without the benefit of technology resources, although online resources and discussions add significant advantages. Handouts can take the place of the online research track, and a debate or Socratic seminar can be substituted for the online discussion.

Resources

ALTEC, "TrackStar." (Lawrence, KS: ALTEC, 2005), http://trackstar.4teachers.org/trackstar/index.jsp

ezboard, Inc. "ezboard." (San Francisco, CA: 2005) http://www.ezboard.com/

"Ancient Egyptian Government." January 25, 2005. http://expage.com/ancientegyptiangovernment (July 15, 2005)

"Democracy." Microsoft Encarta Online Encyclopedia. (2005) http://encarta.msn.com/encyclopedia_1741500781/United_States_(Government).html#p2

"The Democratic Experiment." British Broadcasting Company. January 1, 2001. http://www.bbc.co.uk/history/ancient/greeks/greekdemocracy_01.shtml (October 23, 2006)

Richard Hooker, "Mesopotamia: The Sumerians." June 6, 1996. http://www.wsu.edu:8080/~dee/MESO/SUMER.HTM (July 15, 2005)

"The Middle Ages: Feudal Life." Annenberg Media. 2006 http://www.learner.org/exhibits/middleages/feudal.html (October 23, 2006)

"The Roman Republic." SchoolsHistory.org. July 11, 2004. http://www.schoolshistory.org.uk/republic.htm (July 15, 2005)

Tian Jie, "Dictatorship and Autocracy in Singapore." The Epoch Times (May 3, 2005) http://www.theepochtimes.com/news/5-5-3/28402.html

Engaging Midlevel Learners in Children's Issues Around the World

GAYLE Y. THIEMAN AND KYLE EVANS

SIXTH TO EIGHTH GRADES: GLOBAL STUDIES, CULTURAL STUDIES AND GEOGRAPHY

NCSS Thematic Strands

Ⓘⓧ GLOBAL CONNECTIONS

Ⓧ CIVIC IDEALS AND PRACTICES

NCSS Performance Expectations

Ⓘⓧ GLOBAL CONNECTIONS

   d. Explore the causes, consequences, and possible solutions to persistent contemporary, and emerging global issues such as health, security, resource allocation, economic development, and environmental quality.

   f. Demonstrate understanding of concerns, standards, issues, and conflicts related to universal human rights.

Ⓧ CIVIC IDEALS AND PRACTICES

   b. Identify and interpret sources and examples of the rights and responsibilities of citizens.

   j. Examine strategies to strengthen the common good, which consider a range of options for citizen action.

NETS-S National Educational Technology Standards for Students

3. Technology Productivity Tools
4. Technology Communication Tools
5. Technology Research Tools

NETS-S Performance Expectations

3. Technology Productivity Tools

   ♦ Students use technology tools to enhance learning, increase productivity, and promote creativity.

4. Technology Communication Tools

   ♦ Students use a variety of media and formats to communicate information and ideas effectively to multiple audiences.

5. Technology Research Tools

   ♦ Students use technology to locate, evaluate, and collect information from a variety of sources.

Introduction

Hosford Middle School is a Title I school in Portland, Oregon, which takes pride in the diversity of its student body. For the third year in a row ALL students at Hosford participated in a School-Wide project in their social studies, language arts, math, science, and electives classes. The essential question for this year's project was: How do problems of human rights, hunger, health, environment, and education impact children around the world? Student research culminated in a Global Summit (C) conference (similar to Model UN) in which students presented their resolutions to address children's issues. The lesson in this article focuses on social studies curriculum; however, this was a school-wide project, which required students to integrate research in social studies, math, science, and health classes with writing and persuasive speaking in language arts classes to prepare for the Global Summit.

Objectives

The student will be able to:

1. Locate information from a variety of sources (Internet and print media) regarding his or her country.
2. Use technology tools to organize (Inspiration) and communicate (PowerPoint) information with peers and community.
3. Create an informative poster about his or her country: physical geography, human geography, economic geography, history, and basic facts.
4. Research issues that affect children in an assigned country and choose one as a focus (health, hunger, human rights, education, environment).
5. Write a resolution in support of action needed to resolve the children's issue and support the position with detailed evidence, examples, and clear reasoning.
6. Present the resolution to classmates and potentially to the Hosford General Assembly (student body, staff, and community).

7. Create informative posters regarding children's issues in the Portland, Oregon community and participate in a Children's Awareness March in surrounding neighborhoods.

Time
Three weeks

Instructional Steps

1. In preparation for this school wide project, all teachers met in subject area departments with a university professor/facilitator to plan the overall School Wide Project. Social studies teachers were responsible for teaching their students how to do internet research using a variety of Internet and print media. Social studies teachers chose a region of the world as the focus for their classes. Within the class, each cooperative group of 4-5 students conducted research on a country.

2. To begin the unit all social studies students read and discussed the United Nations Declaration of the Rights of the Child[1] and analyzed the degree to which the United States supports these rights. Some teachers also used the United Nations Convention on the Rights of the Child as a model for the resolutions students would write for the Global Summit.[2]

3. Using Oregon as an exemplar, teachers used the internet with a computer and LCD projector to model how to locate, evaluate, and take notes on Oregon geography, history, economics, political and cultural data and consider a problem affecting Oregon's children, e.g., hunger.

4. Students read and discussed a sample briefing paper on hunger in Oregon, which described the problem, summarized the history, evaluated causes, and proposed solutions. They used the Oregon fact sheet and briefing paper as a model for their own work.

5. Students used mobile Mac labs with wireless internet connections to conduct research on individual countries. Students used a variety of internet sources including Free the Children[3], Country Watch[4], CIA World Fact Book[5], Amnesty International[6], and UNICEF[7]. Hosford purchased a site license for Countrywatch.com, and students were able to log on from school or home to complete their research.

6. Students completed a country fact page. In social studies class, students also created informative posters for display in the school. Then as a group, students researched information about five issues affecting children within that country.

7. Individual students chose one of the issues and wrote a briefing paper. The briefing paper was used in language arts class as the basis for writing a persuasive speech, using the format of a resolution. Resolutions were typed as Microsoft Word documents.

Model for Global Summit Resolution written in Language Arts Class and Presented in the Form of a Persuasive Speech

Topic:

Proposed By:

Introduction (problem)

Alarmed

Acknowledging

Body (facts)

Observing

Considering

Conclusion (action to be taken) "We resolve…"

Requesting

Recommending

"Because we fully believe…"

8. Students presented their resolution/speeches to their classmates in language arts class, and one student from each class was chosen by vote to present the resolution at the Global Summit (which occurred at an all-school 90-minute assembly in the school auditorium.

9. At the Global Summit, nineteen students presented their resolutions to the entire student body and community. Resolution topics ranged from exploitation of girls and women in Bosnia, low literacy rate in Nigeria, and child labor in Egypt, to air pollution in Colombia, and the one-child policy and female infanticide in China. Student musicians and dancers performed an Argentinean tango, a Brazilian Samba, and Native American dances representing five local tribes.

10. After the Global Summit, social studies classes toured the school viewing the informational posters, art projects, and PowerPoint presentations. Students voted for the three posters they felt were most informative, and each social studies class awarded a certificate of excellence to a winner.

Assessment

Social studies teachers developed rubrics to score the informational posters and the briefing papers. The resolutions were scored by language arts teachers, using the Oregon scoring guide for persuasive speech. (See Rubrics, pp. 86-87)

Teachers' Evaluation

Hosford teachers evaluated the strengths and challenges of the School-Wide Project and commented: (a) Student learning was open-ended, divergent, differentiated, and rigorous; (b) Students used technology as a tool for learning; (c) Students developed empathy for children around the world; (d) The complex project required an unusual amount of staff collaboration and additional work. One teacher commented, "When the smoke cleared....students realized that they had learned a great deal about their world."

Student Enrichment

As an alternative to the fact sheet and briefing paper, special needs students used the internet and worked with their group to complete a Country Project worksheet.

SERVICE CONNECTION: While planning for the School-Wide project, Hosford students collected over $1000 for tsunami relief, and a Mercy Corps volunteer in Oregon was the keynote speaker at the Hosford General Assembly. The Hosford students' funds were used to help rebuild a school in Indonesia that was destroyed by the tsunami.

COMMUNITY CONNECTION: During advisory period, students created large signs and informational leaflets comparing children's issues globally and locally (e.g., world fact: 640 children worldwide do not have adequate shelter; community fact: an estimated 1,500 youth are homeless in Portland). At the close of the Global Summit students marched through the Hosford neighborhoods carrying their signs and distributing the leaflets.

Teaching Tips

Teachers met in subject area teams with a university professor who recommended research materials, modeled instructional strategies, and facilitated team planning. Staff also participated in workshops on using technology tools for learning (e.g., Inspiration software).

Technology Resources

HARDWARE
Mobile Computer Lab, Color Printers, LCD projectors

SOFTWARE
Microsoft Word, Inspiration, Power Point, QuickTime

Some of the websites included streaming video, integrating interviews with children about issues affecting them. Some students created PowerPoint presentations, while others learned how to use Inspiration software for note taking. The school obtained a site license for countrywatch.com, and students were able to log in from home or school to complete their research.

Resources

INTERNET
www.unhchr.ch/html/menu3/b/25.htm
www.unhchr.ch/html/menu3/b/k2crc.htm
www.freethechildren.org
www.countrywatch.com
www.cia.gov/cia/publications/factbook/
www.amnesty.org
www.unicef.org

PRINT
UNICEF, *A Life Like Mine: How Children Live Around the World* (New York: D.K. Publishing, Inc., 2002)

Rubric for Informative Poster

Category	4	3	2	1
MAP	Map clearly shows assigned country. Map has key, compass rose, important landforms, neighboring countries, and population density.	Map shows assigned country. Map has most but not all required elements.	Map shows assigned country but lacks most required elements.	Map is not present or lacks all required elements.
GRAPHICS- RELEVANCE AND ORIGINALITY	All graphics are related to topic and support factual data. Graphics reflect an exceptional degree of student creativity.	All graphics are related to the topic but some do not support factual data. Graphics demonstrate student creativity.	Some graphics are related to the topic but do not support factual data. Little demonstration of creativity present.	Graphics do not relate to topic or are not present.
TIMELINE	Timeline contains 10 dates relating to the history of the country and problems affecting children in that country.	Timeline contains 10 dates relating to the history of the country but they do not reflect the problems affecting children in that country.	The timeline contains 8 dates but they do not relate to the history of that country.	Timeline contains fewer than 8 dates.
RESEARCH- USE OF TECHNOLOGY	Students used 4 resources (three websites and a print resource) to gather information on the assigned country. All resources are properly cited.	Students used 3 resources (two websites and a print resource) to gather information on the assigned country. All resources are properly cited.	Students used 2 resources (one website and a print resource) to gather information on the assigned country. All resources are properly cited.	Students did not use a variety of resources to gather information or failed to properly cite resources.

Rubric for Briefing Paper (also available in Spanish)

Category	4	3	2	1
DESCRIPTION OF THE PROBLEM	Precisely explains the problem. Describes where the information was found. Contains statistical information about the country.	Explains the problem and contains some detail about the country but lacks statistical data.	Explains the problem but contains no detailed information about the country.	No evidence of a problem and no description of the country.
HISTORY OF THE PROBLEM	Explains the historical implications of the problem and gives the duration of the problem. Includes dates and factual information.	Explains why this is a problem and the duration but lacks specific detail.	Explains why this is a problem or the duration but not both. Paper has no specific detail.	No history reported.
POSSIBLE CAUSES OF THE PROBLEM	Gives three possible causes of the problem.	Gives two possible causes of the problem.	Gives one possible cause of the problem.	No causes presented.
POSSIBLE SOLUTIONS FOR THE PROBLEM	Offers three developed ideas that could be used to solve the problem.	Offers two developed ideas that could be used to solve the problem.	Offers one developed idea that could be used to solve the problem.	Lacks any possible solutions to solve the problem.

Student Sample of Briefing Paper

STUDENT: *CP*

COUNTRY: *Somalia*

ISSUE/PROBLEM: *Education*

DESCRIPTION OF ISSUE/PROBLEM: *The education in Somalia is very bad. The kids are not going to school or anywhere else where they can get educated. People need to send their kids to school to stop the poverty level.*

HISTORY OF PROBLEM: *In the early 1900's and the mid 1900's the Italians owned Somalia. The Italians set up colonies all over Somalia, and their cities. Only thing they didn't have many public schools for the Somali people. They made plenty of schools for themselves though. Still the Italians made the people more educated than they were when they left. The Italians wanted to educate the Somali people, so they could farm or do work for them as slaves.*

Also the British established elementary administrative posts and positions not previously open to them. They set up a training school for the police and one for medical orderlies.

CAUSES OF PROBLEM: *After World War II there was little demand for west-style education. Moreover the existence of two official languages (English, Italian) is not widely understood by the people. The adults in Somalia, the literacy rate is at elementary school level.*

SOLUTIONS ALREADY TRIED: *Thirty years ago the UN set up a bunch of public education schools. The literacy rate increased 5% of the adult population in 1975.*

WHAT NEEDS TO BE DONE: *Kids need to be involved with the schools, and they need to go to school. Also the government needs to set up more schools and colleges and fund them.*

Other Materials Needed
Posterboard (4' x 6'); magazines for pictures

Student Voices
See the sample student briefing paper on p. 88.

Notes
1. Office of the High Commissioner for Human Rights, "Declaration of the Rights of the Child" (Geneva, Switzerland: UNHCHR, 1959), www.unhchr.ch/html/menu3/b/25.htm
2. Office of the High Commissioner for Human Rights, "Convention of the Rights of the Child" (Geneva, Switzerland: UNHCHR, 1989), www.unhchr.ch/html/menu3/b/k2crc.htm
3. Free the Children, "Child Rights Issues" (Toronto, Ontario: 2005) www.freethechildren.com
4. CountryWatch (Houston,TX: CountryWatch,Inc, 2005), www.countrywatch.com
5. Central Intelligence Agency, "CIA Factbook" (Washington, D.C.: CIA, 2005), www.cia.gov/cia/publications/factbook/index.html
6. Amnesty, International, "Children's Issues" www.amnesty.org (Search for Children's Issues)
7. UNICEF, "United Nations Children's Fund" (New York: UNICEF, 2005) www.unicef.org

Who Cares about State Government? Using the Internet to Research State Legislative Issues

Joe O'Brien, Jeff Strickland and Aaron Grill

Seventh and Eighth Grade and High School: Civics and Government

NCSS Thematic Strands

Ⅵ POWER, AUTHORITY, AND GOVERNANCE

Ⅹ CIVIC IDEALS AND PRACTICES

Ⅷ SCIENCE, TECHNOLOGY, AND SOCIETY

NCSS Performance Expectations

Ⅵ POWER, AUTHORITY, AND GOVERNANCE

a. Examine persistent issues involving the rights, roles and status of the individual in relation to the general welfare.

c. Analyze and explain ideas and mechanisms to meet needs and wants of citizens, regulate territory, manage conflict, establish order and security, and balance competing conceptions of a just society.

Ⓧ CIVIC IDEALS AND PRACTICES

c. Locate, access, analyze, organize, synthesize, evaluate, and apply information about selected public issues—identifying, describing, and evaluating multiple points of view.

d. Practice forms of civic discussion and participation consistent with the ideals of citizens in a democratic republic.

Ⅷ SCIENCE, TECHNOLOGY, AND SOCIETY

b. Show through specific examples how science and technology have changed people's perceptions of the social and natural world.

NETS-S National Educational Technology Standards for Students

4. Technology Communications Tools
5. Technology Research Tools

NETS-S Performance Expectations

4. Technology Communications Tools

♦ Students use telecommunications to collaborate, publish, and interact with peers, experts, and other audiences.

♦ Students use a variety of media and formats to communicate information and ideas effectively to multiple audiences.

5. Technology Research Tools

♦ Students use technology to locate, evaluate, and collect information from a variety of sources.

♦ Students use technology tools to process data and report results.

♦ Students evaluate and select new information resources and technological innovations based on the appropriateness for specific tasks.

Introduction

State government often is an afterthought in the social studies curriculum. This lesson suggests a way for students to research online a state policy issue and to form and communicate a well reasoned position on the issue to a legislator or other appropriate state official. Using the Track Current Events site, www.trackcurrentevents.org, students follow a five step process. First, the site enables the teacher to create an online survey of issues before her or his state legislature. Students rank the issues by their level of interest in each one. The teacher uses the results to assign students to research groups. During the second and third steps, the teacher creates a Tracker on each issue and the groups use the sites linked to the appropriate Tracker to learn both background information on the issue and arguments for and against it. After reviewing the sites on the Tracker, students compose and upload a Top Story, which is an overview of the state policy issue. During the fourth and

Screenshot 1: Editor's Page

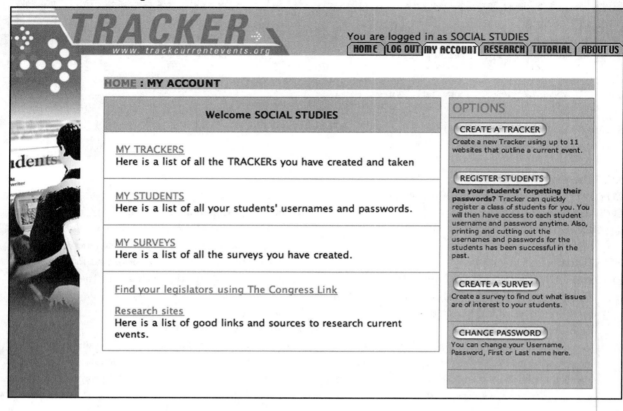

TRACKER
www.trackcurrentevents.org

You are logged in as SOCIAL STUDIES

HOME | LOG OUT | MY ACCOUNT | RESEARCH | TUTORIAL | ABOUT US

HOME : MY ACCOUNT

Welcome SOCIAL STUDIES

MY TRACKERS
Here is a list of all the TRACKERs you have created and taken

MY STUDENTS
Here is a list of all your students' usernames and passwords.

MY SURVEYS
Here is a list of all the surveys you have created.

Find your legislators using The Congress Link

Research sites
Here is a list of good links and sources to research current events.

OPTIONS

CREATE A TRACKER
Create a new Tracker using up to 11 websites that outline a current event.

REGISTER STUDENTS
Are your students' forgetting their passwords? Tracker can quickly register a class of students for you. You will then have access to each student username and password anytime. Also, printing and cutting out the usernames and passwords for the students has been successful in the past.

CREATE A SURVEY
Create a survey to find out what issues are of interest to your students.

CHANGE PASSWORD
You can change your Username, Password, First or Last name here.

---

fifth steps, students use the site's Letter to the Editor feature to post a letter to a state official, which reflects their position on the issue. After reviewing and editing the students' letters, either the student or the teacher e-mails each letter to the appropriate state legislator. The examples discussed in the lesson are drawn from students in Kansas, but the lesson itself is applicable to the study of issues before any state legislature. For samples designed for this lesson, go to www.trackcurrentevents. org and log on using the following information:

User Name: NCSS
Password: STATEGOV

Objectives

1. Students use an online survey to select state legislative issues to research as a group.
2. Working in groups, students locate and use online sites that provide accurate and appropriate background on the policy issue, as well as reasoned and well documented sites that advocate a position on the issue.
3. Students write and upload an overview of the legisla-

tive issue that is an accurate, appropriate, and a well balanced portrayal of the public policy issue.
4. Based on their research, students formulate a well reasoned position on the issue.
5. Students express their position in a letter to a legislator or other state official that each one has researched and individually e mail the letter to that person.

Time

Two to three class periods for an abbreviated version where students research a legislative issue using a teacher-prepared Tracker and use the results of their investigation to draft a letter to e-mail to an appropriate state official. An extended version where students locate the internet sites themselves requires additional days. The number of days depends upon how long the teacher wants students to follow a public policy issue.

Instructional Steps

TEACHER PREPARATION STEP: For a sample Tracker go to www.trackcurrentevents.org and log on with the user name of

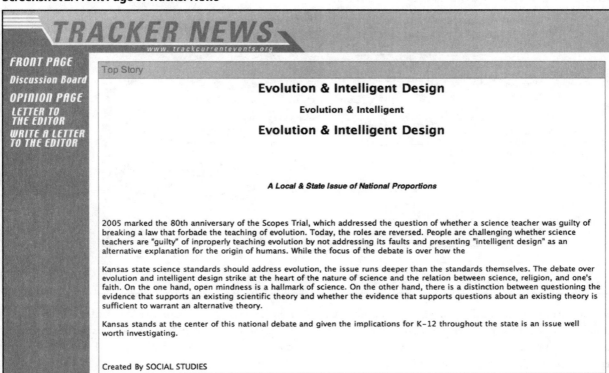

NCSS and the password STATEGOV, a user's account created specifically for this Bulletin. This will take you to the "editor's page." (See Screenshot 1 for an example.) From this page you can: register a class of students and the site will generate a password for each student; create an online interest survey; and create the initial parts of a Tracker. Also, there is a button on this page for a Tutorial, which explains how to use the site and to create your own account. Your account offers the same user name and password features, which ensures the privacy of your students' work.

1. IDENTIFY STUDENTS' INTERESTS: The teacher creates an online interest survey that presents a handful of state policy issues that students can research online and allows them to rate their level of interest in each issue. Based on the results, the teacher assigns students in groups to use the appropriate Tracker to begin researching the issue. Prior to the students accessing the site, the teacher will select several online news stories that provide background on the state policy issue and link them to a Tracker. The example used here is the Kansas Board of Education's consideration of the state science standards and

the role of "intelligent design" in the science standards.

Since issues such as the one here are controversial, this is also a good point to provide students with guidelines on how to address such issues in a civil manner. Such guidelines might include: respect one another's viewpoints; the exchange of different and opposing ideas is healthy; critique ideas, not people; and, expression of opinions is a beginning, reasoned thinking is the end. (See the Resources section for references on teaching and learning about controversial issues.)

2. PROVIDE BACKGROUND TO THE STATE POLICY ISSUE: Using a user name generated by the teacher and a password generated by the site, students access the Tracker created for their issue. As students access their Tracker, they will encounter a "front page," such as the one in Screenshot 2, absent the Top Story article. For the shortened version of this lesson, the Tracker already will contain the links to the news stories, which the students can access either in a sequenced order using the Next Link button or by moving back and forth among the links via the Choose a Link button on the top left. In the sample Tracker, when students click on Next Link button they

Screenshot 3: Sample Page with Link to News Source

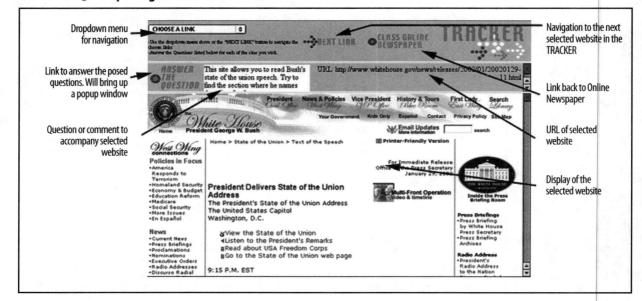

Dropdown menu for navigation

Link to answer the posed questions. Will bring up a popup window

Question or comment to accompany selected website

Navigation to the next selected website in the TRACKER

Link back to Online Newspaper

URL of selected website

Display of the selected website

encounter a news article titled: "New Science Standards May Include Intelligent Design." After they read each report, students can read the question(s) in the text box above the news report posted by the teacher and respond to each one using the Answer the Question button. (See Screenshot 3.) Based on what they learn from each site, students create a summary of the policy issue. They go to the editor's page and to the My Tracker button, where they can access the edit function to upload their Top Story. The teacher can read the student produced Top Story and assess it for clarity, accuracy and completeness to ensure that students comprehend the issue well enough to continue researching it. (For an extended version of the lesson students can locate such online news reports and create the links to a Tracker themselves.)

3. CONDUCT ONLINE RESEARCH TO IDENTIFY DIFFERENT POSITIONS ON THE ISSUE: Students return to their respective Tracker and use the additional links to learn arguments for and against, for example, the inclusion of intelligent design in a state's science standards. Students discuss what they learn at each site and upload their answers to the questions for each site as a group.

4. FORMULATE AND POST THEIR POSITIONS ON THE ISSUE: Working individually, students use the Letter to the Editor feature of the site to post a well-reasoned argument either for or against, a position on an important topic. Students are to draw information from the sites that they used to support their position. Prior to posting the letter, students need to identify a

state legislator or, in this case, a state board of education member as the recipient of the letter and address it accordingly. (See the Print Resources section: Writing an E Mail "Letter" to a Legislator.)

5. REVIEW AND FORWARD LETTER: The teacher reviews each letter and works with each student to edit her or his letter. Once satisfied with the result and according to school or district policy, the teacher and student e mails the letter. (See the Assessment section for criteria to use when reviewing the students' letters.)

Assessment

Assessment criteria for the e-mail message to a state official:

+ Opening paragraph–student introduces self and demonstrates knowledge of legislator.
+ Body of letter clearly and concisely presents issue. Position is clearly and persuasively stated.
+ Arguments, which accurately and appropriately represent two or more positions on the issue, are clearly presented and cause the reader to think more deeply about the issue.
+ Arguments for the student's position are well reasoned, clearly presented and supported with facts and examples.
+ Concluding paragraph thanks legislator and requests a reply.
+ Grammar, spelling and punctuation are accurately and appropriately used.

+ The tone of the letter is professional and mature.

Student Enrichment
Since some groups are likely to finish before other groups, these students can research a second legislative issue by using another group's Tracker.

Resources
INTERNET
Sample Tracker, go to http://trackcurrentevent.org and log on. Username: NCSS; Password: STATEGOV. There also is a Tracker with links to and about state governments.

State of Kansas Track, a collection of Internet sites that serve as a starting point for research on legislative issues and an example for similar Tracks on other state governments: http://trackstar.4teachers.org/trackstar/ts/viewTrack.do?number=263325

PRINT
Writing an E Mail "Letter" To Your Legislator
E-mail makes it easy to communicate your thinking to a state legislator. The purpose of the e-mail "letter" to your legislator is to try and convince that person to support your position on the issue. As a result, make sure to treat both the issue and your communication with the legislator in a serious manner. Below are guidelines to help you prepare your electronic letter.

Tips for writing a good letter:
+ Make a good impression. While most e-mail messages that you receive are very informal, you need to present yourself and your thinking in a serious, thoughtful way.
+ Have someone proofread your letter.
+ Limit the length of your letter to one page and discuss only one issue per letter.
+ Familiarize yourself with the legislator and her or his position on the issue.
+ Take care to be polite and courteous and respect the legislator's viewpoint.
+ Thank him or her for taking the time to consider your viewpoint.
+ Present yourself and your views with a positive, thoughtful, calm and mature attitude.

Letter format:

The Honorable Jane Doe
Legislator's address

Dear Representative/Senator Doe

Contents of Introductory Paragraph
1. Identify yourself completely.
2. Open with a positive note about his or her voting record and the job he or she does.

Contents of the Body
1. Introduce the issue or bill, identifying it by number and popular title.
2. State your position on the issue or bill.
3. Give reasons for your position. Provide facts and examples of how it will affect you and others.

Contents of Conclusion Paragraph
1. Thank your legislator for his/her consideration of your concerns.
2. Ask for a reply.

Close your Letter
1. Type your full name under your signature.
2. Include appropriate and teacher-approved contact information.

Teacher Tip
Here are two logistical matters to consider when selecting Internet sites to link to a Tracker. First, a school's or district's firewall system might affect the choice of sites. Teachers in three different districts, for example, who used the Tracker program to follow the debate in Kansas over a marriage amendment to the state constitution differed in their ability to access dramatically different sites. Second, many news sites either require membership and/or post stories for a limited amount of time prior to archiving them.

Two good references for information on teaching and learning about controversial issues are: Diana Hess and Julie Posselt, "How High School Students Experience and Learn from the Discussion of Controversial Public Issues," *Journal of Curriculum and Supervision* 17, no. 4 (2002), 283-314 and Ronald Evans and David Saxe, *Handbook on Teaching Social Issues*. (Washington DC: National Council for the Social Studies, 1996).

If a teacher is interested in a less interactive site where she or he may collect and link together a host of sites on a state legislative issue and simply focus on the second part of the lesson, the Track Star program is recommended. It is found at http://trackstar.4teachers.org/trackstar/index.jsp.

Technology Resources

Use of the Internet as a research tool and the use of e-mail to communicate with state legislators.

Student Voices

Here are two sample student letters:

Dear (Legislator):

After researching online the issue of gambling in Kansas, I would have to say that a casino would not be a bad idea for the state of Kansas. While there are a lot of addictions and other problems associated with gambling, the good outweighs the bad. Bringing a casino to Wyandotte county would actually be a very good idea economically considering the Kansas Speedway, Cabala's, and Nebraska Furniture Mart are all right there, drawing in big crowds of people who would possibly go to the casino.

What I have to say about the people who are addicted is that it's their own problem just like those who are addicted to smoking, no one made them smoke, and no one will make anyone go and gamble at a casino. I can also see how some people might have a problem with a casino being built by their home, where they want to raise their kids with out a casino nearby. If you build a casino it would be best to build one in an area that is already booming with other businesses, that way it will be better off.

I encourage the Kansas legislature to build a casino in Wyandotte County because the benefits of the casino would greatly outweigh any possible disadvantages.

Sincerely,

Dear Legislator,

I am an avid believer that most people should have the right to possess firearms, but within rea-son. I have grown up around firearms and first fired a shotgun when I was 13. However, I believe there is a difference in owning a shotgun or rifle for recreational use and in carrying a handgun in your pocket. I have no problems with responsible people owning a shotgun. One reason for that is you know when they are armed; there is no way to really hide the weapon.

My opinion on firearms starts to become less open when it comes to concealed weapons. I'm not necessarily comfortable with not knowing whether or not the person standing behind me in the line at the grocery store has a gun in his/her pocket and a very short temper. I, by no means, believe that the right to carry a weapon should be denied to all, because that would be violating the second amendment to the constitution. I just believe that to allow concealed carry, governments need to be more restrictive about who can possess such. Persons must be required to undergo extensive background checks before being granted a permit, and there needs to be a waiting period. If an abusive husband comes in to apply for a permit, the persons issuing the permit need to be able to take into consideration his history of violence and any orders of protection or restraining orders out against him. If there are, it is just common sense why he wants the weapon. The other thing that I have a problem with is persons with mental illnesses being allowed to possess firearms. Yes, people may argue for protection, but you also have to protect society. There is no guarantee that the person will not have a psychotic episode, in which he/she will not fire the weapon out of rage.

I do think that responsible, trained people should have the right to own and possess firearms on his/her person, but I just believe that the government needs to have a strong say in who may. After all it is the government's job to protect its citizens from harm.

Sincerely,

The Youth Vote Initiative

Hilary Landorf and Anthony Reid

Seventh to Twelfth Grades: Civics, Government, Sociology and Cultural Studies

NCSS Thematic Strands
ⓧ CIVIC IDEALS AND PRACTICES
ⓥ INDIVIDUALS, GROUPS, AND INSTITUTIONS

NCSS Performance Expectations
ⓧ CIVIC IDEALS AND PRACTICES
  c. Locate, access, organize, and apply information about an issue of public concern from multiple points of view.
  d. Identify and practice selected forms of civic discussion and participation consistent with the ideas of citizens in a democratic republic.

ⓥ INDIVIDUALS, GROUPS, AND INSTITUTIONS
  g. Apply knowledge of how groups and institutions work to meet individual needs and promote the common good.

NETS-S National Educational Technology Standards for Students
1. Basic Operations and Concepts
5. Technology Research Tools

NETS-S Performance Indicators (Grades 6-8 and Grades 9-12)
1. Basic Operations and Concepts
  + Demonstrate an understanding of concepts underlying hardware, software, and connectivity, and of practical applications to learning and problem-solving.

5. Technology Research Tools
  + Select and apply technology tools for research, information analysis, problem-solving and decision-making in content learning.

Introduction
The Youth Vote Initiative (YVI) is a social studies unit for middle and high school students that is designed to enhance students' understanding of and respect for civic participation by engaging them in original research. Using a local, state, or national election as the context, students create and conduct an attitudinal survey of voters between the ages of 18-25, analyze the results of the survey, and write and present a paper that reflects the results and significance of their research. Technology is an integral part of this unit. Students create surveys using Microsoft Publisher, Adobe Acrobat, and Word. They use Excel software to compile and analyze data, illustrate data with graphs and charts, and present their research with a PowerPoint presentation.

Objectives
Upon completing this unit the student will be able to:
  1. Create a survey to be integrated into a class website or distributed via email.
  2. Perform data entry and analyze data using Microsoft Excel software.
  3. Create graphs and charts based on quantitative data.
  4. Create graphic presentations using a computer, projector and PowerPoint.
  5. Present results of research in the form of a written research paper and a class presentation.

Time
Six block sessions of one hour and forty minutes each.

Instructional Steps
Day 1: Unit Introduction and Goals
Steps:
  + Share with students the importance of youth participation in the voting process, using information from the Rock the Vote website (http://www.rockthevote.com).
  + Explain the purposes of the Youth Vote Initiative unit:
     1. To encourage citizens 18 to 25 years old to vote
     2. To serve as a tool for gaining an understanding of younger citizens' attitudes towards voting and politics
     3. To act as a vehicle for conducting real-world quantitative research
     4. To provide an opportunity for middle and high school students to learn about elections and the voting process through civic participation.

Figure 1: Parental Consent Letter

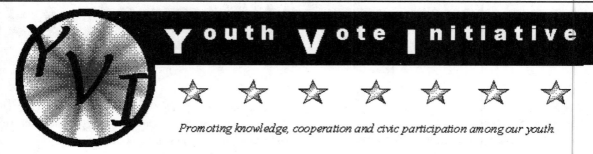

Youth Vote Initiative

Promoting knowledge, cooperation and civic participation among our youth.

Day and Year

Dear Parents:

We are very excited to announce the start of a new unit designed to give our students the opportunity to gain knowledge and experience in and beyond the classroom. **Youth Vote Initiative** is a research project whose goal is to facilitate students' understanding and active participation in the democratic process. Its primary purpose is to combat the apathy among our nation's youngest voters through knowledge, cooperation, action and awareness. YVI encourages middle school students to survey voters from 18 to 25 years old and to record the data for classroom analysis and discussion.

Please review with your child the survey form included in this package.

If you have any questions or concerns regarding this assignment, please call or email me using the information below.

Thank you,

Name of Instructor
Grade and Subject
Phone: Email:

- Explain to students the steps of the unit, as well as the goals and objectives they must meet during the process.
- Distribute the Power to Our People Participatory Research Kit: Creating Surveys (http://datacenter.org under Research Tools) for the class to use as a reference guide.
- Explain and distribute a parental consent letter (Figure 1) for students to take home and inform their parents of the activity.
- Explain and distribute an election survey form for survey participants to complete (see Figure 2).
- Have the class brainstorm a list of possible survey questions to be included in an attitudinal research survey of 18 to 25 year-old voters who are students in a local university. The teacher will make arrangements with social science content and education professors to have their students complete the survey via e-mail.
- Pair students into groups of two to create the survey and do the research project. These pairs will work together for the duration of the project.
- Explain the parameters of the survey.

HOMELEARNING EXTENSION: Have each group use the list of questions, the Power to Our People Participatory Research Kit: Creating Surveys, and the internet to research actual surveys, and create their own surveys using Adobe Acrobat, Publisher, and/or Word.

TEACHING TIPS: Suggest to university professors that they make the completion of the survey a mandatory part of their respective coursework.

Day 2: Survey Presentation and Preparation for Distributing Surveys

- Have each pair take turns presenting their surveys to the class using a computer and projector. The pairs are to discuss the following points:
  - The overall organization of the survey
  - The readability of the survey
  - The design and aesthetic quality of the survey
- Have the class discuss which survey they would like to adopt for the research study. They may decide to modify or combine the characteristics of two or more surveys. Once the class has decided on a survey (through a class vote or general consensus), the teacher will create the final electronic version to be uploaded onto the class website and attached to an email.
- Discuss the protocol for sending surveys via e-mail to university professors, who will distribute surveys to their students. Students will, as a class, write a one-paragraph introduction in which they describe themselves as a class, state their objectives, and ask that the professors have their students complete the surveys using one of the following steps: 1) University students may log onto the class website, complete the survey online, and submit the results electronically, or 2) The teacher can send an e-mail to the university professors, with the survey as an attachment. The university professors will photocopy the surveys and give them to their students to be completed in class. The teacher will pick up the completed surveys.

TEACHING TIPS: Plan on having 10 percent more university students complete the survey than desired in order to make up for unusable surveys containing errors.

Day 3: Survey Inspection and Identification

- Discuss with students the mechanics of survey inspection and identification:
  - Inspect each survey for recording errors (an excessive number of items left blank or unintelligible responses), and decide as a group the criteria for discarding surveys
  - Assign each survey a number
  - Organize surveys in numerical order
  - Staple numbered surveys into sets of five or ten so that they can be easily managed for inputting data
- Break up into pairs and perform survey inspection and identification.

TEACHING TIPS: Before inspection and identification the teacher should have available printed versions of all surveys that university students completed online.

Day 4: Excel Workshop

- Introduce and discuss the basic purpose of a computer spreadsheet program and why it is important for the Youth Vote Initiative research project.
- Assign each student a computer in the computer lab allowing him or her to follow along and repeat the steps that the teacher will model on a projected monitor in front of the room.
- Model the following tasks while the student performs each of them on his/her own computer:
  - Creating a new worksheet
  - Creating and labeling data fields
  - Entering data
  - Creating simple formulas, such as equating cells with

Figure 2: Sample Election Survey

Thank you for participating in this election survey. Are you between the age of 18-25, registered to vote in the upcoming elections, and are you completing this survey for the first time?

☐ Yes to all. You are eligible to complete this survey by responding to the questions below.

☐ No to one or more. You are not eligible to complete this survey.

IDENTIFICATION AND HISTORY

1. Name (optional) _____
2. Age_____
3. Gender: ☐ Male ☐ Female
4. Race/Ethnicity (Please check one)
   ☐ Hispanic   ☐ White/Caucasian
   ☐ Black (non-Hispanic)   ☐ Asian
   ☐ Other
5. Family Origin/Nationality (*Please specify name of country*)
   _____
6. Marital status:
   ☐ Single   ☐ Married   ☐ Divorced
7. Number of children _____

EDUCATION

8. Have you graduated from high school or obtained a degree? ☐ Yes   ☐ No
9. (If the answer to question 8 is yes). What was the highest degree you earned?
   ☐ High school   ☐ Associate   ☐ Bachelor
   ☐ Graduate   ☐ Doctorate
10. Are you presently a student? ☐ Yes ☐ No
    If yes, specify where: ☐ High school   ☐ College
    ☐ University   ☐ Trade/technical school
11. Have you ever participated in JROTC or a military school?
    ☐ Yes   ☐ No

EMPLOYMENT

12. Are you currently employed? ☐ Yes ☐ No
    If yes, please specify type of employment: _____
    _____
13. Have you ever served in the U.S. Armed Forces?
    ☐ Yes   ☐ No

POLITICS AND VOTING

14. Which political party are you currently registered under?
    ☐ Democratic   ☐ Republican
    ☐ Other (please specify) _____
15. Which of the following candidates are you likely to vote for in the upcoming election? (specify candidates)
    _____
16. Is this your first time voting in a local, state, or federal election? ☐ Yes   ☐ No
17. Which is the most important issue influencing your vote this election? (Choose one)
    ☐ Economy/Jobs   ☐ Public/Higher Education
    ☐ Environment   ☐ Foreign Policy
    ☐ Healthcare   ☐ Morals/Values
    ☐ National security   ☐ Other
18. Which is your primary source for gaining political information? (Choose one)
    ☐ Newspaper   ☐ Radio   ☐ Television
    ☐ Internet   ☐ Posters and Billboards
    ☐ Parents/relatives   ☐ Friends
    ☐ Teachers/Professors   ☐ Other
19. Do you feel your vote counts and can make a difference? (Please check one)
    ☐ Not at all   ☐ Somewhat   ☐ Very Much
    ☐ Much more than the average person
20. Do you consider yourself politically informed? (Please check one)
    ☐ Not at all   ☐ Somewhat   ☐ Very Much
    ☐ Much more than the average person
21. What is the name or location of the polling place where you are authorized to vote?
    Please specify _____
    ☐ Don't know
22. Would you be interested in becoming a Youth Vote Initiative Mentor for a future voter presently attending middle or high school?
    ☐ Yes (please provide contact information)
    ☐ No

other cells and adding, subtracting, multiplying, and dividing the numbers in a range of cells.

+ Display a survey template-Excel worksheet as a model for students to learn how the formulas work
+ Model the following tasks while the students repeat on their own computers:
  - Creating formulas for calculating percentages
  - Creating charts and graphs using the information from the spreadsheet
  - Labeling and formatting charts and graphs.

HOMELEARNING: SURVEY DATA ENTRY

+ Have each pair of students copy onto a floppy disk or USB flash-drive copies of the teacher-prepared survey template.
+ Assign each pair a pre-determined amount of surveys to enter onto the spreadsheet.

TEACHING TIPS: Have examples of assignments saved onto a file-sharing computer network for students to access while in the lab. If no network is available, manually create a folder of assignment examples on each lab computer.

Day 5: Youth Vote Initiative Research Paper and Presentation Guidelines

+ Display the completed "Survey Data Results" using a computer and projector for class discussion and analysis.
+ Introduce the group research paper and presentation portion of the unit. Individually or in groups of two, students will complete a research paper and presentation based on the raw data from the Survey Data Results.
+ Review with students the Youth Vote Initiative research paper and presentation guidelines (See Figure 3).
+ Have each pair of students choose a research question for their paper and presentation. They may choose from a list, which the teacher has displayed on the board, or create their own question. No two pairs may have the same research question. The research question must be answerable based on conclusions drawn from the Survey Data Results.
+ Arrange time in the computer lab so that students have the opportunity to do one or more of the following:
  - Use the internet to find ideas for creating their own research question
  - Use Excel to extract data from the Survey Data Results in order to create new spreadsheets aimed at answering their research questions
  - Create charts and graphs based on their own data

sheets
  - Use a word processor to begin an outline for their research papers.

HOMELEARNING: RESEARCH PAPER AND PRESENTATION PREPARATION: Students will write a research paper and prepare a presentation based on their findings using the format stipulated in the research paper and presentation guidelines.

TEACHING TIPS:

+ Reserve sets of relatively easy research questions for students who find the assignment particularly challenging.
+ If available, show the students a model research paper and presentation completed by students from a previous school year.
+ If time permits, have students hand in a rough draft of their research paper, or give time in class for peer review of rough drafts, using rubrics for guidance.

Day 6: Student Presentations and Discussion

+ Have students present research findings to the class.
+ Encourage the class to provide constructive feedback and discussion for each group's research, presentation, and conclusion.

Assessment
See page 100 for a rubric.

Student Enrichment
Extensions
As one extension of the research in which the students engage during the Youth Vote Initiative, students may participate in an Election Day Mentoring Activity. For this activity, students accompany a voting adult to the polls and then interview this adult.

Later the students present their interview responses and reflections on their Election Day experiences as written essays and topics for class discussion.

Once the students have participated in the Youth Vote Initiative unit and have reached its objectives, the teacher can introduce research related assignments where students can apply those skills: (1) Have students survey members of their communities on shared problems or concerns; (2) Survey other students in school on attitudes towards achievement, extra-curricular activities, or other school related issues; (3) Students could also perform long-distance research where they

(Continued on page 101)

Research Paper Rubric

Objective: Upon completing this lesson the student will be able to write an actual research paper based on findings after completing an attitudinal survey analysis.

Criteria	Quality				Total
	4	**3**	**2**	**1**	
Introduction	The paper provides a well-written research question and outline of the main points to be discussed.	The paper provides a plainly written research question and outline of the main points to be discussed.	The paper provides a poorly written research question and outline of the main points to be discussed.	The paper is missing either a research question or outline of the main points to be discussed.	
Hypothesis	The paper provides a well-explained research-based hypothesis.	The paper provides an adequately-explained research-based hypothesis.	The paper provides a poorly explained and researched hypothesis.	The paper provides a hypothesis without a research base.	
Data Collection	The paper provides a clear overview of the following: type of data collection, participants, time and place.	The paper provides an overview of three of the following: type of data collection, participants, time, and place.	The paper provides an overview of two of the following: type of data collection, participants, time, and place.	The paper provides an overview of one of the following: type of data collection, participants, time, and place.	
Data Analysis	The paper shows detailed procedural steps and analytical results, and how they are both clearly linked to the research question.	The paper shows partially detailed procedural steps and analytical results, and how they are both linked to the research question.	The paper shows poorly detailed procedural steps and analytical results, and how either is linked to the research question.	The paper shows poorly detailed procedural steps and/or analytical results with no link to the research question.	
Charts and Graphs	The paper includes clear and concise charts and/or graphs that strongly reinforce the written analytical results.	The paper includes charts and/or graphs that adequately reinforce the written analytical results.	The paper includes charts and/or graphs that poorly reinforce the written analytical results.	The paper includes charts and/or graphs with no link to the written analytical results.	
Conclusion	The paper concludes with the following: a well-written summary of the research, the research findings, and opinion of the overall significance.	The paper concludes with the following: a plainly written summary of the research, the research findings, and opinion of the overall significance.	The paper concludes with only two of the following: a written summary of the research, the research findings, and opinion of the overall significance.	The paper concludes with only one of the following: a written summary of the research, the research findings, and opinion of the overall significance.	
Mechanics	The paper has no more than 2 misspellings and/or grammatical errors.	The paper has 3 or 4 misspellings and/or grammatical errors.	The paper has 5 or 6 misspellings and/or grammatical errors.	The paper has 7 or more spelling errors and/or grammatical errors.	
Paper Guidelines	The paper adheres to all the following guidelines: contains title page with student name, period, date, and title; 1" margins; Times New Roman or Arial 12 Point font; 5-10 pages; double spaced	The paper adheres to all but one of the paper guidelines.	The paper adheres to all but two of the paper guidelines.	The paper adheres to all but three of the paper guidelines.	
Total Points					

study the attitudes of students in another country via e-mail and the internet.

Strategies Addressing the Unique Needs of Students

Throughout the unit lessons encourage students to pair or form groups when performing various activities. Doing so allows greater peer-to-peer assistance when the class is engaged in creating ideas, writing, researching, and working with technology. We believe this approach is invaluable to classrooms with Limited English Proficiency students, students with learning disabilities, and other students with special needs.

Technology Resources

HARDWARE

Computer Laboratory, Laptop Computer, LCD Projector, Computer Network (optional)

SOFTWARE

Microsoft Excel, Word, PowerPoint, Adobe Acrobat, and Publisher

Resources

INTERNET

Data Center. "Power to our people: Participatory research kit: Creating surveys." Retrieved Aug. 15, 2005, from http://www.datacenter.org

Rock the Vote. Retrieved Jan. 8, 2005, from http://www.rockthevote.com/is_whyvote.php

PRINT

Berson, M., B. Cruz, J.A. Duplass, and J.H. Johnston. 2004. *Social Studies on the Internet*, Second Edition. Upper Saddle River: Pearson Education.

Roblyer, M.D. 2003. *Integrating Educational Technology into Teaching*, Third Edition. Upper Saddle River: Pearson Education.

OTHER MATERIALS NEEDED

YVI parent letters; survey form; sample survey template; research paper and presentation guidelines; rubrics; directions for use of Excel.

Student Voices

The following quotations are from students in an 8th grade social studies gifted class in a public middle school in the Miami-Dade County Public Schools. These students were among those who participated in the Youth Vote Initiative research project from September to November 2004. The quotations come from post-research e-mail interviews conducted with the students in July 2005.

"This experience made me more interested in the elections. It made me want to figure out a new way of voting, or at least a way that would make me feel like my vote counted. I guess I have to wait more years to see." – *Grade 8 student.*

"Throughout this assignment I've become very interested in seeing what ethnic group would vote most for what candidate, as well as how people receive their political information, and what issues have more significance in [respect to] their vote than others. As my project came to a finish, I was extremely pleased with the amount of young people, ages 18-25 who decided to vote in the 2004 election. I'm also content knowing that the future of the United States is in the hands of people who care about where this country is headed." – *Grade 8 student.*

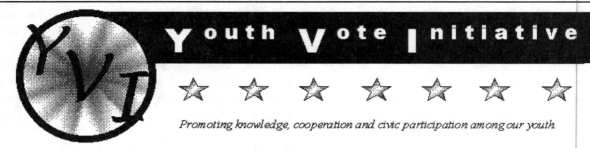

Youth Vote Initiative Research Paper and Presentation Guidelines

Objective: While working in groups of two, the students will devise a research question based on the data they collected from the YVI survey. They will then write a research paper and prepare a presentation based on their findings using the criteria below.

I. Research Question
Have students devise their own research question or list possible questions on the board for them to choose. The questions will depend on the categorical data from the YVI survey. For example, if one of the survey's data categories is gender and another is political party, a possible research question could be: How are the political parties divided based on gender?

2. Research Paper: Format and Contents
   A. *Introduction*: The introduction must contain the research question and an outline of the main points to be discussed in the research paper.
   B. *Hypothesis*: The students will give a hypothesis of what they believe will be the findings of the research. They must also provide concrete evidence as to why they have come to that conclusion. This section should require students to do some research and gather references.
   C. *Data Collection*: The students will give an overview and explanation of how they obtained the research data (research method, participants, time, place, etc.)
   D. *Data Analysis*: The students will explain the steps they will take in order to analyze their targeted data from the raw data provided by the survey. They must show how the procedure is in direct relation to answering their research question.
   E. *Charts and Graphs*: The students will create at least one chart or graph, which fully reflects the outcome of their analysis.
   F. *Conclusion*: The conclusion should contain a brief summary of the research paper, the research findings, and the significance of the research findings within the overall context of voting and citizenship.
   G. *Paper Guidelines*: Title page with student name, period, date, and title; 1" margins on top, bottom, and sides; Times New Roman or Arial; 12 Point font; 5-10 pages; double spaced

3. Student Presentations
   A. The students will share their research findings with the class.
   B. The teacher will encourage the class to provide constructive feedback and discussion for each group's conclusion and presentation.
   C. Presentation Guidelines: 15-30 in duration; must display all charts and graphs from research paper using a projector.

The War of 1812

Chapter **18**

David Calhoun and Simon Meshbesher

Eighth Grade: U.S. History

NCSS Thematic Strands
TIME, CONTINUITY, AND CHANGE

NCSS Performance Expectations
TIME, CONTINUITY, AND CHANGE

b. Identify and use key concepts, such as chronology, causality, change, conflict, and complexity to explain, analyze and show connections among patterns of historical change and continuity.

NETS-S National Educational Technology Standards for Students
1. Basic Operations and Concepts
5. Technology Research Tools
6. Technology Problem-solving and Decision-making Tools

NETS-S Performance Expectations
1. Basic Operations and Concepts
+ Students demonstrate a sound understanding of the nature and operation of technology systems.

5. Technology Research Tools
+ Students use technology to locate, evaluate, and collect information from a variety of sources.
+ Students use technology tools to process data and report results.
+ Students evaluate and select new information resources and technological innovations based on the appropriateness for specific tasks.

6. Technology Problem-solving and Decision-making Tools
+ Students use technology resources for solving problems and making informed decisions.

Objectives
The student will be able to:
+ Create a PowerPoint slide show.
+ Answer why the War of 1812 should or should not be referred to as the Second American Revolution.
+ Identify five major events of the War of 1812.
+ Identify two causes of the War of 1812.
+ Create a research log.
+ Create and use a class-generated rubric.

Teaching Tips
The Task
You are an investigator for FDH, the Foundation for Debatable History. The FDH has conscripted you and your classmates to help solve an extremely debatable history question: Should the War of 1812 be called the Second American Revolution?

For your search you will create a 10-slide presentation using Power Point. The slides are to broken down accordingly:
+ 2 slides for causes of the War of 1812
+ 5 slides explaining some of the major events of the war period of 1812 to 1814.
+ 3 slides answering and explaining the group's answer to the question, should the War of 1812 be called the Second American Revolution?

Each group will also create a research log to present for the group research grade.

The Process
The whole class will construct a Power Point presentation on the War of 1812. This presentation is to be 10 slides in length.

Begin your research by using the sites specifically designated for the War of 1812. However, be sure to also review the general information sites and print sources as well. Here are the web sources:

http://library.thinkquest.org/22916/index.html
http://www.historychannel.com/1812/
http://www.pbs.org/wgbh/amex/presidents/04_madison/printable.html
http://www.dean.usma.edu/history/web03/atlases/atlas_toc.htm
(click on "The War of 1812")

As you research, use the following questions to guide you through the information.

- Who was involved?
- What happened?
- Where did it happen?
- Why did the event occur?
- When did the event occur?
- How did people act or react at that time?
- How can their actions be considered to continue to affect us today?

The group research log should be completed in Microsoft Excel. The directions for completing the log are as follows:

1. Head the first column "Job Completed." In this column, list any job that was completed for the project, i.e. internet research, slide production, etc.
2. Head the second column "Date/Time Completed." Fill in the time and date when the job was completed.
3. Head the third column "Completed by Whom." List the name(s) of the person(s) who worked on this part.

Learning Advice

- Remember to include an illustration, map, drawing, or political cartoon to enhance your slides.
- All internet articles used must be cited. Do not plagiarize!
- Illustrations may be student created, downloaded, or copied from other sources. If using someone else's work, be sure to cite the source.

Assessment

- Each student will complete a research log.
- Each student will critique his/her own and peers' work, by using a class or teacher created rubric.
- Each group will create a slide show as to why the War of 1812 should or should not be referred to as the Second American Revolution.

Technology Resources

HARDWARE

Laptop computers, Microphones, Digital Cameras

SOFTWARE

Microsoft PowerPoint, Internet Browser, Pinnacle, Real Player, Div X, Windows Media Player 🌐

Geography in Action: Locating a Site for a Video and Game Rental Store

19

Frederick W. Koehl

Eighth Grade: Geography and Economics

NCSS Thematic Strands

Ⅲ PEOPLE, PLACES, AND ENVIRONMENTS

Ⅶ PRODUCTION, DISTRIBUTION, AND CONSUMPTION

NCSS Performance Expectations

Ⅲ PEOPLE, PLACES, AND ENVIRONMENTS

d. Estimate distance, calculate scale, and distinguish other geographic relationships, such as population density and spatial distribution patterns.

h. Examine, interpret, and analyze physical and cultural patterns and their interactions, such as land use, settlement patterns, cultural transmission of customs and ideas, and ecosystem changes.

Ⅶ PRODUCTION, DISTRIBUTION, AND CONSUMPTION

b. Describe the role that supply and demand, prices, incentives, and profits play in determining what is produced and distributed in a competitive market system.

NETS-S National Educational Technology Standards for Students

3. Technology Productivity Tools
6. Technology Problem-solving and Decision-making Tools

NETS-S Performance Indicators (Grades 6-8)

3. Technology Productivity Tools

- Use content-specific tools, software, and simulations (e.g., environmental probes, graphing calculators, exploratory environments, Web tools) to support learning and research.

6. Technology Problem-solving and Decision-making Tools

- Select and use appropriate tools and technology resources to accomplish a variety of tasks and solve problems.

Introduction

In this lesson students will use geographic information systems (GIS) software to map and analyze a series of socioeconomic variables. The objective is to use these data to recommend a specific location for a new video and game rental store. Through this exercise students will gain an understanding of available socioeconomic data, their relationship to consumer demand for different kinds of products and services, ways in which these data can be mapped and analyzed, and how such information and analytical processes can be used to make locational decisions.

Objectives

The student will be able to:

1. Identify socioeconomic criteria associated with the successful marketing and operation of a video store.

2. Evaluate data at the census tract level to determine alternatives for a possible store site.

3. Utilize basic GIS software to compare and map alternatives, and ultimately recommend and justify a specific site.

Time

Two to three one-hour sessions

Instructional Steps

Teachers should download the files needed for this lesson from http://www.fredkoehl.com, following the instructions in the Resources section on p. 111 below.

Following are specific instructions for students to implement the lesson. The instructions guide them through use of the software and prompt them to answer a series of interpretive questions.

Questions that students must answer will be highlighted on the left like this: **?** Students should answer in the space provided.

In this activity you will use geographic information systems (GIS) software to examine and analyze different factors that might be important in locating a new retail store. Using the data available, you will recommend a specific store location within a local neighborhood. You will explain the factors you considered most important, and describe how the geographic concentration and/or dispersion of those factors influenced your recommendation.

Step 1. Start ArcExplorer

Left-click on the Start button with your mouse. From your teacher, find where the ArcExplorer Java Edition for Education (AEJEE) program is located on your computer, and double-click on its icon.

The ArcExplorer view window will appear:

Step 2. Add Information to Your Project

Left-click the button that looks like a plus sign: This is what's called the Add Data button, and it lets you add information to your project. Clicking it brings up the Content Chooser dialog box. Using the box, navigate to the computer directory specified by your teacher. You should have three files to choose from. One by one, and in the order that follows, highlight the name of the file and click the OK box in the lower right. Start with 2000_tracts.shp, then majroads.shp, and finally points of interest.shp.

Your window should show these data elements listed on the left, plus they are drawn on the map! Note that each data source has a check box that is currently checked. This means the information is drawn on the map. Try clicking on the check box to un-check it. What happens? The information is not drawn on the map unless that box is checked! Be sure all

three boxes are checked before you move ahead.

OK—we're where we need to be! You should see a base map of sections of Fulton and DeKalb Counties in the Atlanta, Georgia area, with census tract boundaries and a network of major roads. It should look something like this:

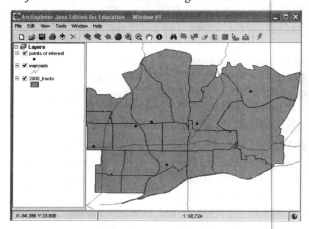

This is the study area we'll use for possibly opening up a new Movie and Game rental store. Census tracts are areas used by the U.S. Census Bureau to categorize their data geographically. These units are generally smaller than zip codes. Information like population (in total and by age range), household income, and educational levels are examples of data provided at the census tract level. We'll explore some of these data elements further in this activity.

First, let's make the roads more visible. Highlight the "Major Roads" ("majroads") theme name, right-click on it, and then left-click on "Properties." You should bring up the Properties dialog box. It will look something like this:

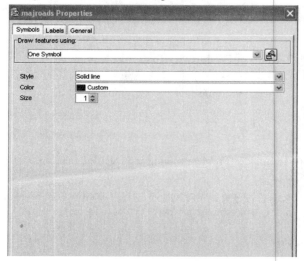

The Symbols tab in the upper left should be highlighted. Be sure that you are "drawing features using One Symbol" and that your Style is "solid line." Click on the down arrow next to Color and choose a color that shows up well, like red. Change the Size to "3," click "Apply," then "OK." Now the roads should be even easier to pick out!

Let's get oriented to the geography covered by this map. This is an area on the east side of the city of Atlanta, Georgia. The road running east-west pretty much through the center of the map is Ponce de Leon Avenue. The road that branches off to the northeast from its intersection with Ponce de Leon in the center of the map is Briarcliff Road. Piedmont Road runs generally north-south through the left side of the study area. To check the names of some of these roads, use the Identify tool that looks like this: **ⓘ** . The cursor will change to the shape of this tool; click on any one of the roads. In the dialog box that comes up the name of the road will be indicated in the "Street" field.

? Identify each of the roads on your map and write the names in on the outline map below.

Now highlight and right-click on "points of interest." Left-click on "Properties," and this time click on the Labels tab. Under "Label features using" select NAME, and click OK. You will now see the names of several points of interest in the study area displayed on the map.

? Locate the Carter Presidential Center, Emory University, and Grady High School on the outline map below. When you're done, go back to "Properties" for the "points of interest," and select "None" as your field, then click "OK." The labels should disappear from your map.

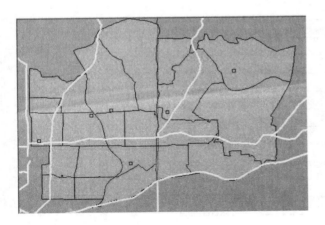

Step 3. Practice Viewing Data Distributions in ArcExplorer

Let's work with some of the data available to us about this area. Using the process you've worked with before, highlight and right-click on the "2000 Tracts" name, and then left-click on "Properties." Use the "Symbols" tab and "Draw features using graduated symbols." Under "Field," select the MFI99 field--you will have to scroll down. (This data element represents the median family income in each tract in 1999. In Step 4 you will see a complete description of all the fields accessible in this project). The number of classes should be "5," classified by "Equal Interval." Click "OK" and your map has really changed!

You are now looking at the distribution of incomes by census tract, with the darker colors representing the higher incomes. The ranges of income associated with each color are now shown in the list to the left of your map.

? What income levels are represented by the lightest color?

? What income range is represented by the darkest color?

? Describe the areas of this part of Atlanta that have the highest incomes on this map. Use compass directions and, if it helps, go back and label the streets and points of interest again.

Go back to the "Properties" box for the "2000 Tracts" theme again. Change the field to "Age_65_up." Click "OK." Now, instead of mapping household income, we have mapped the distribution of people age 65 and older. This map looks quite different from the map of income distribution. This map shows the population density of people age 65 and older by census tract. (Note: Because the area of each census tract is different, instead of the total number of people in a category, we use the number per square mile. This allows us to compare tracts on an "apples-to-apples" basis.)

? Describe (using compass directions or other descriptive ways) where the greatest concentrations of older people are.

Let's review what we've done so far. We've mapped the distribution of two different data elements within our study area. If your teacher wants you to save your work, click "File," then "Save As," and type in a file name once you've navigated to the directory specified by your teacher.

Now let's start to do some real analysis and make some decisions!

Step 4. Start Exploring the Best Locations for Your New Store!

In this exercise you are a young business person who wants to open your own retail store. You love movies and games, and know a lot about them, so you really want to open up your own video store. We'll assume there are no such stores currently open in this study area. You know there is enough demand for such a store in this area; you have many friends who have to travel outside the area to rent or buy movies and games. Your objective now is to determine exactly where within the area is the best location for your store.

Let's review the description of all the data available, by census tract, for you to make your decision. Below is a list of all the information you have available to help make your decision.

These data come from the U.S. Census Bureau (collected during the census conducted every ten years) and from the Atlanta Regional Commission, the regional planning agency for the Atlanta area. The data are included in a key "theme" in our project, the "2000 Tracts" theme.

? Using the list of available data above, identify the four fields of data you think would be most important in determining where to locate your store. In other words, which are the data elements that, if they have high values (or maybe even low values), are the best indicators of success for your store? Is it the greatest population density? The most employees? The households with the highest income? The greatest concentrations of young or old people? Etc.

Data Field	Description
Area	Area of the census tract in square miles
Acres	Area of the census tract in acres
Pop1990	1990 Population Density
Pop2000	2000 Population Density
Pop0015	Forecast change in population density, 2000–2015
White	White Population density, 2000
Black	Black or African American Population density, 2000
Hispanic	Hispanic Population density, 2000
Age_under5	Population density ages 0-4, 2000
Age_5_17	Population density ages 5-17, 2000
Age_18_21	Population density ages 18-21, 2000
Age_22_29	Population density ages 22-29, 2000
Age_30_39	Population density ages 30-39, 2000
Age_40_49	Population density ages 40-49, 2000
Age_50_64	Population density ages 50-64, 2000
Age_65_up	Population density ages 65 and older, 2000
Pop5_29	Population density ages 5-29, 2000
Pop5_29shr	The share of the 2000 population made up of people ages 5-29
Med_age	Median age of the population, 2000
Avg_hh_sz	Average household size (avg. # people per HH), 2000
Families	Number of families per square mile, 2000
Hh	Number of households per square mile, 2000
Mfi99	Median Family Income, 1999
Emp90	Employment density, 1990
Emp99	Employment density, 1999
Emp9099	Change in employment density, 1990-1999
Emp9915	Forecast change in employment density, 1999-2015
Coll_ed	Percent college graduates, 2000 (of all persons 25 years and older)

1. _____

2. _____

3. _____

4. _____

? Now, explain your selections. Why do you think these variables are the four most important for your product and your store?

Using the process and steps we followed earlier, use the "2000 Tracts" theme to create maps showing the distribution of each of the four data elements you think will be most helpful in locating your new store. Highlight and right-click on "2000 Tracts" and then left-click on "Properties" to allow you to select the data fields you think are helpful from the "Field" drop-down box. One-by-one, create maps of each of the four data elements. Before you go on to the next map, see Step 5 for printing your map, or recording key information on a sketch map.

Step 5A. Analyze Maps of Your Data

If you can use a printer, follow these instructions. If not, skip to Step 5B.

With your map view on the screen, click "View" at the top left, then "Layout View." You can modify your map for printing now. Use the "Add Text" button **A** to add a text box to your map view. Right-click on the text box and left-click on "Properties." Then type in a descriptive title for your map. Also include your name in the map title. Click "Apply," then "OK." You may need to use your mouse to move the title to a good place on the map. Now click on "File," then "Print." Be sure the printer you'll use is specified under "Printer." Change the "Page Setup" or "Appearance" settings if your teacher directs you to. Finally, click "Print" and go get your map!

Go through this same process to map each of your four key data elements. When you have maps for each of your variables, lay them side-by-side and examine the patterns. Go to Step 6.

Step 5B.

If you can't use a printer, generate maps on the screen of each of your data variables, making note of the patterns and concentrations you see for each of them. You may want to make sketch maps showing which parts of the study area rank high and low on each of the variables. Go to Step 6.

Step 6. Recommend a Specific Site for Your Store!

Are there census tracts that rank consistently high (or "good") on each one of the maps? Are there "good" tracts that cluster together, or are they scattered around the study area? Think carefully about the distributions and patterns reflected by these maps. On the base map below, put an "X" where you think the best location may be for your store, based on your review and analysis of the maps. Put the "X" as precisely as

possible where you'd locate your store. Below the map, explain your thought process, and explain and justify your decision.

Also, save your project one last time as directed by your teacher.

? Explain why you have selected the specific site for your store. Discuss in detail the influence of the data elements you've focused on.

? Also, think whether there was a kind of information that would have been helpful in conducting this analysis, but was not available to you. Was there any information that could have made your analysis and selection better? Please explain and discuss.

? Finally, in Step 4 we made the assumption there are no such stores currently open in this study area. If there were already other stores in the area, how might that have changed your analysis and your recommendation?

Assessment

Assessment of each student should come from a combination of qualitative review of their work as the exercise progresses, and student responses to the questions contained within the activity sheet. Specifically, examine the students' understanding at two levels. First, at a somewhat "factual" level, evaluate students' ability to identify various features of the study area, and their ability to follow the instructions and prepare thematic maps. Then, at a more advanced level, assess students' critical thinking skills in their selection of data, explanation of that selection, and their justification of their specific site selection. Also assess students' writing skills and their ability to effectively communicate their thought process and recommendations. The assessment rubric for the full evaluation follows.

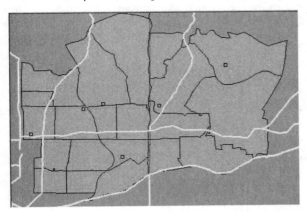

Assessment Rubric

Assessed Content	Advanced	Proficient	Partially Proficient	Does Not Meet Requirements
Identification of various features on base map of study area (20%)	All requested locations were accurately identified and labeled on base map. (20 points)	Most requested locations that are labeled on computer are accurately identified and labeled on base map. (17 points)	Two or three of the locations that are labeled on computer are accurately identified and labeled on base map. (15 points)	Less than two of the locations that are labeled on computer are accurately identified and labeled on base map. (0 points)
Map generation (15%)	Student generates four interpretable maps from selected data. (15 points)	Student produces at least three interpretable maps from selected data. (12 points)	Student produces one or two interpretable maps from selected data. (10 points)	Student is unable to produce an interpretable map from selected data. (0 points)
Selection and justification of data pertinent to site decision (30%)	Student selects data elements that relate to site location for video store AND provides a good explanation for their selection. (30 points)	Student selects data elements that relate to site location for video store AND provides some explanation for their selection. (25 points)	Student selects data elements that partially relate to site location for video store AND provides some explanation for their selection. (15 points)	Student selects data elements that partially relate or are unrelated to site location for video store AND provides limited or no explanation for their selection. (0 points)
Rationale for specific site recommendation (35%)	Student makes a site recommendation that is supported by maps, data, and student's written explanation. (35 points)	Student makes a site recommendation that is generally supported by maps, data, and student's written explanation. (30 points)	Student makes a site recommendation that is only partially supported by maps, data, and student's written explanation. (20 points)	Student makes a site recommendation that is not supported by maps, data, and student's written explanation. (0 points)

Student Enrichment

Students can further explore ways of modifying their maps to make them more effective and interpretable. For example, allow students to experiment with different colors and patterns when they map data from the "2000 Tracts" theme.

Students can also access the "American Fact Finder" site from the U.S. Census Bureau (http://factfinder.census.gov/). If they click on "Maps" they can explore reference and thematic maps, using census data, for their local community.

Teaching Tips

1. The teacher needs to complete the lesson him/herself completely before asking the students to do so. This way, the teacher can anticipate questions and provide additional direction to students.

2. Before beginning the lesson, provide an overview of geographic information systems to give some context to the students. Good background information is found on the GIS.com website (www.gis.com). Other good resources include www.esri.com/mapmuseum, www.gisday.com, www.geographynetwork.com, and http://www.esri.com/industries/k-12/atlas/index.html.

3. Introduce the lesson by giving an overview of the concept and principles of market analysis, with specific reference to decisions of "what goes where." Remind the students that the market influences even the location of their school: where are there enough students to support a school in a given community? Brainstorm with students why certain types of stores are located where they are. For example, where are fast food restaurants typically located—on major streets or in quiet residential neighborhoods? Why?

4. Then transition to the purpose of this lesson, which is to map and analyze factors important in deciding where to locate a particular type of retail store. Describe the procedures the students will follow, the intended result of the exercise, and how the students will be evaluated. Distribute and review the instructions and the assessment rubric. It will probably help if you download the Word document of the lesson (see the Resources section, below). This will permit you to create more space on the student handout for their responses.

5. If appropriate, encourage students to save their work on the computer frequently. This will keep them from losing work in case of a computer problem.

6. Depending on the availability of computers and the room arrangement, this activity is suitable for cooperative work by two or three students.

7. If only a black and white printer is available, have students prepare their maps using grey and black tones.

8. When there are about 10 minutes remaining in the overall exercise, assemble the students for a concluding discussion. Using an overhead transparency of the study area, have students indicate their site recommendations. Plot the student recommendations on the overhead. Picking two or three sites, lead a discussion of the reasons for these particular recommendations. Remind the students of the context for this work: daily, "real world" decisions of how to use real estate and capital in the market. See how knowledge of geography is applied!

Technology Resources

HARDWARE

Windows: Win2000 or WinXP, 100 MB hard drive space, Pentium III or faster processor recommended, and more than 64 MB RAM.

Macintosh: MacOS 10.3 or above, 100 MB hard drive space, G4 or faster processor recommended, and more than 64 MB RAM.

SOFTWARE

The ArcExplorer software is available free from the developer, ESRI. It may be downloaded from http://www.esri.com/software/arcexplorer/download.html. Select the "ArcExplorer – Java Edition for Education Version 2" option. You may also wish to download the "Introduction to ArcExplorer Java Edition for Education" file available from the same page.

Resources

INTERNET

The majority of the data used in this activity were obtained from the U.S. Census Bureau. Census data for other geographic areas can be obtained from http://factfinder.census.gov/. Selected data have been obtained from the Atlanta Regional Commission (http://www.atlantaregional.com).

The following data files need to be loaded on each computer used in the activity. The files may be obtained from http://www.fredkoehl.com. Click on "NCSS Lesson." This provides access to the files, which may be downloaded directly to your computer. Each of these files should be in the same folder on the hard drive. You may also download a Word version of the lesson: Geography in Action Lesson.doc. If there are any difficulties accessing the data, or other questions about this exercise, please contact the author at fred.koehl@comcast.net.

2000_tracts.shp	points of interest.shp
2000_tracts.dbf	points of interest.dbf
2000_tracts.sbn	points of interest.sbn
2000_tracts.sbx	points of interest.sbx
2000_tracts.shx	points of interest.shx
majroads.shp	majroads.shx
majroads.dbf	

PRINT

None

OTHER MATERIALS NEEDED

None 🪨

part 3
For High
Schools

Erie Canal WebQuest

Darci Mitchell, Tom Darrow and Barbara Slater Stern

20

Eighth to Twelfth Grades: U.S. History and Geography

History/Social Science Discipline
American History

NCSS Thematic Strands
Ⅲ PEOPLE, PLACES, AND ENVIRONMENTS
Ⅷ SCIENCE, TECHNOLOGY, AND SOCIETY
Ⅱ TIME, CONTINUITY, AND CHANGE

NCSS Performance Expectations
Ⅲ PEOPLE, PLACES, AND ENVIRONMENTS

h. Examine, interpret, and analyze physical and cultural patterns and their interactions, such as land use, settlement patterns, cultural transmission of customs and ideas, and ecosystem changes.

i. Describe ways that historical events have been influenced by, and have influenced, physical and human geographic factors in local, regional, national, and global settings.

Ⅷ SCIENCE, TECHNOLOGY, AND SOCIETY

b. Make judgments about how science and technology have transformed the physical world and human society and our understanding of time, space, place, and human-environment interactions.

Ⅱ TIME, CONTINUITY, AND CHANGE

d. Systematically employ processes of critical historical inquiry to reconstruct and reinterpret the past, such as using a variety of sources and checking their credibility, validating and weighing evidence for claims, and searching for causality (High School).

c. Identify and describe select historical periods and patterns of change within and across cultures, such as the rise of civilizations, the development of transportation systems, the growth and breakdown of colonial systems, and others (Middle Grades).

NETS-S National Educational Technology Standards for Students
2. Social, Ethical, and Human Issues
3. Technology Productivity Tools
5. Technology Research Tools

NETS-S Performance Expectations

2. Social, Ethical, and Human Issues
- Students practice the responsible use of technology systems, information, and software.
- Students develop positive attitudes toward technology uses that support lifelong learning, collaboration, personal pursuits, and productivity.

3. Technology Productivity Tools
- Students use technology tools to enhance learning, increase productivity, and promote creativity.
  Students use productivity tools to collaborate in constructing technology-enhanced models, prepare publications, and produce other creative works.

5. Technology Research Tools
- Students use technology to locate, evaluate, and collect information from a variety of sources.
- Students use technology tools to process data and report results.

Introduction
This lesson is a ninety minute multimedia WebQuest on the Erie Canal. The students work independently on wireless laptops to watch mini videos, look at panoramic photographs of the growth of cities, read mini histories, and listen to folk songs in order to enrich their understanding of the Erie Canal and its impact on the surrounding area. The WebQuest structures the students' exploration of the website and asks the students critical thinking questions to monitor their comprehension of the content.

Objectives

Students will be able to:

1. Locate the Erie Canal on a map: the region and state, its cities of origin and terminus, and the two bodies of water it connects.
2. Use multimedia to enrich their understanding of the time period surrounding the building of the Erie Canal.
3. Critically analyze why the Erie Canal was created and decide whether they think it would still be useful today.
4. Explain, in their own words, how canal locks operate.
5. Examine how the creation of the Erie Canal led to population growth in the cities surrounding its banks.
6. Compare the economic impact of the Canal with that of the Transcontinental Railroad (later lessons).

Time

Ninety minutes. More time may be needed if students are not comfortable with the technology.

Instructional Steps

+ Assign students to individual computers and show them where to access the WebQuest. Each school's network is different, so the teacher should load the file onto each computer, load it into the students' network folders, or upload it onto a website, such as PortaPortal.
+ When the students have opened the WebQuest, explain that the students will answer the WebQuest questions on the Word document on their screens. They should put their names on the top of their documents, and send their files to the printer when they are finished. Distribute headphones to students so that they can complete the WebQuest and listen to the videos and songs at their own pace without disturbing other students. Students should be informed that the directions are detailed step-by-step on their WebQuest screen, but that the teacher would be happy to assist them. Students can also assist one another in getting started as long as they understand that their questions are to be worked on independently. (Usually it takes about five minutes for the students to get the hang of it, but beyond that, even the most computer illiterate could handle the assignment independently.)
+ Circulate around the room, making sure that the students understand the instructions and are finding the information they need. Also, since this is a web based assignment, it is important to monitor that the students

are only visiting Erie Canal websites.
+ As students finish, make sure they print their completed WebQuest. It helps to read aloud the names of WebQuests the teacher receives to insure that each student has printed his or hers before closing their Word documents. Depending on the lab setup students may want to print their completed WebQuests without saving to insure that they do not save their answers on the WebQuest template, which may be used by other classes.
+ Note: If some students finish their WebQuests with class time remaining, encourage them to further explore the Erie Canal websites, listen to the songs, look at more panoramas, photos, etc. that were not selected by the teacher.

Assessment

The WebQuest works best when graded in terms of participation and completion, rather than analyzing the responses. Teachers may assess the content later in a unit test, where the students will have to know the physical location of the Canal (cities and bodies of water) and answer questions about economic and population impact.

Differentiation

This WebQuest is intended for average or above-average performing students. The website used features some activities, such as history for kids, which are aimed at students with lower reading levels. Also, if the teacher has fewer than ninety minutes available, he or she can select specific parts of the WebQuest, depending on the needs of the class.

Student Enrichment

Students could further research one or more of the boom town cities along the Canal to determine how many of them continued to grow after the peak of the Canal, and which ones suffered and shrunk when the Canal lost its popularity. Advanced students might enhance their knowledge by researching current plans for redevelopment of decaying sites along the Canal as a future tourist destination.

Teaching Tips

As with any use of technology, try accessing the website, playing the movies, and exploring the 360° panoramic views prior to teaching this lesson to ensure that the computers have the software needed. Also, installing the WebQuest Word document onto the computers prior to this activity is necessary.

Erie Canal Computer Activity Instructions and Questions

Read the following instructions and then answer the questions, as prompted, in this Word document.

1. Go to the website http://www.epodunk.com/routes/erie-canal/

2. Click on the link "This Journey Through History"

3. Watch, and answer questions on information from the introductory video.
   The Erie Canal originates at what city and terminates at what city?
   How many years did it take to build?
   What two bodies of water were connected by the canal?
   What city became the economic city of the new world?

4. From the link "History" click the option "Erie Canal History"

5. Read the Erie Canal History and answer the history questions below.
   Who was the governor of New York who supported the project?
   What were some barriers to the creation of the canal?
   How much did the canal cost to build?
   What are the cities and bodies of water at the start and end of the canal?
   How many miles long was the canal?
   How much did the elevation change?
   What year was the canal opened?
   List five products shipped along the canal.
   What did the Erie Canal do to the populations of the cities around it?
   How did the canal influence the outcome of the Civil War?

6. Click on "Canal Tour". Pick two towns (dots) from each section of the canal (East and West) and answer the questions below.
   City on the east side (name):
   Elevation:
   One interesting fact:
   Population:
   City on the west side (name):
   Elevation:
   One interesting fact:
   Population:

7. Click on "Panoramas." Select "Albany: 1909 view" and then "Albany: 1911 view".
   Write what has changed during these two years and why you think this has happened.

8. Go to the website www.eriecanal.org/locks.html
   Watch the animation of how canal locks work. (Watch it once and then click refresh for it to start at the beginning again.)
   Write down the major steps involved in raising a barge up in elevation.

Critical Thinking

Now that you've learned so much about the Erie Canal, explain in your own words why you think it was built. Would it still be useful today?

Technology Resources

HARDWARE

Any computer lab or mobile wireless lab will work, as long as each student has his or her own computer, the computers are capable of playing audio files, and the computers are connected to at least one networked printer or individual printers.

SOFTWARE

Internet Explorer or another web browser that can play the videos and songs. Teachers should preview the WebQuest activity before using it in their classes to ensure that their software and web browser works with the website. Any word processing software should be adequate for the students to record their answers to the WebQuest.

Resources

INTERNET

The Erie Canal, "Locks on the Erie Canal" (2005), http://www.eriecanal.org/locks.html.

Epodunk, "The Erie Canal: A Journey Through History" (2005), http://www.epodunk.com/routes/erie-canal/.

OTHER MATERIALS NEEDED

Each student will need headphones in order to watch the videos and listen to the songs at his or her own pace without disturbing other students. Most school computer labs have a class set of headphones available.

Student Voices

The students who piloted this WebQuest were 8th graders. They were thrilled to use the mobile lab in the classroom. They were absolutely silent and enthralled throughout the ninety minutes, and numerous students commented on how much fun this lesson was and how they'd love to do more activities like this in the future.

Ex Nihilo: Creating a Civilization

21

ROBERT COVEN AND BILL VELTO

NINTH AND TENTH GRADES: WORLD HISTORY, GLOBAL STUDIES AND GEOGRAPHY

NCSS Thematic Strands

❶ CULTURE

Ⅶ PEOPLE, PLACES, AND ENVIRONMENTS

Ⅷ SCIENCE, TECHNOLOGY, AND SOCIETY

NCSS Performance Expectations

❶ CULTURE

c. Apply an understanding of culture as an integrated whole that explains the functions and interactions of language, literature, the arts, traditions, beliefs and values, and behavior patterns.

Ⅶ PEOPLE, PLACES, AND ENVIRONMENTS

e. Describe, differentiate, and explain the relationships among various regional and global patterns of geographic phenomena such as landforms, soils, climate, vegetation, natural resources, and population.

Ⅷ SCIENCE, TECHNOLOGY, AND SOCIETY

b. Make judgments about how science and technology have transformed the physical world and human society and our understanding of time, space, place, and human-environment interactions.

NETS-S National Educational Technology Standards for Students

4. Technology Communications Tools
5. Technology Research Tools

NETS-S Performance Indicators (Grades 9-12)

4. Technology Communications Tools
5. Technology Research Tools

+ Routinely and efficiently use online information resources to meet needs for collaboration, research, publication, communication, and productivity.

+ Collaborate with peers, experts, and others to contribute to a content-related knowledge base by using technology to compile, synthesize, produce, and disseminate information, models, and other creative works.

Introduction

This is a long-term project that is done in components. In the end, the students will have taken part in developing a nascent civilization. They will learn some of the difficulties that faced every society and what it took to overcome them. Of course, they are doing it in miniature—something that took millennia and involved thousands of people—in one semester and combining the efforts of a small group. The civilizations may be based anywhere in the world, but the time frame may be no more recent than 500 BCE. The four components of the project are:

1. *Ecce Homo* (the students establish the geography, environment, technology, economy, government, social structure, and culture of their civilization);

2. *Lingua Nova* (the students create an alphabet, syntax, and grammar for their civilization—the basic components of an oral and written language);

3. *Fiat Lux* (the students develop a creation myth for their civilization); and

4. *Terra Incognita* (the students create art, architecture, and an urban plan for their civilization).

All materials are presented on websites developed by the students. The students present the civilization to the class as though they were at a professional conference and they were the archaeology team who discovered the civilization.

Objectives

The student will be able to:

1. Work in a collaborative manner, i.e., negotiate a fair distribution of labor.

2. Define "civilization" and formulate its constituent elements.

3. Show how geography and the environment (climate, topography, resources, location) affect the evolution of civilizations.

4. Establish how people define themselves (identity), and determine who belongs to the group and who is an outsider.

5. Show how civilizations demonstrate their identity

through art, myth, language, and conceptions of race.

6. Demonstrate an understanding of the elements and structure of language and its importance in the development of a civilization.

7. Write a myth that shows an understanding and sensitivity to world folklore and demonstrates an understanding of the elements of a myth, and the importance of myth in creating group identity and transmitting a group ethos.

8. Make presentations orally and through written, electronic, and videographic media.

9. Conduct library and electronic research.

10. Develop an informative, accessible, and attractive website.

Time

We do this lesson in stages over a fourteen-week trimester. We typically use twelve class periods (forty five minutes in length) scattered through the term to work, along with outside homework time. The time schedule could certainly be expanded or compressed, however.

Instructional Steps

Students receive the following instructions:

LESSON 1 (ECCE HOMO): In the first stage of this project, your group must establish the basic identity of your civilization. You will need to figure out:

+ The kind of environment in which your people live (topography, geographic location, climate, ecology and resources, flora and fauna, and geology, i.e., minerals and metals);

+ What kinds of technology your civilization possesses (stone, metal, agriculture, transportation, war);

+ The structure of your society (kind of government—e.g., despotic tyranny, open democracy)—be careful to keep it to systems that existed then;

+ Laws and legal structure;

+ Social organization, gender roles, whether there are classes (hierarchy) based on status (wealth, education, military and religious standing) ;

+ Economy (barter, coinage, agriculture, "industry");

+ Style of art and architecture;

+ Values and beliefs; role of religion – ritual, control of society, morals and values; mythology;

+ Education (practical and moral).

Each group should decide how to manage the work. Try to split the load fairly and evenly, so that students can share their ideas and talents and have an equal share of the responsibility. Each group should present its material in the form of a well-organized expository essay—no more than two pages long.

LESSON 2 (LINGUA NOVA): All you know has come to you through language. Man is capable of language, both spoken and written. It is this evolutionary advantage that is responsible for our success as a species. Language is also a prerequisite for civilization. People need to be able to communicate in order to maintain our lives in increasingly complex societies.

For this phase of the Civilization Project, your group is to develop a new language. The focus will be on creating a system of writing, though many civilizations functioned with only an oral language.

You will present an alphabet of no fewer than twenty (20) characters. You will need to provide consonants and vowels. The vowels can be written as letters or as diacritical marks. You will need to show the evolution of at least five characters of your alphabet from pictograph to ideograph and from ideograph to alphabet. You may do this through the use of computer software, like Photoshop, or through a series of sketches.

Written languages require an alphabet, but all forms of language have a grammar and vocabulary. Therefore, you will need to provide these elements for your language. The table below provides the required and optional elements expected of your group's language.

Required

Number	Singular and plural
Tenses	Past, Present, and Future
Possessive	My cat. Peter's book.
Nouns	Dog. Tablet.
Pronouns	His, Her, I, You
Verbs	Walk. Talk. Eat.
Indications for questions, ends of sentences, exclamations.	What are you doing? None of your business. Stop!
Indications for subject and object.	The boy bought the book.

Optional

Adjectives (including superlative and comparative)	Blue, large, larger, largest
Adverb	Slowly, happily.
Prepositions	Up, down, in
Conjunctions	And, or, with
Complete set of punctuation	, . -- - ? !
Articles	A, the
Formal, informal	Tu, usted, you/thee
Inflection and accents	È, È, é

LESSON 3 (FIAT LUX): Creation myths are the key to understanding a culture's identity and sense of purpose. These legends are attempts to bring meaning to our lives and to our universe. Science provides us with progressively clearer explanations of the world around us. We have been able to explore and study stars billions of light years distant, to the atomic structure of our cells. But much remains outside our grasp. It is here, in the unknown, that myth becomes our guide.

In this phase of the Civilization Project, your group will develop a creation myth—a tale which will evoke what is most important to your society: who you are and what you value. Your group's myth will be modeled on the stories told by other civilizations. However, you should avoid following someone else's tale too closely; your story should be as distinctive as your culture.

Your creation myth should address how you, as a people, and your world came into being. The tale should be written as a story of two-to-three pages.

For extra credit, you may choose to present a copy of your myth written in your civilization's language. It may also be possible for you to produce a copy of your film in your language, with subtitles, as well.

LESSON 4 (TERRA INCOGNITA): This phase of the project will provide your group a final opportunity to enhance the work you submitted in previous phases and to add three new components to the description of your civilization: architecture, art, and city planning. For the architecture component, you are to design a minimum of two buildings—at least a temple and an ordinary person's house must be included. Other buildings can be added to your sites at your group's discretion. For this section you will need to produce both images and a description. The description should include: number, type, and size of rooms; materials; how the designs reflect cultural norms, geography, and social status; and, for the temple, how the design reflects rituals.

You will need to present at least two types of art, one performing (e.g., drama, music, or dance) and one visual (e.g., painting, sculpture, jewelry, or pottery). As with the architecture, you will need to show how these works reflect the culture (customs and beliefs) of your civilization. One of your challenges is to find a way to communicate this information through your web pages.

Finally, you will need to create a visual representation of the layout of your city (this might be presented in the form of a model, drawing, or sketch, for example). This image must appear on your web page. In addition, you will be required to post a one- to two-page description of the main features of your city plan. All cities take their form because of a combination of cultural, social, political, intellectual, economic, and geographic factors. You might want to address these in your description.

You will, as a group, present the total project in front of the class. This should be thought of as though you are before your colleagues at an academic conference. You can use your website to illustrate your talk, but you will need to go beyond simply reading from the site. It is expected that each member of the group will contribute equally to this oral presentation.

Assessment

Observations of group dynamics; student self-evaluation; grade individual steps as well as final projects.

Student Enrichment

Many of the lessons include extensions for students who want to go beyond the expectations of the assignment. For example, students can provide additional complexity to this language by doing the optional parts. They may also write and film the myth in the language they create. Obviously, other possibilities exist. Students could build a 3-D model of their city using clay or other art materials. They could also build it using computer modeling software, if available. Students could design coins (if applicable) or other cultural items to bring in for the presentation. If you have a tolerant principal, you could even have students from one class "excavate" items from cultures created by a different class. The team would have to see if they could accurately figure out what the object was and how it would be used.

Teaching Tips

Have fun! In our experience, the kids really enjoy this. We do too. Feel free to contact us with questions or suggestions.

Technology Resources

HARDWARE

Computers (1 per group); video cameras or digital cameras that take video

SOFTWARE

Ideally: web design and video editing software; can be done with PowerPoint instead of web design and the video shown unedited.

Resources

INTERNET

Kilmon, Jack. The History of Writing. http://www.historian.net/hxwrite.htm.

Learn English. "English Grammar: Nouns." http://www.learnenglish.de/grammar/nountext.htm#BOTTOM.

Library Spot. "Grammar/Style" http://www.libraryspot.com/grammarstyle.htm.

Quinon, Michael. World Wide Words. http://www.worldwidewords.org/pronguide.htm.

Ryan, Donald P. Ancient Languages and Scripts. http://www.plu.edu/~ryandp/texts.html.

PRINT

Campbell, Joseph. *The Hero with a Thousand Faces*. Princeton: Princeton University Press, 1949.

Campbell, Joseph. *The Masks of God: Primitive Mythology*. New York: Penguin, 1987.

Campbell, Joseph. *The Power of Myth*. New York: Random House, 1988.

Conrad, Geoffrey, and Arthur Demarest. *Religion and Empire: The Dynamics of Aztec and Inca Expansionism*. New York: Cambridge University Press, 2001.

Diamond, Jared. *Collapse: How Societies Chose to Fail or Succeed*. New York: Viking, 2005.

Diamond, Jared. *Guns, Germs, and Steel: The Fates of Human Societies*. New York: W.W. Norton, 1999.

Rosenberg, Donna. *World Mythology: An Anthology of the Great Myths and Epics*. 2nd ed. Lincolnwood, IL: National Textbook Company, 1994.

Sacks, David. *Letter Perfect: The Marvelous History of Our Alphabet from A to Z*. New York: Random House, 2003.

Schultz, Emily, and Robert H. Lavenda. *Cultural Anthropology: A Perspective on the Human Condition*. 3rd ed. Mountain View, CA: Mayfield, 1995.

Scupin, Raymond. *Cultural Anthropology: A Global Perspective*. Englewood Cliffs, NJ: Prentice Hall, 1992.

Comparing and Contrasting U.S. Presidential Campaign Ads from the Cold War

22

Brian P. Collins, Rand J. Spiro and Aparna R. Ramchandran

Ninth to Twelfth Grades: US History, Civics and Media Studies

NCSS Thematic Strands
Ⅱ TIME, CONTINUITY, AND CHANGE
✕ CIVIC IDEALS AND PRACTICES

NCSS Performance Expectations
Ⅱ TIME, CONTINUITY, AND CHANGE

b. Apply key concepts such as time, chronology, causality, change, conflict, and complexity to explain, analyze, and show connections among patterns of historical change and continuity.

c. Identify and describe significant historical periods and patterns of change within and across cultures.

d. Systematically employ processes of critical inquiry to reconstruct and reinterpret the past, such as using a variety of sources and checking their credibility, validating and weighing evidence for claims, and searching for causality.

✕ CIVIC IDEALS AND PRACTICES

c. Locate, access, analyze, organize, synthesize, evaluate, and apply information about selected public issues— identifying, describing and evaluating multiple points of view.

NETS-S National Educational Technology Standards for Students
5. Technology Research Tools

NETS-S Performance Indicators (Grades 9-12)
5. Technology Research Tools

+ Select and apply technology tools for research, information analysis, problem-solving and decision-making in content learning.

Introduction

In this lesson, students use EASE History, an online learning environment that supports the teaching and learning of U.S. History. EASE History has three entry points: Campaign Ads, Historical Events, and Core Democratic Values. The three organizing themes are interdependent and supportive. Students can better understand the complexities of campaign issues and their historical context by looking at associated historical events, develop deeper understanding of historical events by looking at campaign ads, and explore the meanings of core values by examining how these values have been applied in both historical events and campaign ads. The richness of the learning that results derives in part from the ability to apply varying conceptual or thematic perspectives to the same material. In EASE History learners can work with hundreds of rich cases in three different viewing modes. The lesson plan includes a guide to comparing and contrasting campaign ads.

Objectives

The student will be able to:

1. Examine historical cases from multiple perspectives.
2. Analyze cases and their related resources.
3. Place historical cases in context.
4. Examine the reliability of sources.
5. Reflect on the connections between campaign ads and historical events.
6. Compare and contrast Cold War campaign ads.
7. Develop a deeper conceptual understanding of the Cold War, the 1960s, and 1960s presidential campaigns.

Time

One 50-minute class period.

Instructional Steps
Dealing with Complexity
The Cold War is a complex concept. Understanding a complex concept like the Cold War is difficult, but fortunately there are habits of mind that can help us to better understand the concept.

Here are a few habits of mind that support conceptual understanding:

+ Look at multiple cases: In order to get a deeper understanding of the Cold War we need to see a lot of cases related to the Cold War.
+ Place events in context: Since context is always changing, no Cold War case is exactly like another. Cold War cases will be sort of similar and sort of different.
+ Multiple Perspectives: Cases are multi-faceted, so you need to look at events from multiple perspectives. A single perspective will not help you fully understand the Cold War.

1. Pair up students. Each pair of students will need a computer w/ high-speed internet connection and two sets of headphones.

2. Go to EASE History at http://www.easehistory.org/ Point out key features.

3. Give each team a "Guide to Comparing and Contrasting Campaign Ads." (See Appendix A: Guide to Comparing and Contrasting Campaign Ads)

4. Have teams examine at least twelve Cold War ads from the 1960s.

5. Give each team a slip of paper with the names of two campaign ads. (See Appendix B: Campaign Ad Pairs)

6. Students should use the guide to compare and contrast their two ads.

7. Come back together as a whole group and discuss how teams compared and contrasted the campaign ads and how their understanding of the Cold War has changed.

Assessment
1. Students can be assessed for their participation in class discussion and small group work.
2. Students can be assessed for their work on the guide.

Student Enrichment
1. Have students ask their relatives what they remember or know about the historical events that surrounded the 1960s ads.

2. Have students use the Historical Thinking Guide, available online in the EASE History Learning Guide, to compare and contrast historical events.

3. Have students compare and contrast historical events or campaign ads across/within different decades.

4. Have students write more formal essays about the Cold War.

Teaching Tips
To become familiar with EASE History's content and features, take the EASE History tour and spend time exploring the system. Throughout the lesson use the language of historical thinking and flexible habits of mind: multiple perspectives, multiple cases, looking again, revisiting, it depends, context dependent, making connections.

Technology Resources
HARDWARE
Computers: PCs or Macs. High speed internet connection. Digital projector.

SOFTWARE
EASE History requires Flash 7 or higher.

Resources
INTERNET
EASE History is available to the general public and can be viewed at http://www.easehistory.org/

PRINT
History textbook for background information.

OTHER MATERIALS NEEDED
Copies of the "Guide to Comparing and Contrasting Campaign Ads." Headphones.

TECHNOLOGY APPLICATIONS
High speed Internet connection and Flash 7. EASE History can be viewed at http://www.easehistory.org/ 🖼

Guide to Comparing and Contrasting Campaign Ads

Instructions:

+ Go to EASE History — http://www.easehistory.org/
+ Search on Cold War Ads in EASE History. [Search: EASE History Campaign Ads>Issues>Cold War Ads]
+ Examine at least 12 Cold War ads from the 1960s.
+ Find the two ads that are on the slip of paper given to you by the teacher.
+ Complete the guide.

Ad #1

+ Title:
+ Candidate:
+ Year:
+ Party:
+ Do you think that this source is reliable?
  Rate from 1 2 3 4 5 6 7 (circle one)
+ Why did you give the source this rating?

Ad #2

+ Title:
+ Candidate:
+ Year:
+ Party:
+ Do you think that this source is reliable?
  Rate from 1 2 3 4 5 6 7 (circle one)
+ Why did you give the source this rating?

Watch the two ads.

1. First Impressions

+ What is the first ad about? What is the second ad about?
  Ad #1 is about:

  Ad #2 is about:

It is important to look again. We see more when we continue to revisit cases.

2. Looking Again

Look at the two ads again.

+ After looking again at the videos, what did you notice that you didn't notice the first time around?
  I noticed that in Ad #1:

  I noticed that in Ad #2:

The circumstances in which an event occurs is called context. Since context is always changing, each case will be sort of similar and sort of different from other cases.

3. Placing Cases in Context

Think about the context that surrounds each case (i.e. situation, time period shown, people and objects). Use the resources available through each case, prior knowledge, and information from your textbook, to help you place these cases in context.

+ Thinking about context, how are the cases sort of similar and sort of different?

Similarities	Differences
1.	1.
2.	2.
3.	3.

Campaign ads often highlight their candidate's strengths and compensate for their candidate's weaknesses.

4. Each Campaign Ad has Multiple Goals

+ How does each ad highlight the candidate's strengths and compensate for the candidate's weaknesses? In EASE History, candidate profiles include information on the candidate's strengths and weaknesses.

	Case 1	Case 2
How are the candidate's strengths highlighted?		
How does the ad compensate for the candidate's weaknesses?		

Campaign ads are complex because one single theme or perspective cannot tell its whole story. Your ability to look at cases from multiple perspectives can help you have a deeper understanding of the ad.

5. Viewing Cases from Multiple Perspectives

+ Describe each case from four different perspectives.

Perspective #1: National Security	Perspective #2: Patriotism
Perspective #3: Common Good	Perspective #4: Freedom

Campaign Ad Pairs
See EASE History at http://www.easehistory.org

Group 1. Richard Nixon's 1960 "Important" ad and John F. Kennedy's 1960 "Issue" ad. *Search on "1960" in the Campaign Ads Menu to find these two ads.*

Group 2. John F. Kennedy's 1960 "Issue" ad and Richard Nixon's 1968 "Leadership" ad. *Search on "1960" "or" "1968" in the Advanced Theme Search to find these two ads.*

Group 3. Richard Nixon's 1968 "Leadership" ad and Hubert Humphrey's 1968 "Ahead" ad. *Search on "1968" in the Campaign Ads Menu to find clips.*

Group 4. Hubert Humphrey's 1968 "Ahead" and John F. Kennedy's 1960 "Kennedy". *Search on "1960" "or" "1968" in the Advanced Theme Search to find these two ads.*

Group 5. John F. Kennedy's 1960 "Kennedy, Kennedy" ad and Barry Goldwater's 1964 "March" ad. *Search on "1960" "or" "1964" in the Advanced Theme Search to find these two ads.*

Group 6. Barry Goldwater's 1964 "March" ad and Barry Goldwater's 1964 "Reagan" ad. *Search on "1964" in the Campaign Ads Menu to find these two ads.*

Group 7. Barry Goldwater's 1964 "Reagan" ad and Lyndon Johnson's 1964 "Daisy" ad. *Search on "1964" in the Campaign Ads Menu to find these two ads.*

Group 8. Lyndon Johnson's 1964 "Daisy" ad and Richard Nixon's 1968 "Chicago" ad. *Search on "1964" "or" "1968" in the Advanced Theme Search to find these two ads.*

Group 9. Richard Nixon's 1968 "Chicago" ad and Hubert Humphrey's 1968 "Bomb" ad. *Search on "1968" in the Campaign Ads Menu to find these two ads.*

Group 10. Hubert Humphrey's 1968 "Bomb" ad and Lyndon Johnson's 1964 "Cone" ad. *Search on "1964" "or" "1968" in the Advanced Theme Search to find these two ads.*

Group 11. Lyndon Johnson's 1964 "Cone" ad and Richard Nixon's 1960 "Important" ad. *Search on "1964" "or" "1960" in the Advanced Theme Search to find these two ads.*

Group 12. Hubert Humphrey's 1968 "Ever Done" ad and John F. Kennedy's 1960 "A Week" ad. *Search on "1968" "or" "1960" in the Advanced Theme Search to find these two ads.*

Group 13. Richard Nixon's 1968 "Percy" ad and Lyndon Johnson's 1964 "Poverty" ad. *Search on "1964" "or" "1968" in the Advanced Theme Search to find these two ads.*

Lights, Camera Action: Using Digital Movies to Study History

23

Cheryl Mason Bolick and Eddie Gray

Ninth to Twelfth Grades: U.S. History and World History

NCSS Thematic Strands
Ⅲ TIME, CONTINUITY, AND CHANGE

NCSS Performance Expectations
Ⅲ TIME, CONTINUITY, AND CHANGE

d. Systematically employ processes of critical historical inquiry to reconstruct and reinterpret the past, such as using a variety of sources and checking their credibility, validating and weighing evidence for claims, and searching for causality.

NETS-S National Educational Technology Standards for Students:
4. Technology Communications Tools
5. Technology Research Tools

NETS-S Performance Indicators (Grades 9-12)
4. Technology Communications Tools
5. Technology Research Tools
   + Routinely and efficiently use online information resources to meet needs for collaboration, research, publications, communications, and productivity.
   + Select and apply technology tools for research, information analysis, problem-solving, and decision-making in content learning.

Introduction

This lesson uses a digital movie to present a justification of why it is important to study history. Students watch a teacher-created digital movie that explores the notion that "History should be studied because it is essential to individuals and to society, and because it harbors beauty" (Stearns, 1998). After watching the movie, students use iMovie (Mac OS) or MovieMaker (Windows) to construct their own digital movie that explores a dimension of history. In this lesson, students will develop an understanding of why they should study history and develop technical skills that will allow them to create a digital movie.

The historical and technical skills learned in this lesson can be applied throughout the curriculum.

Objectives
The student will be able to:
1. Obtain an understanding of why it is important to understand history.
2. Create a digital movie that demonstrates competence in conducting historical inquiry.
3. Develop the technical skills required to create a digital movie.

Time
3 days

Instructional Steps
Begin class by asking students to brainstorm a list of reasons why it is important to study history? Once students have had the opportunity to reflect on the question, engage students in a whole class discussion about why students feel it is important to study the discipline.

Show students the teacher-created movie based on Stearn's 1998 essay, "Why Study History" (See Resources on p. 129) Stearn's essay is founded on the premise that history helps us "understand people and societies" and "understand change and how the society we live in came to be." He states, "When we study it reasonably well, and so acquire some usable habits of mind, as well as some basic data about the forces that affect our own lives, we emerge with relevant skills and an enhanced capacity for informed citizenship, critical thinking, and simple awareness."

The 6-minute video we developed and showed students was created using copyright free photographs, maps, instrumental music, and text. We prepared the video by writing a script, identifying images that helped illustrate the script, and selecting music that accompanied the script and images.

After playing the video for the class, ask students to reflect on the video by brainstorming a second list of reasons why it is important to study history. Engage the students in a class discussion that explores what they included in their second brainstorm and why they included it.

Ask students to individually prepare a brief essay that responds to the question, why study history? After presenting a rationale for the discipline, students should consider what time period, event or person they would like to know more about. The essays should be collected and assessed by the teacher.

The students will now create their own digital movie that helps them begin to answer the question(s) they posed in their essay. Movies should be 3-5 minutes in length.

Demonstrate the skills necessary to create a digital movie in either iMovie or MovieMaker. Provide students with handouts that lead them through the basic steps required to create a movie. The web pages provided at the end of this lesson have helpful guides on using the programs.

Direct students towards helpful online collections of primary sources [a list of helpful resources is included later in this lesson]. Demonstrate how to effectively search for images and primary sources using search engines such as Google.

It is essential to address copyright issues with students at the start of the assignment. Students should be instructed only to use documents that are copyright free or documents they have received permission to use. (A helpful resource is included at the end of the lesson.)

As students identify copyright free digital history resources to be included in their movie, they should save the document to a designated area (network space or disk). To save, students should click on the document and select "Save As."

Once students have collected the digital historical resources, they should create a storyboard of their movie. The storyboard should include the titles of the historical documents, narration, and song titles.

Students should submit their storyboard to the teacher or to a peer for review. It is helpful to get feedback at this point of the development process.

Students should make any suggested revisions and then begin constructing their digital movie. Using either iMovie or MovieMaker, students should import images and audio, and record narration.

Depending on amount of time and student skill, students may add creative transitions or effects.

Demonstrate how to insert the title page and credits page.

Students should save their projects to a designated area.

Assessment

The assessment is three-fold: reflective essay, movie storyboard, and completed movie.

The reflective essay should be read for conceptual understanding of the importance of studying history. Provide narrative feedback for each student.

The final movie storyboard should be submitted and assessed using a rubric. It is important to assess the movie script to emphasize the importance of the content of the movie. Otherwise, students may get carried away with the technical bells and whistles. The movie script should include the full script of the movie narration with titles of the images that will be displayed and the music to be played.

Teaching Tips

We recommend that the teacher model a digital movie before asking students to create one. This not only provides a model for the students, but also ensures the teacher is familiar with the technology. A collection of digital movies that was created by teachers using an online collection is available for viewing at http://docsouth.unc.edu/classroom/narratives/.

We used this lesson on the first day of school. It was an exciting way to welcome students back to school and engage them in the study of history. After watching the video on the first day, the students broke into a round of applause.

Students can work in teams or individually to make their digital movie. The teacher should decide whether to assign the movie topic or to let students select their own topic. To insure all students complete a movie, we suggest assigning a topic and limiting the resources from which student can select. When students create movies later in the school year, the topic and resources may be broadened. This helps focus the students on the technical skills.

If working on teams, each student should have an assigned role to insure all students contribute to the development of the movie. If students do not have equal access to computers, teachers should allow ample class time or make arrangements for students to have access to computers.

A computer lab full of students can be a noisy place to record movie narration. By having students prepare a script in advance, it reduces the amount of recording time needed for each student. The teacher should arrange a specific place for recording. Students may record in the library, hallway, or empty classroom.

When teaching a unit, the teacher could require all students to create a digital movie. Or, the teacher could assign one or two students the task of creating a movie to share with the class. This provides each student with the opportunity to create a movie throughout the school year. A compilation of the movies could be used to help review material covered at the end of the school year.

Technology Resources

HARDWARE

Internet-connected computer for each student or team of students; projector to demonstrate the teacher-created movie; microphones to record audio, CDs to save the movies (unless they are saved to a network space)

SOFTWARE

Apple iMovie or Windows MovieMaker

Resources

INTERNET

"Copyright resources." *Learning & Leading with Technology,* 32, no. 7 (2005), 22-23. Accessible at http://www.iste.org/Template.cfm?Section=Publications

The Digital History Inquiry Project. Retrieved August 19, 2005, from http://www.historicalinquiry.com/links/index.cfm

Digital History: Using New Technologies to Enhance Teaching and Learning. Retrieved August 19, 2005, from http://www.digitalhistory.uh.edu/music/type_noncopyright.cfm

Documenting the American South. Retrieved August 19, 2005, from http:docsouth.unc.edu

iMovie HD in the Classroom. Retrieved August 19, 2005, from http://www.apple.com/education/imovie/

The Library of Congress Learning Page. Retrieved August 19, 2005, from http://memory.loc.gov/learn/

Magnatune. Retrieved August 19, 2005, from http://www.magnatune.com/

New York Public Library Digital Collection. Retrieved August 19, 2005, from http://www.nypl.org/digital/

The Perseus Digital Library. Retrieved August 23, 2005 from http://www.perseus.tufts.edu/

Stearns, P. (1998). Why Study History. American Historical Association. Retrieved August 28, 2005 from: http://www.historians.org/pubs/Free/WhyStudyHistory.htm

U.S. National Archives and Records Administration. Retrieved August 19, 2005, from http://www.archives.gov/

Using Digital Media with Windows XP: A Guide for Educators. Retrieved August 19, 2005 from http://www.microsoft.com/education/MovieMaker.mspx

The Virginia Center for Digital History. Retrieved August 19, 2005 from http://www.vcdh.virginia.edu

OTHER MATERIALS NEEDED

None 🖼

Beg and Borrow: A Consumer Credit Case Application

24

SPENCER MORRISON

NINTH TO TWELFTH GRADES: ECONOMICS

NCSS Thematic Strands
Ⓥ PRODUCTION, DISTRIBUTION, AND CONSUMPTION

NCSS Performance Expectations
Ⓥ PRODUCTION, DISTRIBUTION, AND CONSUMPTION
b. Analyze the role that supply and demand, prices, incentives, and profits play in determining what is produced and distributed in a competitive market system.
c. Consider the costs and benefits to society of allocating goods and services through private and public sectors.

NETS-S National Educational Technology Standards for Students
4. Technology Communications Tools
5. Technology Research Tools

NETS-S Performance Indicators (Grades 9-12)
4. Technology Communications Tools
5. Technology Research Tools
   + Select and apply technology tools for research, information analysis, problem-solving, and decision-making in content learning.
   + Collaborate with peers, experts, and others to contribute to a content-related knowledge base by using technology to compile, synthesize, produce, and disseminate information, models, and other creative works.
   + Routinely and efficiently use online information resources to meet needs for collaboration, research, publication, communication, and productivity.

Introduction
Understanding the financial responsibility of obtaining a loan can be a daunting task. While most students have a general idea of what a loan is, this lesson provides an opportunity to discuss this issue in more detail. This activity will not only expose students to the process of obtaining credit, but it will provide them with a better understanding of the fundamental principles of consumer credit, such as character, capital, and capacity. Students will also

be challenged to utilize their knowledge of choices and trade-offs to role-play the task of approving or declining a loan request as if they were a loan officer at a bank. The case is a fictional scenario based on an actual loan application. Although this lesson was designed for use in an online learning environment via an asynchronous discussion board, it could be easily adapted in the traditional setting as well. Incorporating an electronic discussion board engages all students in the discussion, allows time for reflections and multiple responses, archives the discussion for future reference, and frees up traditional class time.

Objectives
The student will be able to:
1. Understand the process of obtaining credit for general loans.
2. Role-play the banker's side of the lending process to demonstrate an understanding of the principles of consumer credit.
3. Evaluate a loan application and justify approving or denying the loan request by participating in an online chat and writing a letter justifying the group's decision.
4. Compare their perceptions of acceptable risk with standards used by bankers.

Time
Two one-hour sessions (face-to-face).
Four fifteen minute sessions (online).

Instructional Steps
1. Prior to participating in this lesson, the students should have successfully completed the activities for lessons 6-8 located on the Practical Money Skills for Life/At School web site, http://www.practicalmoneyskills.com/index.php (PMSFL). These activities will give students the foundation needed to prepare for this activity challenging them to apply what they have learned in a real life scenario. Tell the students that the activity they are about to participate in is the culminating activity of the unit focusing on obtaining and using credit.

2. The teacher should review with the students the essential elements of the Three Cs of Credit: Character, Capacity, and Capital, and the 20/10 Rule (Does the payment exceed 10% of the borrower's monthly net income? Does the potential borrower have more than 20% of his or her yearly income going towards credit debt?) Project on overhead the 20/10 Rule and the 3 Cs of Credit to use as a reference during the review. These visuals are also posted on the PMSFL website. The review should focus on the reliability of a potential borrower, the availability of assets to be used if income is insufficient, and if the client has enough income to repay the loan.

3. Introduce the activity by distributing Handout 1, "Beg and Borrow," (included with this article) and discussing the procedure for the activity. Explain to the students that they will role-play the task of approving or declining a loan request as if they were loan officers at a bank by applying the 3 Cs and the 20/10 Rule. Inform them that the case they are about to review is a fictional scenario based on an actual loan application. The interest rate used may not reflect the current interest rates at your local bank, but it will provide a realistic estimate for this case. Explain that the activity is not designed to teach them how to run a bank or be a banker. It is designed to teach the fundamental principles of consumer credit by putting the student on the banker's side of the lending process.

4. After the introduction discuss the job description of a loan officer. Students will also have this information in Handout 1. Explain to the students that banks are in business to make money, and the interest earned on loans is a primary and important source of income. Therefore, your job as loan officer is to make as many safe loans as possible. A safe loan is one that is paid on time as agreed on by the borrower. Ask the students, "How do bankers determine which applications will lead to safe loans?" Lead students to the following response: a loan officer needs to look at the potential borrower's loan application, credit history, and financial situation for clues of his or her creditworthiness. Discuss additional details bankers have to consider when reviewing loan requests, such as:

   a. What evidence suggests this applicant will be successful in repaying the loan?
   b. Do any facts signal it may not be in the borrower's best interest to take on more debt at this time?
   c. Will this loan help the person make more money, improve or preserve assets, or meet long-term financial goals?

5. Organize students into groups of four or five and inform them that they will conduct an asynchronous chat over the next five days based on the discussion board titled "Beg and Borrow." The students will use this forum to discuss their decision for approving or declining the loan. If they all agree on approving or declining the application, then discuss the points that lead to that conclusion. If they have reached different conclusions discuss why and what caused the difference. The ultimate goal is for the group to reach a consensus to approve or deny the loan request and justify their decision. One group member is responsible for summarizing the decision and the key points to defend the group's position. This information will be used in the whole class discussion at a later date.

6. Distribute one copy of Handout 2, which shows the background of the applicant for a loan, and Handout 3, which provides a sample of a loan application form. Tell the students that for homework they are to review the loan application and additional background information carefully. From the information provided, they are to determine whether the applicant meets the requirements for all of the Three Cs of credit: character, capacity, and capital, as well as the 20-10 rule (see above). Based on this review, the students are to make a recommendation to approve or decline the loan and justify their reasons for reaching those conclusions and place this response to the discussion board titled "Beg and Borrow."

7. Remind the students to refer to Handout 2 for a general description of the applicant, his financial situation and goals, and the purpose of the loan. The discussion should include the relevant facts and conditions that lead to the decision of approving or denying the loan. They should also refer to the discussion board at least once each day for four out of the five days to add any comments, respond to other postings, or to answer questions based on their responses. Every student needs to post an initial response to the teacher's prompt and reply to at least two different students' posts. Also remind students that the teacher will view the discussions on a daily basis but will only intervene as needed.

8. At the end of the five-day period, the teacher will use one class period to lead a whole class discussion to help the class reach a consensus on the recommendation for approving or denying the loan application. During the debriefing period, the class should discuss the quality of the discussions and the

Continued on page 135

How Much Can You Afford? The 20/10 Rule

never borrow more than 20% of your yearly net income

- If you earn $400 a month after taxes, then your net income in one year is:

    12 x $400   = $4,800

- Calculate 20% of your annual net income to find your safe debt load.

    $4,800 x 20% = $960

- So, you should never have more than $960 of debt outstanding.

- Note: Housing debt (i.e., mortgage payments) should not be counted as part of the 20%, but other debt should be included, such as car loans, student loans and credit cards.

monthly payments shouldn't exceed 10% of your monthly net income

- If your take-home pay is $400 a month:

    $400 x 10% = $40

Your total monthly debt payments shouldn't total more than $40 per month.

- Note: Housing payments (i.e., mortgage payments) should not be counted as part of the 10%, but other debt should be included, such as car loans, student loans and credit cards.

The Three Cs

character—will you repay the debt?

From your credit history, does it look like you possess the honesty and reliability to pay credit debts?

- Have you used credit before?
- Do you pay your bills on time?
- Do you have a good credit report?
- Can you provide character references?
- How long have you lived at your present address?
- How long have you been at your present job?

capital—what if you don't repay the debt?

Do you have any valuable assets such as real estate, savings, or investments that could be used to repay credit debts if income is unavailable?

- What property do you own that can secure the loan?
- Do you have a savings account?
- Do you have investments to use as collateral?

capacity—can you repay the debt?

Have you been working regularly in an occupation that is likely to provide enough income to support your credit use?

- Do you have a steady job? What is your salary?
- How many other loan payments do you have?
- What are your current living expenses? What are your current debts?
- How many dependents do you have?

"Beg and Borrow": A Consumer Credit Case Application

Overview

In this activity, you will role-play the task of approving or declining a loan request as if you were a loan officer at a bank. The case presented to you is a fictional scenario based on an actual loan application. The interest rate used may not reflect the current interest rates at your local bank, but it will provide a realistic estimate for this case. This activity is not designed to teach you how to run a bank or be a banker. It is designed to teach the fundamental principles of consumer credit by putting the student on the banker's side of the lending process. This activity will expose you to the process of obtaining credit and a better understanding of the fundamental principles of consumer credit.

Guidelines/Directions

As a banker you are in business to make money, and the interest earned on loans is a primary and important source of income. Your job is to make as many safe loans as possible. A safe loan is one that is paid on time as agreed by the borrower. But how do you tell which applications will lead to safe loans? To answer this question you need to look at the potential borrower's loan application, credit history, and financial situation for clues on their creditworthiness. When reviewing the loan request, ask questions such as:

+ What evidence suggests this applicant will be successful in repaying the loan?
+ Do any facts signal it may not be in the borrower's best interest to take on more debt at this time?
+ Will this loan help the person make more money, improve or preserve assets, or meet long-term financial goals?

Be sure to review the loan application carefully. From the information provided, determine whether the applicant meets the requirements for all of the Three C's of credit: character, capacity, and capital, as well as the 20-10 rule.

To successfully complete this activity you need to follow the procedure listed below:
1. Carefully review the loan application (Handout 2) and additional background information (Handout 3),
2. From the information provided, the students are to determine whether the applicant meets the requirements for the Three C's of credit: character, capacity, and capital, as well as the 20-10 rule to approve the loan,
3. Based on this review, the students are to make a recommendation to approve or decline the loan and justify their reasons for reaching those conclusions and place this response to the discussion board titled "Beg and Borrow,"
4. The discussion board will be organized for groups of students to interact with one another. The ultimate goal is for each group to reach a consensus on approving or declining the loan request,
5. All students are required to post to the initial teacher prompt and to respond to at least two different student postings during the discussion period.
6. After the face-to-face discussion, the students are to write a one-page letter to the applicant explaining the bank's decision of approving or denying the loan.

"Beg and Borrow": A Consumer Credit Case Application

The Applicant

John Doe, a college graduate, is in need of a computer for personal organization and communication as well as continuing his education. John would like to buy a new computer for $1,200. His monthly net income is $931.00 and monthly expenses are $714.00. John has a checking account and savings at his local bank worth $960.00. Although his savings account could be used to supplement his income and pay for the computer, he is saving it for a specific purpose and does not plan to use it for purchasing the computer. He received a flyer from his bank offering an Any-Reason Loan of up to $3,000 for a 90-day term with an interest rate of 16.05%. The total interest expense to be paid out towards the loan for the 90-day period would be $47.49. This would set the total amount to be repaid at $1,247.49.

significance of understanding the topic of credit. This face-to-face discussion and debriefing period will allow the students to reflect on their asynchronous discussion and prepare them for the final element of this activity.

9. Tell the students that for homework they are to submit to the teacher a one-page letter addressed to the applicant explaining the class's decision of approving or denying the loan. Remind students to refer to the archived discussion board and to include the key facts and conditions that led to the ultimate decision.

Assessment

1. Evaluate the quality of students' contributions to the discussions (face-to-face and electronic discussion board) and the extent to which they demonstrated knowledge, key terms, and concepts obtained from the Practical Money Skills for Life/At School web site regarding credit during chat and the teacher's debrief session.
2. Evaluate the students' letter to the applicant explaining the group's decision, including the key facts and conditions that led to the ultimate decision.
3. A rubric will be used to assess the asynchronous discussions as well as the letter to the applicant. It will be based on Subject Knowledge, Organization of Ideas, and Netiquette. (The rubric is included with this article.)

Student Enrichment

1. As an extension activity, the students could be required to explain under which conditions they might have approved the loan if they decided to deny the request (e.g., a longer period of time). This could be conducted via an online discussion board. This would allow an opportunity for the students to reflect on their decision-making process.
2. Students who were absent or unable to significantly contribute could review the archive of the discussion board to reflect on the discussion to evaluate and list what they could have added to the quality of the discussion and explain if it may have influenced the final decision.

Teaching Tips

1. Possess the skills and equipment needed to facilitate online discussion boards.
2. If you have never used a discussion board in class with your students, to ensure success you may want to hold an initial session in the school computer lab. Have all of the students log in and connect to a discussion forum and interact with one another. This will allow the teacher to model appropriate online discussion techniques and encourage successful contributions.

Continued on page 138

"Beg and Borrow": A Consumer Credit Case Application

CONSUMER CREDIT APPLICATION

IMPORTANT: Read these Directions before completing this Application.

☑ If you are applying for individual credit in your own name and are relying on your own income or assets and not the income or assets of another person as the basis for repayment of the credit requested, complete only Sections A and D. If the requested credit is to be secured, also complete the first part of Section C and Section E.

☐ If you are applying for joint credit with another person, complete all Sections except E, providing information in B about the joint applicant. If the requested credit is to be secured, then complete Section E.

☐ If you are applying for individual credit, but are relying on income from alimony, child support, or separate maintenance or on the income or assets of another person as the basis for repayment of the credit requested, complete all Sections except E to the extent possible, providing information in B about the person on whose alimony, support, or maintenance payments or income or assets you are relying. If the requested credit is to be secured, then complete Section E.

Amt. Requested: $1,200⁰⁰   Pmt. Due Date: 1/15/03   Term: 90 day   Rate: .1605   Purpose: Computer Purchase

Credit Insurance	SGL. C/L _____	SGL. C/L&A/H _____	JT. C/L _____	JT. C/L&A/H _____	NO INS _____

SECTION A- INFORMATION REGARDING APPLICANT

Telephone No. XXX-XXX-XXXX

Full Name John Doe   Birthdate: 4/20/80

Present Street Address: 123 Crescent Avenue   Years There: 1

City: Beaver   State: PA   Zip: 15009   Twp., Borough: Beaver

Social Security No: 123-45-6789   Driver's License No.: _____

Previous Street Address: 689 Langley Street   Years There: 22 years

City: Pittsburgh   State: PA   Zip: 16902   Twp., Borough: _____

Present Employer: Pittsburgh Paints   Years There: 1   Telephone: 412-123-4567

Position or Title: Sales Manager Tra   Name of Supervisor: Jim Barnes

Employer's Address: 2501 Navigation Blvd.

Previous Employer: Best Buy   Years There: 2   Telephone: 412-651-3456

Previous Employer's Address: 6522 Junction Street

Present gross salary or commission: $1,377⁰⁰ per Mt.   No. Dependents: ____   Ages: _____

Alimony, child support, or separate maintenance income need not be revealed if you do not wish to have it considered as a basis for repaying obligation. Alimony, child support, separate maintenance received under: court order ☐   written agreement ☐   oral understanding ☐

Other income: $ None per _____ . Source(s) of other income: _____

Is any income listed in this Section likely to be reduced before the credit requested is paid off?   Yes ☐ (Explain in detail on separate sheet.) _____   No ☐

Have you ever received credit from us? No   When _____   Office _____

Checking Account No.: 8900-1246789-1   Institution and Branch: AIG

Saving Account No: 8900-1246789-3   Institution and Branch: AIG

Name of nearest relative not living with you Jack Doe   Telephone: 412-681-2346

Relationship: Father   Address: 689 Langley Street, Pitsburgh, PA 16902

SECTION B–INFORMATION REGARDING JOINT APPLICANT OR OTHER PARTY (Use separate sheets if necessary.)

Are you a co-maker, endorser, or guarantor on any loan or contract?   Yes ☐   No ☑   If "Yes" for whom?   To who _____

Are there any unsatisfied judgements against you?   Yes ☐   No ☑ Amount $ If "Yes" to whom owed? _____

Have you been declared bankrupt in the last 10 years?   Yes ☐   No ☑ where?   Year _____

Other obligations–E.g., liability to pay alimony, child support, separate maintenance. Use separate sheet if necessary.) No

SECTION E–SECURED CREDIT (Complete only if credit is to be secured.) Briefly describe the property to be given as security:

and list names and address of all co-owners of the property.

Name   Address

Everything that I have stated in this application is correct to the best of my knowledge. I understand that you will retain this application whether or not it is approved. You are authorized to check my credit and employment history and to answer questions about your credit experience with me.

John Doe   10/1/03   _____   _____
Applicant's Signature   Date   Other Signature   Date
(Where Applicable)

Evaluation Rubric for Written Assignments and Asynchronous Postings

	Exceptional - 5	Good - 4	Average - 3	Fair - 2	Minimal - 1	Score
Subject Knowledge Demonstrates learning and understanding	Student addresses all necessary information and demonstrates full knowledge by including all necessary details with explanations and elaboration.	Student addresses the information required, displays knowledge with explanations, but fails to elaborate.	Student addresses information required, displays knowledge with partial explanations.	Student addresses some of the information required, inadequately explained.	Student addresses some of the information required, off task	
Organization Information is well thought out.	Student addresses all necessary information in a logical, interesting sequence which the reader can easily follow	Student addresses information in a logical, interesting sequence; gets point across well.	Student presents information in a logical manner. Easy to follow.	Student shows some evidence of presenting information in a coherent manner; difficult to follow	Student does not present information in a coherent manner; disorganized and/or poorly planned.	
Mechanics Sentence structure Spelling Grammar Neat and orderly	Presentation has no misspellings or grammatical errors and sentences are complete without flaw. Professional appearance, followed directions	Presentation has no more than two misspellings and/or grammatical errors and sentences are complete. Quality appearance, followed directions	Presentation has more than two misspellings and/or grammatical errors, but not enough to distract. Neat and orderly, followed directions	Presentation has fragmented sentences and too many errors. Lacks neatness & orderliness	Illegible Unreadable, did not follow directions	
Netiquette Asynchronous Postings	Contributes by answering questions and posting reflections and responding to others in an encouraging manner. Answers are insightful.	Contributes by answering questions and posting reflections and responding to others in an appropriate manner. Answers are insightful.	Contributes by answering questions and posting reflections and responding to others in an appropriate manner. Answers are not original in thought.	Does not consistently contribute to the discussion by answering questions or posting reflections and is insensitive to others.	Does not contribute to the discussion or postings are insufficient with one or two word responses.	

Total out of (20) = _____

Comments:

3. Provide enough guidelines and information to empower the students with their learning. To accomplish this goal, make sure they know appropriate netiquette, such as criticizing the ideas, not the person posting them. They should also understand what a quality posting should include, such as supporting opinions with facts.

4. The use of a rubric is very beneficial for evaluating student's work during an online chat as well as any performance piece such as the letter. It allows them to focus on specific areas that may need improvement as well as reflect on their growth as a student.

Technology Resources

HARDWARE

PCs with Windows 98 – XP (Minimum requirements.)
Macs with OS 9.X – 10.X (Minimum requirements.)

SOFTWARE

Microsoft Corporation, "Internet Explorer 5.2" (Redmond, WA: Microsoft, 2005), www.microsoft.com/windows/ie/default.mspx.

Blackboard Inc., "Blackboard Academic Suite" (Phoenix, AZ: Blackboard, 1997-2004), www.blackboard.com/us/index.aspx.

Resources

INTERNET

Practical Money Skills For Life, "Practical Money Skills For Life – At School, Student Activities, Lessons 6-8." (San Francisco, CA: Visa Inc., 2000-2004), www.practicalmoneyskills.com/english/at_school/students/teens.php.

PRINT

Bruce E. Larson, "Considering the Move to Electronic Discussions," *Social Education* 61, no. 3 (April 2005): 162 – 166.

Student Voices

The teacher can use the following prompt:

For this task, you are role-playing the part of a loan officer at a bank. After carefully reviewing an applicant's loan application and his background information, post to this discussion board your recommendation to approve or deny the loan request. You will have five days to interact on this discussion forum. Be sure to include the reasons for your decision. The ultimate goal is for your group to reach a consensus on approving or declining the loan request.

You will only be able to view and interact on your group's discussion forum.

Student A: "I would approve the loan request. The applicant's 'character' qualities are very positive and he demonstrates responsibility. He has also held a job for over a year and he has a checking and savings account at the bank."

Student B: "Well, he has a good credit history I guess, but he doesn't make that much money so we should decline the application. He does not have the income capacity to cover the loan over a three-month period. He also has a very short credit history."

Student C: "I agree that he may be responsible enough to pay it back on time but he might not have the money to do it. Therefore, I can't approve the loan. If it were that important to him, he would be willing to use some of his savings for it."

Student A: "I agree with what you said. But he does have the capacity to repay the loan by using his savings account if needed."

Student B: "He could use his savings, but he specifically stated that he intends on using that money for something else and he does not want to use it for this loan."

American Revolution: A Digital Timeline Analysis

Ann-Marie Peirano, Elizabeth K. Wilson and Vivian H. Wright

Tenth Grade: U.S. History

NCSS Thematic Strands
❷ TIME, CONTINUITY, AND CHANGE
❺ INDIVIDUALS, GROUPS, AND INSTITUTIONS

NCSS Performance Expectations
❷ TIME, CONTINUITY, AND CHANGE

b. Apply key concepts such as time, chronology, causality, change, conflict, and complexity to explain, analyze, and show connections among patterns of historical change and continuity.

c. Identify and describe significant historical periods and patterns of change within and across cultures, such as the development of ancient cultures and civilizations, the rise of nation-states, and social, economic, and political revolutions.

NETS-S National Educational Technology Standards for Students
2. Social, Ethical, and Human Issues
3. Technology Productivity Tools
5. Technology Research Tools

NETS-S Performance Expectations
2. Social, Ethical, and Human Issues
- Students practice responsible use of technology, systems, information, and software.

3. Technology Productivity Tools
- Students use technology tools to enhance learning, increase productivity, and promote creativity.

5. Technology Research Tools
- Students use technology to locate, evaluate and collect information from a variety of sources.
- Students use technology tools to process data and report results.

Introduction
This lesson is a culminating activity for an American Revolution unit. Students will create a digital timeline of the American Revolution using Microsoft Photo Story 3. Using the Internet, books, other instructional materials, and concepts/information they have learned in class, students will produce a timeline of the major events and ideas that took place during the American Revolution. They will then collect photographs and drawings either from Internet sources or originally produced work. Drawings done by students will be scanned to convert them to digital format. As a final step they will insert their photos and information, as well as music appropriate for the time period, into Microsoft Photo Story 3, creating a digital timeline presentation. The finished project will be presented to the class.

Objectives
The student will be able to:

1. Recognize and evaluate the causes of the American Revolution, how America won independence, and the significance of the American Revolution. (NCSS Thematic Strand: ❷ TIME, CONTINUITY, AND CHANGE; ❺ INDIVIDUALS, GROUPS, AND INSTITUTIONS)

2. Create a digital timeline of the American Revolution using Microsoft Photo Story 3. (NCSS Thematic Strand: ❷ TIME, CONTINUITY, AND CHANGE)

Time
One 45-minute session; Two 98-minute sessions; One 60-minute session.

Instructional Steps
Day 1 (45 minutes)

1. Students will complete this project as a culminating assignment for a study of the American Revolution. On day one, students will be introduced to the project,

American Revolution: A Digital Timeline Analysis Handout

Using the Internet, books, information from class, music, drawings, and artwork, you are to create a digital timeline in Photo Story 3. Your timeline will include major events and ideas that took place during the American Revolution.

Create your timeline according to the following components and guidelines:

+ The timeline must have nine events or people significant to the American Revolution arranged in chronological order. These events or people must include the following:

  — Three events or ideas or documents that were important to bringing about the American Revolution.

  — Three major battles during the American Revolution.

  — Three important leaders during the Revolutionary period.

+ Each event or person you choose will represent one frame in your Photo Story 3 timeline. For each one of these frames you must include a picture that represents the event or person (nine total pictures). You may draw your own artwork or use images from approved Internet sites.

+ The timeline must have original written text explaining each event or person.

+ Music appropriate to the Revolutionary time period must be included.

+ The Photo Story 3 presentation should be between one and two minutes long.

+ Use correct grammar and spelling.

+ Follow copyright and fair use guidelines.

For additional instructions on how to use Photo Story 3, access the following website:
http://www.microsoft.com/windowsxp/using/digitalphotography/photostory/tips/create.mspx

"American Revolution: A Digital Timeline Analysis," and given an outline of when tasks must be completed (see handout).

2. The instructor will demonstrate the software, Microsoft Photo Story 3, and will show examples of previously produced Photo Stories.

3. Copyright and fair use guidelines will be discussed detailing what material is acceptable for use in the project and how to locate information and secure permission if needed. See the following websites for information on fair use and copyright policies: http://www.copyright.gov/; http://thecopyrightsite.org/.

4. Instructor will also share basic design principles (e.g., use limited text and ensure readability).

Day 2 (98 minutes)

1. Students will develop their storyboards on paper, frame by frame, and include how they want their final Photo Story 3 project to look. In the storyboard they will include the following: the events that will make up their timeline (i.e., The Molasses Act, Proclamation of 1763, Sugar Act, Tea Act, Boston Tea Party, First Continental Congress, etc.), the order of events they will use, the text that will accompany each event, where music will be inserted, and where pictures will be inserted.

2. Students will research each event they have chosen to include in the timeline, using print and electronic resources. See "Resources" section for suggestions.

3. Students will write short event summaries and describe the significance of the event to the American Revolution. Portions of these summaries can be the text or narration for the Photo Story 3 project. This portion of the assignment will encourage the students to utilize critical thinking skills as they select each event.

4. While in a computer lab or media center in which each student (or pairs/groups of students) has access to the Internet, students will choose pictures to accompany the events in their timeline. Students must follow the copyright and fair use guidelines presented earlier in the lesson when using pictures from Internet websites. See "Resources" for websites which offer copyright free images or sites that have specific policies allowing for educational use of material.

5. Students may also choose to produce their own artwork, which will be scanned and saved for use in the Photo Story 3 project.

6. Students will save images, both scanned and downloaded, to removable storage or student server space for use in the Photo Story 3 timeline.

7. Students will choose and save music appropriate to the time period, remembering fair use guidelines. Students may also use the create music tool included in the Photo Story 3 software.

Day 3 (98 minutes)

1. While in a computer lab or media center, a tutorial will be given by the instructor on how to use Photo Story 3 (see tutorial on Microsoft web page at http://www.microsoft.com/windowsxp/using/digitalphotography/photostory/tips/create.mspx).

2. As a final step the students will insert their previously prepared summaries of events, photos/pictures, and music into Photo Story 3 creating a digital timeline.

Day 4 (60 minutes)

1. Students will present their finalized Photo Story 3 projects.

Assessment
See the Photo Story 3 grading rubric.

Student Enrichment
The instructor for this lesson should provide individualized accommodations, as needed, for students with special needs. Modification of the lesson should be based on academic needs and may include, but not be limited to, giving more time to complete the timeline, establishing peer partner pairs, and adjusting required components in the digital timeline. In addition, special needs students may be provided with specific websites from which to find research material and content that are appropriate to academic ability and reading level.

Teaching Tips
1. Coordinate with the school's media specialist in advance of the project start date to ensure that Photo Story 3 is downloaded on appropriate computers.

2. Ensure that media center/lab computers are compatible with Photo Story 3 software (Requires Microsoft Windows XP operating system and Windows Media Player 10).

Photo Story 3 Grading Rubric

Category	Unsatisfactory (0)	Satisfactory (2)	Superior (4)	Comments/Score
Accuracy of Historical Content Research	Inaccurate content; student did not complete research requirements; Photo Story sequence and story were not clear	Some content was incorrect and out of sequence; research was adequate; some content unclear	Content was correct; student supported content with research; student presented Photo Story with clarity; student met all research requirements	
Explanation of Historical Significance	Events selected for the Photo Story were not explained	Some explanation of the historical significance of the events selected was provided	A thorough, clear explanation of the historical significance of the events selected was provided	
Graphics/Images and Text	Appropriate graphics/images were not used throughout the Photo Story; text was not readable; images did not contribute to the tone of the story	Most graphics and images used were appropriate for the content; most text was readable; overall tone was not established	Appropriate graphics/images were used, helping to establish tone that matched the story with images that communicated appropriate story, symbolism and/or metaphors; text was readable	
Narration/Music	Appropriate music of time period was not used; Sequencing within Photo Story was not fluid	Appropriate music was used; however, not fluid	Appropriate music of time period was used; music flow appropriate to Photo Story scenes	
Grammar/Spelling	Photo Story had major (5+) grammar and/or spelling errors	Photo Story had 3-5 grammar and/or spelling errors	Photo Story was free of grammar and spelling errors	
Ethics	Copyright/Fair Use guidelines were not followed; student did not make informed decisions	Copyright/Fair Use guidelines were followed for most of the presentation; student did not fully understand guidelines in making decisions	Copyright/Fair Use guidelines were followed throughout presentation; student made informed and ethical decisions	
Application Process	Student did not follow assignment guidelines; student did not progress along timelines; student did not meet deadlines; backups of work were not evident	Student completed most guidelines at or before requested deadlines; student had backup of work	All processes and procedures were followed and all deadlines met by the student; student made routine backups	
Overall design and appeal	Student ignored design principles discussed/presented; poor use of multimedia elements including color, text, and music	At least three design principles were followed from color, text, music, and other multimedia elements	Student followed basic design principles; good overall design and use of color, text, music, and other multimedia elements	
Duration	Assignment was more than :30 below or above requested time duration	Assignment was within :30 of the desired duration; however, Photo Story seemed "padded" with unclear content and sequences	Assignment was within requested range and appropriate content was used in a clear presentation	
Creativity	Obviously student followed design modeled by teacher with no creative presentation of self	Demonstration of adequate degree of creativity	Student expressed several creative ideas in the Photo Story	

Total /40

Teacher comments:

3. Be aware that the Photo Story 3 projects can become large digital files. Ensure that students have adequate space on a school server, or appropriate removable storage such as a USB storage device (e.g. jump drive, thumb drive, flash drive) or CD-RW.
4. If using CD-RWs, formatting may be required.
5. To save time students may work in pairs or larger groups.
6. Before having students work with Photo Story 3 the teacher should become familiar with the program so that student questions may be answered.
7. When introducing the project, briefly review the basics of technology use, such as saving files to a certain location and saving images from the Internet.

Technology Resources

Hardware
Removable storage device, scanner, Windows XP compatible sound card; audio headphones (see website for detailed information   http://www.microsoft.com/windowsxp/using/digitalphotography/photostory/sysreqs.mspx)

Software
Microsoft Photo Story 3; Windows Media Player 10, other software (e.g. scanning software) as determined by specific class needs

Resources

Internet
Photo Story 3 Download, tips, tutorials: http://www.windowsmoviemakers.net/PhotoStory3/Index.aspx

Copyright/Fair Use: http://www.copyright.gov/
http://thecopyrightsite.org

Library of Congress: http://www.loc.gov/

National Archives: http://www.archives.gov

Photos: http://classroomclipart.com/
http://www.lauriefowler.com/graphics1.htm

Print
Phillip Hoose, 2001. *We Were There Too!* New York: Farrar Straus Giroux.

Ravitch, Diane, ed. 2000. *The American Reader.* New York: Perennial.

Compston, Christine, Rachel Seidman, eds. 2003. *Our Documents.* Oxford: Oxford University Press.

Student Voices

"It was a lot more interesting to make a timeline using Photo Story [3] rather than just writing it on paper." *Amelia*

"I usually don't like to make presentations in class, but this time I wanted people to see my project." *Renato* 🖼

The Saffron Scourge: Society, Politics and Disease

26

Diane Luke and Ann Winkler

Tenth and Eleventh Grades: U.S. History and Sociology

NCSS Thematic Strands
Ⓘ **PEOPLE, PLACES, AND ENVIRONMENTS**
Ⓥ **INDIVIDUALS, GROUPS, AND INSTITUTIONS**

NCSS Performance Expectations
Ⓘ **PEOPLE, PLACES, AND ENVIRONMENTS**
  j. Analyze and evaluate social and economic effects of environmental changes and crises resulting from phenomena such as floods, storms, and drought.

Ⓥ **INDIVIDUALS, GROUPS, AND INSTITUTIONS**
  a. Apply concepts such as role, status, and social class in describing the connections and interactions of individuals, groups, and institutions in society.

NETS-S National Educational Technology Standards for Students
3. Technology Productivity Tools
5. Technology Research Tools

NETS-S Performance Indicators (Grades 9-12)
3. Technology Productivity Tools
5. Technology Research Tools
  ✦ Select and apply technology tools for research, information analysis, problem solving, and decision making in content learning.
  ✦ Investigate and apply expert systems, intelligent agents, and simulations in real-world situations.

Introduction
Until Walter Reed discovered the source, Yellow Fever ravaged the Americas and was responsible for throwing cities into desolate wastelands of fear. Today we know that Yellow Fever is caused by the specific mosquito, *Aedes aegypti*, and can be contained. This lesson will allow your students to explore aspects of the illness from infection to possible death. Students will also learn about the societal, governmental, and economic

effects epidemics have upon cities. The study is conducted by choosing a city where a major outbreak occurred; two such cities are Philadelphia (1793) and New Orleans (1853). However, if you research a bit you may find that an epidemic happened in your city or close to your home. After an informational session, ten digital pictures will be supplied to the students (see Teaching Tips for complete information). Students will be divided into groups and asked to write newspaper style headlines for each picture as it pertains to the Yellow Fever outbreak they have studied. Students will then compile the pictures in a PowerPoint presentation to show to the class.

Objectives
  1. The student will be able to understand how natural causes, such as disease, can affect the population of a society.
  2. The student will be able to evaluate the role of political and social city models during a time of specific hardship.
  3. The student will be able to illustrate his/her learning through the use of computers and relevant software.

Time
Three 1 hour sessions.

Instructional Steps
Session 1
Preparation ahead of time will include learning the basic facts of Yellow Fever and the information you wish to present to your students regarding the city you have chosen. By looking through the resource list you should be able to obtain excellent information, especially if you choose a major city. The lesson plan originally focused on Tampa, Florida and an outbreak that occurred in 1887.

This first session will be the base content session. Activating prior knowledge of epidemics will help get this lesson rolling. Have students divide into groups and brainstorm words that relate to epidemics. A great graphic organizer for this is to give students a large piece of butcher paper, or poster board, write the word "epidemic" in the middle, and then write their brainstorming words around this central word. Bright colored markers are essential for such an activity!

A vocabulary review would also be helpful in starting the lesson. Some words of importance that students may not be familiar with include:

Yellow Fever: a viral disease transmitted between humans by a mosquito

Miasma: a poisonous atmosphere formerly thought to rise from swamps and putrid matter and cause disease

Quarantine: enforced isolation or restriction of free movement imposed to prevent the spread of contagious disease

Aedes aegypti: the mosquito that carries the Yellow Fever virus

Jaundice: yellowish discoloration of the whites of the eyes, skin, and mucous membranes caused by deposition of bile salts in these tissues; it occurs as a symptom of disease

Hemorrhage: excessive discharge of blood from the blood vessels

Boosters: community organizations designed to help promote a city's popularity for the benefit of increase in population and commerce

Epidemic: an outbreak of a contagious disease that spreads rapidly and widely

Immunity: inherited, acquired, or induced resistance to infection by a specific pathogen

Your content presentation follows next. You can choose to use any presentation device you feel best suited for your students to present the content. Ideas include lectures with graphic organizers, jigsaw activities where students read parts of information and come together to assemble the complete picture, or perhaps even a mini-drama where the Yellow Fever epidemic is played out using a pre-written teacher narration. Regardless of your approach, it is important to include the following concepts:

1. The definition of an epidemic.
2. The basic facts of Yellow Fever and its disease course.
3. The specific facts of Yellow Fever in relation to the city you chose, i.e. date of epidemic, number of people involved, number of people killed, etc.
4. How governmental and societal institutions responded to the epidemic.
5. General population view of epidemic, i.e. great fear, relaxed attitude, etc.

6. Surrounding cities' view of the besieged city and their response.
7. Major changes that occurred in the government, society, medical profession, and everyday life, because of the epidemic.

Session 2

This will be the day your students form into their groups and either use computers in your classroom (if available) or visit the computer lab. Be sure that you reserve the lab ahead of time and make sure that Power Point is on the computers you wish to use. Have students divided into heterogeneous groups. The group size will be based upon the number of students in your class and the number of computers available. Depending on group size, have students rotate the role of "computer operator" throughout the hour so that all students have a chance to work hands-on with the computer and software. Designate other roles—recorder, time-keeper, etc.—so that all students are involved. Be sure to remind students that actions and behavior during this creative process will be taken into account on the final assessment. Help students budget their time by giving them an approximate per minute slide time; for example with forty minutes and ten slides, each slide must be completed in approximately four minutes in order to finish the project. Also, keep the rubric handy and make notations regarding each group to help in final scoring.

This lesson is not suggested for first time Power Point users. Be sure that your students have basic Power Point experience. They do not need expertise to create these slides. Encourage creativity with backgrounds and colors so that they can individualize their projects. Prepare the computers ahead of your scheduled class. We used a USB/thumb drive device to load the pictures onto the computers so that they would be ready for student use. When students were finished with their project we saved it on the USB/thumb drive so that it could then be accessed for presentation purposes.

Session 3

Presentation Day! Student groups will present their slideshow using a projector and computer. You should predetermine how long each group has for their presentation. An approximate time range should be given on the rubric. As each presentation occurs allow a short time for questions. After the presentations are finished wrap up the lesson with a discussion debriefing. Some questions to consider: Could an epidemic like this happen today? What improvements have been made since the time period studied to help people out during periods of crisis? How would you have reacted if faced with this situation?

Assessment

Students will be assessed by taking into account participation on the content session day, how well they worked as a group in the computer lab, and the effectiveness of their headlines. The assessment can be best graded by using a rubric involving a check list and a rating scale. The check list should cover required elements, i.e., ten headlines, ten photos, length of presentation, etc. The rating scale should be used for more esoteric items, i.e., success of group interaction, quality of presentation, creative use of PowerPoint, etc. Be sure your rubric includes an individual score and a group score. Copies of the rubric can be handed out to students before assembly of the slideshow. This way the students will know exactly what is expected.

Student Enrichment

To further understand the effects of Yellow Fever students can be encouraged to read one of two books. They both deal with the outbreak of Yellow Fever in 1793. A novel by Laurie Halse Anderson regarding the outbreak, entitled *Fever 1793*, is a terrific way to introduce students to the trauma. A second alternative is called *An American Plague*, by Jim Murphy. This story presents the facts in an enjoyable format perfect for students of this age group.

Regardless of the book you choose, a great project to help adapt the lesson to students of all abilities would be to divide the students into groups, with each group having a section of the story as their responsibility. They would then draw a story board representing their section. These story boards can be presented to the class. The graphical representation of the story is a way to enhance kinesthetic and visual learning.

TAMPANS LEAVE TOWN, CAMP IN WILDERNESS!

FUNERALS OCCURING DAILY IN OAKLAWN CEMETERY!

Teaching Tips

Obtaining photographs can be done in several ways. Since the outbreak upon which we originally based this lesson took place in our city, we drove to historic sites and took pictures of actual places we had spoken about during the content portion of the lesson. We also staged scenes (a husband became a Yellow Fever victim attempting to recover) to cover some ideas that were impossible to find. We used the sepia setting on the digital camera, which gave the pictures an "old-fashioned" tone. However, since you may not be in the city you are covering, there are still many ways to find ten excellent pictures.

For example, if you know that the disease

came from a boat through a port and you happen to live in an area where there is water available, then take a picture of that spot. It will serve as a substitute for the "real" area. If you are concerned that students will have no idea what to do with a scene of water, remember that this lesson requires active and creative thinking. Even if their headline is not exactly what you envisioned as a possibility when you took the picture, you may be surprised by how fitting it is to the epidemic regardless.

You can also stage your pictures as we did. This just requires imagination, perhaps a few participants, and very little time. We spread a quilt in the backyard, and placed a couple of wooden stools, an old cooking pan and some apples to create a "camp spot." This was to denote the idea that many people fled the city and were forced to camp away from their homes during the time of an epidemic. If you are truly looking for realism then use the internet to find pictures of the actual places in the city you are studying. A bit of caution in doing this third form of picture hunting: be careful not to pick a picture that will be pigeon-holed into one possible headline. Remember to allow for student creativity and not to be completely obvious with your choices. Also be cautious of copyright information and make sure you are using a picture open to the public.

If you have networked computers, you can upload your pictures onto a central site that all students can access. This will save time over using a USB/thumb drive device. You can also designate a folder where all students can save their projects. On presentation day students can simply access this folder on the network. If you are able to burn CDs, you can also use this method to save and load the pictures to available computers. Due to file size, the average floppy will not work for this exercise. Students will need a larger file space to save their work.

One last note on pictures: "Ten" pictures is the number that worked for this class. If you need to make it less or more, by all means change the lesson to suit your needs!

Technology Resources

HARDWARE
Computers (including one computer in classroom capable of projection of PowerPoint presentations), projector, digital camera, USB/thumb drive (optional), compact discs (optional)

SOFTWARE
Microsoft PowerPoint

Resources

INTERNET
Centers for Disease Control. Yellow Fever Disease and Vaccine. http://www.cdc.gov/ncidod/dvbid/yellowfever/.

Bresnahan, Patrick. Yellow Fever. http://web.bryant.edu/~history/h453proj/spring_01/yellow_fever/index.html.

Bronzell, Patrisha and D'Agostino, Patricia. Philadelphia Yellow Fever Epidemic 1793. http://www.libweb.org/sls09/.

Eyewitness to History. Yellow Fever Attacks Philadelphia 1793. http://www.eyewitnesstohistory.com/yellowfever.htm.

The History Channel, search under "yellow fever." http://www.historychannel.com.

PRINT
Anderson, Laurie Halse. *Fever 1793*. Simon and Schuster: New York, 2000.

Duffy, John. *Sword of Pestilence; the New Orleans Yellow Fever Epidemic of 1853*. Louisiana State Press: Baton Rouge: 1966.

Ellis, John H. *Yellow Fever & Public Health in the New South*. University Press of Kentucky: Kentucky, 1992.

Murphy, Jim. *An American Plague: The True and Terrifying Story of the Yellow Fever Epidemic of 1793*. Clarion Books: New York, 2003.

Pierce, John and Writer, James. *Yellow Jack: How Yellow Fever Ravaged America and Walter Reed Discovered Its Deadly Secrets*. Wiley: Hoboken, 2005.

Savitt, Todd L. and Young, James Harvey, Eds. *Disease and Distinctiveness in the American South*. University of Tennessee Press: Knoxville, 1988.

Tomes, Nancy. *The Gospel of Germs*. Harvard College: USA, 1998.

Other Materials Needed
Screen or equitable blank wall for projection, ten digital photos placed in a file that is accessible to students. ▨

Using Documentary Filmmaking to Explore and Preserve Our Past

27

Perry McLeod and Charles Vaughan

Tenth and Eleventh Grades: World History and U.S. History

NCSS Thematic Strands

Ⅱ TIME, CONTINUITY, AND CHANGE
Ⅸ GLOBAL CONNECTIONS
Ⅳ INDIVIDUAL DEVELOPMENT AND IDENTITY

NCSS Performance Expectations

Ⅱ TIME, CONTINUITY, AND CHANGE

d. Systematically employ processes of critical historical inquiry to reconstruct and reinterpret the past, such as using a variety of sources and checking their credibility, validating and weighing evidence for claims, and searching for causality.

e. Investigate, interpret, and analyze multiple historical and contemporary viewpoints within and across cultures related to important events, recurring dilemmas, and persistent issues, while employing empathy, skepticism, and critical judgment.

Ⅸ GLOBAL CONNECTIONS

b. Explain conditions and motivations that contribute to conflict, cooperation, and interdependence among groups, societies, and nations.

Ⅳ INDIVIDUAL DEVELOPMENT AND IDENTITY

a. Articulate personal connections to time, place and social/cultural systems.

NETS-S National Educational Technology Standards for Students

4. Technology Communications Tools
5. Technology Research Tools
6. Technology Problem-solving and Decision-making Tools

NETS-S Performance Indicators (Grades 9-12)

4. Technology Communications Tools
5. Technology Research Tools
   - Select and apply technology tools for research, informa-

tion analysis, problem solving, and decision making in content learning.

4. Technology Communications Tools
5. Technology Research Tools
6. Technology Problem-solving and Decision-making Tools
   - Collaborate with peers, experts, and others to contribute to a content-related knowledge base by using technology to compile, synthesize, produce, and disseminate information, models, and other creative works.

Introduction

Using constructivist pedagogy, students become experts in facets of history of an identified personal interest. Working individually and collaboratively, students explore time periods in U.S. and World History by conducting ethnographic research to produce their own documentary films. The final products are shared in school and among members of the community, and have potential use in other area schools.

Objectives

1. Using resources in print and on the Internet and the World Wide Web, the student will employ critical historical inquiry to research information from any given time period (i.e., World War II—combat and home front, Korean War, Vietnam, Civil Rights Movement, etc.).

2. Using research material, the student will develop a list of interview questions pertaining to the assigned time period.

3. Using a Digital Video camera and interview questions, the student will conduct an interview of a community member.

4. The student will construct a timeline/storyboard for his or her video.

5. The student will transcribe the interview.

6. Using iMovie, the student will edit the interview to create a 10 minute movie, including titles, transitions, background music, still photos, and video segments from the interview.
7. Student will use appropriate documentation.
8. The student will render the completed video to appropriate media (VHS tape, DVD) for the purpose of sharing the finished project with the class and the interview subject.

Time

One to two class periods for Media Center/Internet research, multiple class periods or time after school for video editing, and multiple days for class presentations.

Instructional Steps

+ Introduce and study a Unit on the World War II era or another recent era of history. This will serve as the basis for the entire Oral History interview project. Students will gain necessary skills both to research and complete this project.
+ To familiarize students with this process, use videos that contain Oral History segments and first hand accounts of events from the era to be studied. These will serve as excellent models for later interviews.
+ Introduce students to the five characteristics of documentaries. Using readily available documentaries (e.g., Ken Burns's "The Civil War"), help students identify the five elements of documentary film-making (see Appendix A).
+ Show students a documentary completed in a previous class (if available). Discuss and review the collecting of Oral Histories through the video interview process.
+ Assign students to read Tom Brokaw's *The Greatest Generation*. Students will complete a specific assignment from this book (See Appendix B). They will develop questions from this book as practice for actual interviews. Students will read *The Greatest Generation* to broaden their background knowledge of the World War II era and develop sample interview questions from what they have read.
+ Students should research World War II and other eras on the Internet or other printed material to create a file of images and sites to use as sources for research when developing questions for interviews and for editing.

+ In pairs, students should practice interviewing skills. It is crucial that students have numerous opportunities to practice interviewing before they go out and conduct their interview (see Appendix C, Elements of a Good Interview).
+ Introduce, discuss and practice the use of digital video and digital video editing technology. A simple oral test could be given so that students can exhibit use of a video camera, iMovie software, the process of capturing video, etc.
+ Describe the five roles (Reporter, Screenwriter, Producer, Camera Operator and Grip/Lighting) the students will play during the interview process. These roles will rotate to ensure each group member will have the opportunity to play each role when planning, conducting and completing an Oral History interview. Each of these roles has specific duties (see Appendix D).
+ Set up the initial interview and conduct the pre-interview (students will have practiced this prior to first contact). Interviews can be conducted at school or in the subject's home.
+ After completing the interview, students will break into small production groups to complete the documentary. Scripts will be written (Appendix E) and storyboards will be developed (Appendix F). Microsoft PowerPoint can also be utilized to construct the storyboard. In the storyboard, the student should include basic descriptions of the audio and video, and what images will be used.
+ Using an assessment tool (Appendix G), evaluate the documentary.
+ Once the documentaries are completed and compiled, hold an event at school and invite the interview subjects to see their stories.

Assessment

+ Offer unit tests on historical eras. This assessment is used to determine comprehension of the historical time-period.
+ Evaluate students' research techniques. Accurate research is important to insure that students have the background knowledge to be able to ask the right questions. This research also forms a framework for the documentary.

- Give practical tests on video and editing technology. Performance assessments are used where students display their working knowledge of the technology.
- Students should maintain an ongoing checklist with research questions, pre-interview contact and other deadlines.
- Assess the completed Oral History documentary based on the assigned era. This must show interview segments, real time video footage, images from the era and scanned images of artifacts or photos from the interviewee (see sample assessment, Appendix G).

Student Enrichment

- Students gain valuable experience using digital video technology.
- Students learn history from the source—they have the opportunity to hear and see history from men and women who lived it—they will learn the personal side of history that is not in an average textbook.
- Students get a chance to meet men and women from a different generation and have the opportunity to develop an better understanding and appreciation of older Americans.
- Students experience patriotism—they hear stories from veterans from different conflicts and get a better understanding of the personal side of war.
- It is important for all students to experience each area of production. While going through this process, students will identify a role that best addresses individual abilities. Students will naturally gravitate to an area of the production that best meets their area of interest. For example, students who are extroverted tend to feel most comfortable conducting the interview, while introverted students are more comfortable being in the background, operating the technology, editing the product, writing the script, etc.
- After students have completed one documentary subject, they should feel comfortable replicating this assignment in an area of personal interest (e.g., the Civil Rights Movement). This could be done with the entire class, or students could opt to complete this assignment independently.

Teaching Tips

- This unit is ideally suited to differentiated instruction. Students finish this unit having explored areas in which they have the most interest.
- All levels of students can feel success with this project. Even the most reluctant writers and talkers become engaged in this process.
- After participating in this project, interviewees go out into our community and describe the wonderful things that are going on in our high school. This is invaluable public relations and has helped attract more veterans to participate in Our Local Greatest Generation Oral History Project.
- Give yourself a lot of time to plan and implement this project. You might have to clear time in your curriculum to accomplish this unit, giving students outside assignments to complete to ensure coverage of required content. When changes in curriculum content are not possible, our department has created an Oral History class. This year-long course provides students with a chance to spend longer amounts of time developing documentaries. Future plans include adding a Documentary Film-making course to our journalism program.
- Practice interviews — in front of and behind the camera. The more experience students get with this skill, the better they will be when conducting live interviews.
- If you do not have digital video — do the Oral Histories with a tape recorder and then transcribe them.
- Make sure the students know the era of history before starting the interview process. Research will be much more meaningful if they have a clear understanding of this process.

Technology Resources

HARDWARE

+ Digital video camera, Lavalier microphone
+ Digital still camera
+ Scanner
+ PC or eMac with Internet access
+ External hard drive
+ Flash drives
+ DVD burner
+ CD burner

SOFTWARE

+ iMovie (for Macintosh only)
+ Microsoft Office

Resources

INTERNET

Oral History Sites:

http://www.authentichistory.com/

http://www.eyewitnesstohistory.com/

http://memory.loc.gov/ammem/ndlpedu/lessons/oralhist/ohhome.html#student

http://www.rootsweb.com/

http://www.genealogy.com/index_r.html

http://www.rootsweb.com/~lineage/famhist.htm

http://www.rootsweb.com/~flgso/intvwqus.htm

http://historymatters.gmu.edu/mse/oral/what.html

http://www.dohistory.org/

Apple Education provides an excellent resource for doing student documentaries. Many ideas that we employ (Appendices C-G) are adapted to our student needs from the publication *Stories Worth Telling: A Guide to Creating Student-Led Documentaries* (Palmer and Lee, 2004), which is available at http://www.apple.com/education/documentary/.

Document, Photo and Artifact Sites

http://www.archives.gov/education/lessons/worksheets/artifact_analysis_worksheet.pdf

http://www.archives.gov/education/lessons/worksheets/written_document_analysis_worksheet.pdf

http://www.archives.gov/education/lessons/worksheets/photo.html

http://www.polytechnic.org/faculty/gfeldmeth/USHistory.html

PRINT

Tom Brokaw, *The Greatest Generation*. New York: Random House, 1996.

Donald A. Ritchie, *Doing Oral History — A Practical Guide*. New York: Oxford University Press, 2003.

Tim O'Brien, *The Things They Carried*. New York: Broadway, 1998.

Other Materials Needed

Partnership with a local veterans group is a valuable tool.

Student Voices

"When I first listened to an interview, my junior year, the first thought that came across my mind was the amount of emotion in the room. Every interview since then, I have realized how real it was for these veterans to have to leave their families, not knowing if they would ever return, and fight for their country."
> —*John*
> *Senior, Class of 2005*

"I thought that interviewing Mr. Haller was a once in a lifetime experience. I learned so much about the war from his interview. Listening to him was more beneficial to me because I got to hear his experience first hand. Mr. Haller and his wife talked about some of the same things that I learned about in Mr. McLeod's class. I now have more of an appreciation for older people. I think that all older people may have a story to tell."
> —*Kim*
> *Senior, Class of 2005*

"Every time we interviewed a veteran, my appreciation for veterans grew and continued to grow, until I began to view these veteran's from another perspective. I will never forget what these veterans said or the experiences they related to me in each interview."
> —*Josh*
> *Senior, Class of 2005*

The Five Elements of a Documentary

1. Interviews

+ Frame the person using negative space (space around the subject), leave room behind the subject, and never stand the subject right in front of a wall. Background influences the way the person is perceived
+ Three types of interview techniques are:

  (a) *Structured Interview.* This is an interview in which you have a standard set of questions, progressing straight through the questions in a designated order. This is good if you have an interview team that is interviewing a number of subjects at different times, insuring that you have some consistency and reliability.

  (b) *Open-ended Interview.* This is an interview in which you start out with a few questions and build follow-up questions from people's answers. (Hint: repeat their last few words, and ask "open ended questions," ones that can not be answered with a "Yes" or "No," such as, "Can you describe?" or "Tell me about this...")

  (c) *Semi-structured Interview.* This is an interview that employs both structured and open-ended interview principles. You might start out with set questions, but the subject takes you into areas where you were not thinking, thus you ask more open-ended questions.

2. Cutaways

+ These are "stand-alone" shots, i.e., like still photography. Each shot has its own meaning in the visuals and sound.
+ With two cutaways together, you can create an idea from the juxtaposition of the two images
+ Shoot tons of Cutaways, i.e., store signs, close ups of objects, a clock on the wall, people's faces, a candle, a shot of a highway. This is the time you can squeeze some visual poetry out of the documentary. Always keep your eyes open for little "shots" that evoke something about the truth of the situation you are filming.

3. Chill Footage

+ This is also known as Live Action footage. Film whatever is going on with your subjects.
+ Do not talk or interact with them; just try and hope that a really cool moment happens while you are filming.

4. Process Footage

+ This is when you film the making of your documentary. You can be on-camera (i.e., like Michael Moore or the History Detectives).
+ Film the process of making of your film (i.e., shoot when you are walking up to someone's door—for real, don't fake it)

5. Archive

+ Always ask your subjects for old photos, film or video. Government agencies also have free footage

Adapted from Aron Ranen, "The Five Elements of Documentary." June, 2004. http://www.dvworkshops.com/newsletters/fiveelements.html (10 January 2006) DV-workshops Newsletter.

Local Greatest Generation Oral History Project

Assignment: Read *The Greatest Generation* by Tom Brokaw

This book is an integral part of our project. It is a collection of oral histories of men and women who were part of the World War II-era of American history. The stories are told from many perspectives and will help you understand the personal side of this world-changing era. While you are reading, we will begin our project. We will interview war veterans and home front veterans about their experiences during the war. You will see how many of these stories you have read in the book will be similar to the stories you will actually hear during the interviews. It is imperative that you read this book carefully and learn from the stories.

Assignment
1. Read the entire book.
2. Create a journal. Your electronic journal will be posted in Blackboard.
3. What is a journal entry?
a. After you read a chapter, record the name of the chapter in your journal (i.e., "Ordinary People") and create three questions for each person covered in the chapter. (These are practice interview questions that you would ask these people if given the opportunity.) These questions must be specific to the person in the chapter. General questions will receive no credit.
b. After you have read the chapter, you will write a reflection. Explain how the stories affected you and why you think Mr. Brokaw chose the titles for each chapter. In other words, explain why the title fits. Use at least three specific examples from the chapter to support your explanation.

Elements of a Good Interview

The interview shapes the story and it is the interview that builds trust, rapport, and the relationship. Mature communication skills make an interview work.

1. First, you will make an initial contact with your interview subject. This can be accomplished with a phone call, a letter, or a personal contact. Remember the old adage, "you never get a second chance to make a first impression." Be sure that you explain the project and help your subject feel at ease. This step is very important in helping you establish credibility and rapport with your subject. If your interviewee feels comfortable with you, you are going to get better information.
2. When you and the subject meet, you are expected to act professionally. Again, introduce yourself and the purpose of the interview. Provide the subject with an idea of what to expect (equipment that you are going to use, how long you would like to talk, etc.). While the equipment is being set up and checked, provide expectations or make small talk to make the subject feel more at ease. Try not to be nervous. This is contagious.
3. Once the equipment is ready to go, getting the basic facts behind the story is important: the full name and title of the person being interviewed, and the person's involvement in the topic. This establishes the facts and the foundation of the story.
4. A sound story is a mix of facts and reactions to those facts. To get good, emotional reactions, make sure you exhibit concern, passion, and knowledge about the subject. You should find a way to show the interviewee that you are interested in what is being shared.
5. Remember to ask appropriate follow-up questions. Be sensitive to the situation. Listening is all about silence. Your subject may get emotional recalling events from the past. Try and gauge if it is appropriate to ask follow-up questions about it. Let

your interviewee decide if he or she wishes to continue down this path. There is nothing the matter with you if you show emotion as well. If anything, this gives you even more credibility.

6. Make certain you have enough knowledge about the event to be able to ask questions. Remember to include open-ended questions. Avoid "yes" and "no" questions. Your goal is to probe for deeper understanding. Ask questions that will elicit the essential Who? What? When? Where? Why? How? These questions should trigger emotion and produce powerful sound bites. Create a list of interview questions and bring it to the interview.

7. When concluding the interview, remember the power of a thank-you and a handshake. Anticipate your interviewee's "what next" question, telling him or her what will happen with the interview and when he or she should expect to see himself or herself on film. Write thank-you letters and send invitations to the screenings of your documentary.

Interview Guidelines

- Set up the interview.
- Act and look professional, but be personable.
- Be prepared—do background research.
- Define and state the purpose of the interview.
- Ask the easy questions first.
- Be a good listener and be sensitive.
- Throughout the interview, take mental or written notes regarding nonverbal communication, which can reveal much about an interviewee's feelings or attitudes.
- Don't talk too much.
- Probe behind answers and ask follow-up questions. Ask for details—ask concrete questions.
- Save the tough questions for last.
- Ask about photos, public relations material, letters, awards to use as background material for B-roll, and then film or photograph these items and let the subject tell you about this material.
- Conclude the interview.

The Post-Interview Process

After you complete the interview, you should have a strong feeling about the direction your documentary will take, the sound bites to use, and what message you want to present based on the interview. Immediately after your interview, write a journal entry in which you reflect on this process. You might include disaster stories, successes, reactions your subject had to the questions, or your reactions to what you learned. The day after the interview, feel free to discuss with the class how the interview went. Other students can learn from mistakes made and be motivated by great stories captured.

Transcribing the Interview

The next crucial step in the documentary process is transcribing the interview. Listen to the filmed interview and write down the responses and the times. Although this is a time-consuming process, it is important for two reasons: (1) It helps speed up the writing and editing process as you will not have to guess and spend time looking for those five sound bites you want to use in the story or the documentary; (2) These interviews will be stored for posterity, so the transcriptions will be beneficial for people doing research in the future.

Transcribing the interview will take at least one hour for every ten minutes of interview. While some information can be summarized or categorized, it's best to have a verbatim transcript.

After you have transcribed your interview, make two printed copies: one clean copy for cataloging and one for writing on that can used for highlighting and brainstorming story ideas.

Student Roles in the Documentary Process

Reporters

The reporters are responsible for doing the interviews (usually in groups of three).

+ This group listens to the taped interview and logs it.
+ They gather research information on the topic using various resources from the library to the internet, and find photos, documents, and internet video clips and images (B-roll), as well as music from the time period that can be used in the documentary, and log each resource.

Screenwriters

This group should consist of strong writers. Using the tapes and the logs from the reporters, screenwriters should watch the videos looking for sound bites, and study the logs for guidance. They write the script and complete the storyboard for the documentary.

Producers

This group does the computer editing work. Using their technology skills, producers put together the final product that will be the documentary. After getting the script and storyboard from the screenwriters, the producers input the sound bites in their designated place. The producers also match up the narration and music with the script and do all the other work on the editing system to make a professional-looking documentary.

Camera Operator

The camera operator should employ the "rule of thirds." In order to understand this concept, show students interviews from TV newscasts. Point out that the person being interviewed is not right in the middle of the screen. The subject is always slightly off to the right or left. Whatever the side is, the subject should be looking into the other two-thirds of the shot to make it appear that he or she is looking into space or at a person, and not at a wall. The student conducting the interview should be positioned slightly to the side so that the subject is not looking directly into the camera.

A good shot can start with one to two inches of space above the subject's head (negative space), with the lower portion cut off at the waist. This gives the cameraperson a chance to pull slowly into the subject's face during the interview. As the cameraperson zooms in, he or she should zoom in tighter on the top of the interviewee's head, rather than his or her chin. An effective technique is to zoom in even tighter on the face to bring out the eyes during an emotional part of the interview. The key to a good-looking interview is to focus on the eyes—there should be points of light visible in the subject's eyes. If backlighting cannot be avoided, more light should be placed in front of the interviewee's face to avoid shadows and dark, emotionless images.

Grip/Lighting

A grip is a member of a film production crew who adjusts sets, lighting, and props, and assists the camera operator. The grip should help the camera operator to locate the best lighting for the interview. Move the tripod around and take the time to look at the subject through the camera and check for good lighting. Good light, but not direct light, should come in from a slight side angle, so that one third of the subject's face is in a subtle shadow.

Appendix E

Steps in the Writing Process

1. As you begin to develop the script, decide on the major theme on which you want to focus. What is each interview subject's story? What do you want the audience to say after viewing each subject's story?

2. Write a lead, or an introduction, for the whole documentary or your portion of the class documentary. A lead is a journalistic term for the opening statement made in a story. It should capture the attention of the audience as well as capture the direction and mood of the story. The lead for the whole documentary should portray its purpose or mission.

3. What sound bites will you use to complement your lead or angle? Go through your transcription log and select possible sound bites by making notations on the log. Try to use at least one to two quotes from all interviewees.
   As you review the interviews, keep notes on what reactions you're lacking and those that you feel will be necessary to get from another source, such as another interview.

4. Examine the background information gathered during the research and determine any additional research that needs to be done. Divide the research among team.

5. Construct an outline/Thinking Map prior to writing the script. You should decide where to begin, what segments flow together logically and chronologically, and where and how to end. Consider a theme that will tie it all together, and a title for your segment.

6. Write a rough draft for your documentary, complete with transitions, quotes, and a conclusion. Write the script in a journalistic style—one that is conversational, capturing a cadence. This script should be complete with facts, reaction, and emotion. A typical setup for documentaries and news stories is news, news, reaction to that news, news, reaction, news, reaction, news, news, reaction, and so on.

7. Share the script with your team members for peer editing.

8. Hand in your rough draft.

Storyboard Template

Title of Project _____

Group Member Names _____

Audio	Video	Notes

Sample Oral History Project Assessment

Title of Project _____

Group Member Names _____

Video Interview (100)

_____ Camera setup: angles, fill frame, lighting

_____ Sound: quality sound bites, working microphones

_____ Interview: questions, follow-up and timing, completeness of interview

_____ / 100

Transcription (50)

_____ Appropriate amount of verbatim transcription

_____ Accuracy of time and quotes

_____ Typed

_____ / 50

Filler or B-roll (50)

_____ Amount: enough to complement the story

_____ Quality: steady camera, lighting, background

_____ / 50

Written Feature Story and Storyboard (100)

_____ Storytelling: strong lead, focus on an angle, development of story/depth, capturing the subject's personality and life
event, letting him or her talk

_____ Flow: use of transitions, logical flow between facts and reaction quotes, consideration of pace

_____ Accuracy of historical and personal facts

_____ / 100

FINAL PRODUCT (100)

_____ Use of sound: natural sound, narration, choice of music

_____ Overall effect: match between audio and video, effects used

_____ Completion of story and meeting deadline

_____ / 100

Any deductions: missed deadlines

TOTAL FOR THE WHOLE PRODUCT

_____ /400

The End of Optimism? The Great Depression in Europe

28

Melissa Lisanti, Jane Lehr, E. Thomas Ewing, David Hicks

Tenth to Twelfth Grades, AP, IB: World History, Economics, U.S. History and Government

NCSS Thematic Strands
Ⅱ TIME, CONTINUITY, AND CHANGE
Ⅵ POWER, AUTHORITY, AND GOVERNANCE
Ⅶ PRODUCTION, DISTRIBUTION, AND CONSUMPTION

NCSS Performance Expectations
Ⅱ TIME, CONTINUITY, AND CHANGE
b. Apply key concepts such as time, chronology, causality, change, conflict, and complexity to explain, analyze, and show connections among patterns of historical change and continuity.
d. Systematically employ processes of critical historical inquiry to reconstruct and reinterpret the past, such as using a variety of sources and checking their credibility, validating and weighing evidence for claims, and searching for causality.

Ⅵ POWER, AUTHORITY, AND GOVERNANCE
f. Analyze and evaluate conditions, actions, and motivations that contribute to conflict and cooperation within nations.

Ⅶ PRODUCTION, DISTRIBUTION, AND CONSUMPTION
h. Apply economic concepts (depression, unemployment) when evaluating historical development.

NETS-S National Educational Technology Standards for Students
3. Technology Productivity Tools
5. Technology Research Tools

NETS-S Performance Expectations
3. Technology Productivity Tools
+ Students use technology tools to enhance learning, increase productivity, and promote creativity.
+ Students use productivity tools to collaborate in constructing technology-enhanced models, prepare publications, and produce other creative works.

5. Technology Research Tools
+ Students use technology to evaluate, and collect information from a variety of sources.
+ Students use technology tools to process data and report results.

NETS-S Performance Indicators (Grades 9-12)
3. Technology Productivity Tools
+ Use technology tools and resources for managing and communicating personal/professional information.

5. Technology Research Tools
+ Routinely and efficiently use online information resources to meet needs for collaboration, research, publications, communications, and productivity.

Introduction
This lesson is designed to blend both content knowledge and historical skills development as students examine the essential question: To what extent did the economic crisis cause people in Europe to question the effectiveness and sustainability of democratic institutions, and how did these concerns, doubts, and fears translate into political action? Using an online Digital History Reader module, *The End of Optimism? The Great Depression in Europe*, students examine the context of the Great Depression in Europe and analyze a range of selected primary and secondary sources, including cartoons, speeches, photographs, and charts in order to answer the historical question at hand. Upon completion of a mini lecture, providing the context to the Great Depression in Europe, students utilize group work, a jigsaw sharing/teaching process, and original PowerPoint presentations to educate their peers on:
1. Unemployment: Causes, Comparisons, & Interpretations
2. Demonstrations, Reactions, and Protests
3. Crisis and Conflicts: Elections & Extremism.

Objectives

Students will:

1. Examine the causes and impacts of the Great Depression in Europe.
2. Analyze primary documents, including newspaper reports, photographs, cartoons, tables/charts, and diplomatic reports using the SCIM-C Model. (This model contains five phases: Summarizing, Contextualizing, Inferring, Monitoring, and Corroborating. A sample application is available at http://www.dhr.history.vt.edu/eu/mod04_depression/lessonplan.html)
3. Compare and contrast significant ideas, events, and political reactions to the impact of the Depression in Europe, with special focus on Britain, France, and Germany.
4. Create a PowerPoint outline and "Jeopardy" game questions, and a written narrative that details the extent to which the Great Depression impacted the social and political structures of European countries.

Time

Two 90-minute blocks

Instructional Steps

Anticipatory Set

At the beginning of class students are asked to: 1) define economic depression, and 2) brainstorm a concept map that details the effects of economic depression on society.

During debriefing the teacher may use Inspiration to capture student responses before transitioning into an explanation of today's lesson by introducing the question for inquiry:

To what extent did the economic crisis cause people in Europe to question the effectiveness and sustainability of democratic institutions, and how did these concerns, doubts, and fears translate into political action?

1. Using the PowerPoint presentation provided, the teacher conducts a mini lecture to introduce students to the topic, historical context, and historical question. The PowerPoint presentation is designed to transition from historical content/context into the classroom research tasks.

(Teacher notes for the mini lecture, the PowerPoint Slide show, and student skeleton notes to support the mini lecture are available at http://www.dhr.history.vt.edu/eu/mod04_depression/lessonplan.html.)

2. Using the PowerPoint presentation to focus attention on the directions, students will be divided into groups of three that will draw or be assigned a topic related to the historical question in which they are responsible for becoming experts. The areas of expertise are: (1) Unemployment–Causes, Comparisons, and Interpretations; (2) Demonstrations, Reactions and Protests; and (3) Crisis and Conflict–Elections and Extremism. Within each group the following roles must be filled: group leader (reminds all members to fulfill roles and facilitate discussion), navigator/computer driver (follows site links and describes source titles, etc.), and note taker (takes notes to prepare for presentations).

3. Working with the digital history module *The End of Optimism? The Great Depression in Europe* (http://www.dhr.history.vt.edu/eu/mod04_depression/index.html), groups will collect and analyze a range of historical sources related to their expert topics as assigned in step 2, in order to reconstruct the past from the perspective of their expertise. The historical context/background information included in the module will lend additional support for students as they analyze sources in order to answer the historical question.

4. After allowing students sufficient time to analyze sources and consider their answers to the historical question, ask students to take responsibility for group products. Two members will assume ownership of the task to develop the PowerPoint presentation, and one member should assume the task of developing five questions for the Jeopardy review game. While products are developed, discussion should continue to flow freely among all expert group members so that everyone is capable of presenting both products. Because the primary sources are already well organized and in electronic form, they can easily be pasted into presentations. Doing so will allow students to make powerful visual connections that illustrate their key points and interpretations of the sources. (Please note: model student slides are included in the PowerPoint Presentation.)

5. Once products are complete, student groups are reconfigured into teaching groups. Each teaching group includes one member from each of the three expert groups, for a total of three members. Students will utilize the Jigsaw method to teach their assigned area of expertise to their teaching groups. Upon completion of teaching each of the key areas, the teaching groups will merge their PowerPoint slides in order to reconfigure and create a comprehensive presentation/outline for the historical

question. Teaching groups will then share and discuss their Jeopardy questions, designed in expert groups. These may be submitted to the teacher to create a PowerPoint Jeopardy game to be played with the whole class. (Template available at http://www.dhr.history.vt.edu/eu/mod04_depression/lessonplan.html)

6. Students will use their completed PowerPoint slide shows to individually produce a written narrative to answer the historical question that is supported by the sources. In their analysis, students should be encouraged to consider how these sources illustrate the experience of living through the Depression in Europe, and in particular the causal relationship between economic conditions, political attitudes, and the response of governments. (Rubric available at http://www.dhr.history.vt.edu/eu/mod04_depression/lessonplan.html)

7. Teaching groups are chosen to present their combined PowerPoint presentations, which is followed by playing the teacher-led Jeopardy game.

8. To bring closure to the lesson the teacher hands out/projects the conclusion to the module (http://www.dhr.history.vt.edu/eu/mod04_depression/conclusion.html) and asks students, "What was the legacy of the changes wrought by the Great Depression in Europe?"

Assessment

It is important to monitor group discussions and PowerPoint presentations for understanding. Written narratives should be assessed according to the rubric. (Rubric available at http://www.dhr.history.vt.edu/eu/mod04_depression/lessonplan.html)

—assistants issuing the daily ration of a litre for each member of the family, at one penny per litre.

Student Enrichment

Because this assignment integrates primary source analysis, the consideration of a historical question, presentation design, jigsaw teaching, and a written narrative, it should challenge many students. Some students may require some additional supports to succeed. Some suggestions include: providing additional focus questions specific to each area of expertise that elicit essential understandings, providing document analysis worksheets to guide groups through their sources, and/or pre-selecting specific documents that are essential to the content and most appropriate for the audience.

Those students who are comfortable working with primary evidence should be given the following scaffold through which to analyze all sources: the SCIM-C Historical Evidence Chart (Figure 1) available at http://www.dhr.history.vt.edu/eu/mod04_depression/lessonplan.html. It is essential that students recognize both the context and the perspectives embedded in each kind of primary source. They must also recognize

Figure 1: Historical Evidence Chart
Unemployment during the Great Depression in Europe

Country	1929	1930	1931	1932	1933
Austria	225,000	239,000	304,000	417,000	456,000
Belgium	28,000	42,000	207,000	350,000	383,000
Czechoslovakia	50,000	88,000	340,000	634,000	878,000
France	9,000	14,000	72,000	347,000	356,000
Germany	2,484,000	3,041,000	4,744,000	6,034,000	5,599,000
Norway	24,000	23,000	29,000	38,000	42,000
Poland	177,000	289,000	373,000	360,000	280,000
Sweden	44,000	42,000	73,000	99,000	121,000
United Kingdom	1,204,000	1,694,000	2,666,000	2,660,000	2,821,000
Yugoslavia	12,000	10,000	12,000	23,000	23,000

Figures from: Lionel Robbins, *The Great Depression* (New York: Macmillan, 1936) p. 213.

how possible political biases of the author, intended audience, and format of the presentation reflect the context in which the source was produced while also shaping the way these events are understood historically.

For further enrichment, students may use Inspiration concept mapping software to illustrate key ideas and concepts within their final PowerPoint presentations—e.g. reactions to the Depression, motivations for strikes and demonstrations and protest factors that foster extremist movements.

Finally, depending on the time and level of engagement with the module, a series of assignments are available (http://www.dhr.history.vt.edu/eu/mod04_depression/assignments.html). Optional assignments include writing prompts to examine economic causality in the Depression, an interactive quiz, and questions for further discussion and written response.

Teaching Tips

We have provided a great deal of material to support the historical investigation as designed. However, we believe teaching requires a creative mind, and as a result there are many opportunities to expand or condense this lesson, as necessary, in order for the teachers to make it their own. Whatever the structure and direction of the lesson, we have found that it is important and necessary always to pose the historical question at the opening of the activity and refer to it frequently. Use the accompanying PowerPoint presentation to frame the context and direction of the lesson. Model a historical source analysis and share samples of student slides before students engage with the material (found in the PowerPoint presentation). Be willing to be flexible with student presentations in order to avoid repetition. Prepare and discuss rubrics prior to the written narrative assignment. We generally like to use the PowerPoint Jeopardy game on the second day before students complete their writing narratives.

Technology Resources

INTERNET

Link to "End of Optimism" module: http://www.dhr.history.vt.edu/eu/mod04_depression/index.html

The Digital History Reader is made up of eighteen modules, each of which explores a key event in United States or European history (see "About DHR" webpage for a complete list of modules). By presenting compelling historical questions, the DHR forces students to

deal with conflicting accounts and interpretations that they must weigh and use to develop reasonable conclusions. Each module includes the following sections: an Introduction, which defines the historical questions and learning objectives; a Context section that provides the narrative for the historical material; an Evidence section with textual, visual, audio, and video primary source materials; an Assignment section with analytical questions that allow students to evaluate their comprehension; a Conclusion that integrates the evidence with the historical questions; and a Resource section that directs students to additional published and online materials on this historical topic. By presenting a more sophisticated range of responses to historical questions, students learn to consider the power that individuals have to make choices and effect change, thus deepening their understanding of the continuing significance of the past.

ADDITIONAL SOFTWARE

Shockwave Flash is needed for the animated chart. (Download from the following site: http://www.macromedia.com/shockwave/download/download.cgi)

Inspiration (concept mapping software) is helpful for organizing key details relating to the causes and significance of the Depression in Europe, the social impact of depression (demonstrations and strikes), and the rise of extremist forces in Europe. A trial version can be found at http://www.inspiration.com/home.cfm

Microsoft PowerPoint will be used for student presentations and jeopardy game.

Microsoft Word is optional for written narratives.

Resources

It is important to stress that all online materials are downloadable and printable for use in classes. Printed versions will need the free Adobe Acrobat Reader software: http://www.adobe.com/products/acrobat/readstep2.html 📧

ELEVENTH GRADE: U.S. HISTORY

NCSS Thematic Strands
Ⅱ TIME, CONTINUITY, AND CHANGE

NCSS Performance Expectations
Ⅱ TIME, CONTINUITY, AND CHANGE

   d. Identify and use various sources for reconstructing the past, such as documents, letters, diaries, maps, textbooks, photos, and others.

NETS-S National Educational Technology Standards for Students
4. Technology Communications Tools
5. Technology Research Tools

NETS-S Performance Expectations
4. Technology Communications Tools

   ✦ Students use telecommunications to collaborate, publish, and interact with peers, experts, and other audiences.

5. Technology Research Tools

   ✦ Students use technology to locate, evaluate, and collect information from a variety of sources.

   ✦ Students use technology tools to process data and report results.

Introduction
In this lesson, students work in groups to examine primary sources from the Library of Congress about one of three pioneers of the American Conservation movement, Theodore Roosevelt, Gifford Pinchot, and John Muir. The students work in groups of 3-4 to examine and analyze photographs of these individuals. Students have questions that guide them in their analysis of the photographs and are encouraged to note details. Students then examine the writing of the individual they are studying. Students use the writing to develop a definition of conservationism and then explain the viewpoint that the author likely had about conservationism. Students will then participate in an online threaded discussion examining the definitions and viewpoints

of Roosevelt, Pinchot, and Muir on conservation. The online discussion will allow two different classes within Lynden High School to discuss what they have investigated during the lesson. Students will be required to make a certain number of posts and adhere to standards for posting comments.

Objectives
1. Students will be able to analyze details of a photograph and draw conclusions by examining photographs of Roosevelt, Pinchot, or Muir.
2. Students will be able to draw conclusions from the writings of an individual by examining the writings of Roosevelt, Pinchot, or Muir.
3. Students will be able to define the concept of conservationism and compare different viewpoints by evaluating the writings of Roosevelt, Pinchot, and Muir.
4. Student will be able to demonstrate the ability to use a threaded discussion and their knowledge of the etiquette of online discussions by participating in an online threaded discussion whereby they evaluate the definitions and viewpoints developed during the investigation of Roosevelt, Pinchot, and Muir.

Time
Several class periods depending upon the amount of class time allocated to the online discussion.

Instructional Steps
Step One: Student Activity Website
This lesson can be done individually or in groups. Divide the students into groups of 3 or 4. Assign each group Theodore Roosevelt, Gifford Pinchot, or John Muir to study. Guide students to the following student activity website: http://www.lynden.wednet.edu/lhs/staff/richins/US%20History%20 Units/Conservation%20Activity.htm. At this site you will find specific directions and links for the lesson. In the following "Steps" we focus on an example of what you will find at the student activity website under the Theodore Roosevelt link.

Overview of the Lesson for Students

There were three figures who helped to define conservationism in the beginning of the 20th century. These three people were President Theodore Roosevelt, Gifford Pinchot, and John Muir. Each of these men was dedicated to conserving the natural world, but they had different ideas about what that meant and how it should be done. Through examining the writings of these three men, the student can gain a better understanding of the conservation movement and the definition of conservationism. In the end, the student should be able to answer the question, "who is a conservationist?"

Students will do steps one through three using this webpage. Step 4 will be an online discussion held over a few days for students to evaluate and discuss what they have learned.

Sources

The sources for these selections will be from Project Gutenberg and from the American Memory collection of the Library of Congress. The document and photo analysis worksheets come from the National Archives Online Collection.

Step Two: Analyze Photographs

Each group will click on the appropriate link to access the primary sources, worksheets, and questions to answer. Students will examine two photographs, using the photo analysis worksheet from the National Archives. Students are expected to answer a broad question about the person they are studying based on the photographs. For example, the section at the website on Theodore Roosevelt looks like the following:

After examining the following photographs, use the photo analysis worksheet to answer the question:

1. What do these photographs tell us about the personality and character of Theodore Roosevelt?

Theodore Roosevelt and the "Rough Riders"

Theodore Roosevelt

Step Three: Analyze Documents

In the next part of the lesson, students will read selections from the writing of Roosevelt, Pinchot, or Muir and analyze them using the document analysis form from the National Archives. Students are given the freedom to review any part of the document; this means that they could choose a part that does not help them answer the question. However, giving students the freedom to look at the entire document maintains the authenticity of the activity. For example, the following is from the Theodore Roosevelt section at the website.

Read selections from the following: Theodore Roosevelt's *Autobiography* or *Hunting the Grizzly and Other Sketches*.

Read a few pages worth to get a feeling for Roosevelt. Read from any part of the text that you like. Use the following worksheet to examine the document. After reading, use the information you have reviewed to answer the question at the bottom of Part Two. You may need to search different parts of the document to find information to help you answer the question:

1. What would Theodore Roosevelt say is the reason that conservationism is important?

Step Four: Respond to Questions

In this part of the student activity website, students are directed to answer two questions that prepare them for the discussion. They are then asked to individually write several paragraphs on each question. They will use these paragraphs as a springboard for an online discussion that will follow. For example, a student may discuss how Roosevelt was a hunter who would have seen conservation as a way to preserve his opportunities to use nature for recreation. The following is an example of the prompting questions used at the website:

1. What should be the definition of conservation?
2. How is Theodore Roosevelt a true conservationist?

Step Five: Online Discussion

Students are provided with the URL of the discussion (see "Technology Resources" for some online discussion sites) Students will have an initial thread to discuss. Possible topics could be: what should be the definition of conservationism be?, or which one of the people researched was the most authentic conservationist? Students should be given expectations for the online discussion. For this lesson students should:

+ Use their real name when they sign up for the discussion
+ Post respectfully of others
+ Respond to posts by asking questions and evaluating the statements made by others

- Consider starting new threads for new lines of thought.
- Use evidence to back up their statements.

Assessment

	100 %	80%	60%
Participation	Posts at least one new statement and responds to two others. Responds to all questions that are posted to his or her own posts. Posts at least once each of the three days.	Posts at least one new statement and one response to another post. Responds to most questions to his or her own posts. Posts on two of the three days.	Posts at least one response to another post. Responds to some of the questions about his or her own posts. Posts on only one day.
Quality	The posts and comments advance the discussion and make insightful observations.	The posts and comments fit into the discussion and make good observations.	The posts are repetitive or do not fit into the discussion. Observations are unfounded or weak.
Use of evidence	The statements and questions explicitly refer to solid evidence.	The statements and questions refer to evidence but are not specific.	Makes unsupported comments.

Student Enrichment

EXTENSION: Students may research conservation pioneers in greater depth and breadth beyond the sites given at the student activity website. This could be reflected in the quality of responses during the discussion.

ADAPTATIONS: ESL students could use web resources provided in a variety of languages. Students that may have a difficult time quickly following or responding to a face-to-face discussion are given much more time to respond in an asynchronous discussion.

Teaching Tips

Consider these guidelines for leading online discussions:

1. Demonstrate the discussion in class or have students participate for the first time in the lab. You could do this with a projector and one computer, or if in a lab, every student could participate in a mock discussion.

2. Provide access options such as home, during lunch, during class, after school, before school.

3. Allow several days for the asynchronous discussion to develop but don't drag it on more than a few days. Unless you require daily postings, students tend to wait until the last day to post. We have had discussions that ran two weeks where only one or two posted the first week and a half, and then the others were posting on the last couple of days.

4. Discuss your expectations for the online discussion with the students during class. Explain how your expectations may be similar to face-to-face discussions or how they may be different. Consider expectations such as number of postings, supporting opinions with facts, treating classmates with respect (e.g., not "flaming"), being careful of text based misunderstandings (Comments such as, "I'm smiling when I say this" or "I'm just kidding," are necessary and appropriate), having students show they are thinking about and responding to another's comments rather than merely posting their ideas. You probably don't require a certain number of times for students to talk during face-to-face discussions, but we have found requiring a certain number of postings (2 or 3) per student to be helpful. It is interesting to see some of the quiet students begin to "shine" in a text-based environment.

5. Be willing to step in to the discussion just as you might for a face-to-face discussion. There may be a need at times for re-direction or clarification. However, just as with face-to-face discussions, the teacher's inserted opinion might stifle the discussion.

6. Debrief during class. We have found the important debriefing time is more beneficial if conducted face-to-face than if done online. This could also be a good time to discuss with the class how the discussion format itself worked and to comment on some of the things you observed while "observing". More than likely you'll pick up needed feedback to improve the discussion for the next time.

Technology Resources

Internet connected computer—this could be at the student's home or a computer provided at school.

RESOURCES

Lynden High School. U.S. History Lesson Home Page for Mr. Richins can be found at his website, http://www.lynden.wednet.edu/lhs/staff/richins/US%20History%20Units/Conservation%20Activity.htm

The following are sites that provide online discussion software and server space. (Please understand that this does not constitute an endorsement.)

Blackboard, http://www.blackboard.com

Chatspace, http://www.chatspace.com

The Digital Learning Commons. Information for hosting online discussions through the DLC is available to schools in Washington State and can be found at their website, http://www.learningcommons.org.

DiscusWare, http://www.discusware.com.

Freeboards. Information about free message hosting can be found at their website, http://www.freeboards.net

QuickTopic. Information about acquiring online discussion space can be found at their website, http://www.quicktopic.com/.

Webcrossing. Information about acquiring online discussion space can be found at their website, http://www.webcrossing.com.

Presidential Hostage Crisis Simulation: An Interdisciplinary Case Study

Eliot Waxman and Erica Jacobs

Twelfth Grade: Government, Civics, American History and English Literature

NCSS Thematic Strands
Ⓥ POWER, AUTHORITY, AND GOVERNANCE
Ⓥ INDIVIDUALS, GROUPS, AND INSTITUTIONS

NCSS Performance Expectations
Ⓥ POWER, AUTHORITY, AND GOVERNANCE

c. Analyze and explain ideas and mechanisms to meet needs and wants of citizens, regulate territory, manage conflict, establish order and security, and balance competing conceptions of a just society.

Ⓥ INDIVIDUALS, GROUPS, AND INSTITUTIONS

g. Analyze the extent to which groups and institutions meet individual needs and promote the common good in contemporary and historical settings.

NETS-S National Educational Technology Standards for Students
4. Technology Communication Tools
5. Technology Research Tools

NETS-S Performance Indicators (Grades 9-12)
4. Technology Communication Tools
5. Technology Research Tools

+ Routinely and efficiently use online information resources to meet needs for collaboration, research, publications, communications, and productivity.

+ Collaborate with peers, experts, and others to contribute to a content-related knowledge base by using technology to compile, synthesize, produce, and disseminate information, models, and other creative works.

+ Select and apply technology tools for research, information analysis, problem-solving, and decision-making in content learning.

National Council of Teachers of English Standards
Performance Expectations

8. Students use a variety of technological and information resources (e.g., libraries, databases, computer networks, video) to gather and synthesize information and to create and communicate knowledge.

1. Students read a wide range of print and non-print texts to build an understanding of texts, of themselves, and of the cultures of the United States and the world; to acquire new information; to respond to the needs and demands of society and the workplace; and for personal fulfillment. Among these texts are fiction and nonfiction, classic and contemporary works.

Introduction
The purpose of this interdisciplinary simulation of a hostage crisis is to examine and analyze the factors involved in presidential decision-making as well as to examine how motive and personality can contribute to the outcome. Students read the novel *Bel Canto*[1] before participating in the fictional simulation. *Bel Canto*, by Ann Patchett, follows a hostage crisis in an unnamed South American country over several months, and humanizes both hostages and terrorists through their daily interactions. By the end of the novel, the line between good and evil has been blurred.

The goal of this multi-class lesson is to replicate some of the grey areas and difficult decisions surrounding all hostage crises. To do this, we look at Presidential politics, media coverage, and column writing as ways for students to comprehend the nuances and hard choices inherent in such a situation. As part of a unit on the Presidency, students learn that the President considers many competing goals and pressures on a daily basis, and an international "event" such as a hostage crisis raises the stakes considerably. The President is confronted with a fictional hostage crisis in this simulation that is based loosely on the 1979 Iranian hostage crisis.[2] She or he calls a prime time press conference as a way to calm the country and the world, as well as to buy some time to plan an appropriate response. Students act as members of the White House press corps by researching and developing relevant questions for the President. At the conclusion, students are required to write a 300-400 word commentary on the situation that includes advice to the President and their insight into potential outcomes for the crisis. After posting their commentaries on an electronic discussion board, students are required to read several and respond to four student columns.

Objectives
Students will be able to:
1. Conduct research to determine relevant current events questions.
2. Role-play a member of the White House press corps.
3. Write an opinion column.
4. Read and respond to several opinion columns in an online forum.

Time
Four 90 minute blocks plus 2-4 hours of homework (Not counting the time it takes to read *Bel Canto*.)

Instructional Steps
Day 1: Column writing workshop
Ask students to bring to class examples of columns from newspapers or magazines. In small groups, have students read each others' columns and list characteristics of these columns. Review the characteristics with the class and brainstorm good column topics. Develop another list of qualities that distinguish a good introduction for a column. Have students write 50-100 words of a column and share their writings in small and large groups. Students should complete their first column for homework and post it on the electronic discussion board.

Day 2: Press conference preparation
Allow students to choose the type of news organization for which they wish to work, e.g. daily print press, weekly print press, electronic press, internet news outlet, and discuss with them the different demands and goals that each type of journalist faces. Explain that the President's main goal for the press conference will be to calm the country and the world without revealing too many specifics. Inform the students that asking the President a tough question that causes him/her to squirm or reveal top secret information will gain the journalist notoriety. This would earn kudos from their editors and could lead

to a promotion, a book advance, or a spot as a "talking head" on a television news program. If possible, show a clip from one of President Bush's press conferences and discuss his performance.

Day 3: Press conference preparation
Ask the students to develop at least three questions that they want answered by the President during the press conference. Explain that the questions should be in-depth, relevant, and thought-provoking. After each question, have students write a brief explanation of why the question is important for the President to answer and what the journalist hopes to achieve by asking the question. Provide class time for students to conduct current events research and to learn more about White House press conferences.

Day 4: White House press conference
The teacher may choose to conduct one or more press conferences simultaneously or concurrently. Students and/or the teacher can play the role of President. If more than one press conference is to be held, then divide the class into 2-3 groups of journalists. Depending on the number of Presidents there are, some students will be observers. Once the President is ready, she or he is in charge. She or he may or may not begin with an opening statement, choose the journalists to recognize, and answer any way she or he wishes. The press conference continues until all questions are answered or until the President chooses to finish (20-30 minutes). Depending on the President's response, journalists may ask follow-up questions and/or pursue new lines of questioning. Repeat the procedures with new Presidents and journalists until everyone has participated. Debrief the Presidents' performance with the class, highlighting notable responses or non-responses. Assign for homework a 300-400 word commentary (second column) on the hostage crisis situation, including basic facts, recommendations for the President, and potential outcomes. Have students post their columns on the electronic discussion board.

Once the columns are posted, have students read several of their classmates' columns and respond with thoughtful comments on the discussion board to four other columns.

Assessment
There are several possible assessments within this unit. A simulation activity rubric for the press conference might focus on factual accuracy, the use of resources, the use of skills and participation, while the rubric for written columns might

concentrate on clarity, logical argument, and inclusion of apt references. Formal assessments based on content knowledge of the Executive Branch and *Bel Canto* may be developed and used as well. Finally, students can receive credit for successfully posting and commenting on one another's columns.

Student Enrichment

EXTENSIONS: Following the press conference, students may be asked to switch perspectives and adopt the role of a White House staffer assigned to advise the President on his/her policy options regarding the hostage crisis situation. Working in small groups, students should develop an action plan for the President and brief him/her. Students should be prepared to answer any questions that may arise.

Students may assume the role of Ann Patchett, author of *Bel Canto*, as she is writing the book. Students might write a monologue of her thoughts as she is deciding which characters will live and which will die. Emphasis should be placed on different alternatives and weighing their effects on the reader.

ADAPTATIONS: Teachers may choose to develop different hostage crisis scenarios, e.g., embassy takeover, hijacked plane, hostages taken during the War on Terrorism, to see how the President would handle different situations. This simulation may be applied to state and local issues by substituting the President's role with that of Governor or Mayor and focusing on a state or local issue.

A simulation is an excellent method to use to reach all types of learners. Simulations require students to solve problems by using higher-order critical-thinking skills. Finally, simulations allow students to learn the content better and retain it for a longer period of time.

Teaching Tips

This simulation works best when students play the role of President. The teacher should discuss the intricacies of the role with the student in advance. The President might want to make brief remarks regarding the crisis prior to answering the journalists' questions. This simulation can be completed without the connection to *Bel Canto*.

Technology Resources

HARDWARE
Computer access for students.

SOFTWARE
Electronic discussion board program such as Blackboard, or web log interface such as TypePad.

Resources

INTERNET
Access to research databases, search engines, www.americanpresident.org, www.cspan.org.

Other Materials Needed

Hostage crisis scenario, clips of presidential news conferences.

Student Voices

Examples of students' columns are provided in two appendices. Students were encouraged to write columns on any of the hostage crisis scenarios—fictional or real. Some linked the fictional situation with current events. Erica Jacobs published a column about this lesson in her weekly education column in *The Washington Examiner*. It may be accessed at http://erica_jacobs.typepad.com in "Archives" for February, 2005. 🔊

Notes

1.   Ann Patchett, *Bel Canto* (New York: HarperCollins Publishers, 2001).
2.   Mira Cohen, "You Decide: Iranian Hostage Crisis," *The American President*, www.historywire.com/lp_iranhostage.htm.

Student Column on a Hostage Crisis Scenario

Adapting to Illyria

Two weeks ago terrorists took 66 embassy workers hostage. They are still being held in a small country halfway across the world. People have died, it is likely more will.

Last night I went to the movies and ate pizza.

Think back two weeks ago, what were you doing? What was America doing? We were glued to the television set, watching the news for updates. We were discussing the events in Illyria with our family, friends, coworkers, even people we had never met. We swore we would never forget what was going on there, that this would change our lives.

How can we sit at home watching self absorbed drama queens make fools of themselves on American Idol while chuggin' down a bottle of Sprite while somewhere people are held against their will. People like you and me. They have families and desires. They enjoy a good nap on the couch just like everyone else. Now they are prisoners to a rebellious faction. We can't miss our 8 o'clock crime drama.

Have we forgotten what has happened? What is happening? Most would be appalled by the thought. No. Of course not. How could we? But, the reality is, the Super Bowl is the top news story tonight. Any mention of the hostages will be cursory and generalized in less than thirty seconds.

Of course there are those who are directly affected by the events. The families, the government workers, the negotiators. They will never forget. They can't forget.

But all of us here two weeks ago considered the rebellion as a personal attack on America and its citizens. A situation of utmost importance.

Now Illyria sits in the back of our minds. It is a passing thought between radio stations on the way to Starbucks.

So is it good to forget the hostages in Illyria? No, absolutely not. They are in fact letting the terrorists win.

Americans are not ignorant (although we may be stupid) because we watch American Idol. It is our natural defense mechanism, keeping us moving and working. Keeping us happy.

I am no strategist. I can't say what the chances are the hostages are freed or killed. Whether or not we go to war. I can't present a plan to save mankind. So I'm not going to try, nor obsess about it. All I can do is pray for a peaceful resolution, support those working to develop it, and live my life grateful I am only hostage to my own actions.

But never forget.

Student Column: Background to a Possible Future Hostage Crisis

Suppose We Traded Places For A Moment?

For all you breast-beating, "everything is beautiful" types out there, allow me to ask you a few simple questions.

Suppose America had been invaded and occupied—pardon me, "liberated" ... yeah, "liberated," that's the ticket—by a foreign power.

And suppose our new leader this foreign power had helped into office killed tens of thousands of innocent civilians.

And suppose this growing force practically controlled large swaths of our land that were rich in oil, areas now known to us as the Triangle of Pain, the Octagon of Nastiness and the Rectangle of Evil-Doers.

And suppose intelligence analysts for the occupying—sorry, "liberating"—force had concluded that as a result of their new leader, our country was no longer a "haven for terrorist organizations," but a promising hope in the quest to spread their government.

And suppose our only national army was made up of hurriedly trained and poorly equipped students who, if they avoided getting blown up, were more skilled at retreating than Monty Python's Knights of the Round Table.

And suppose our new leader that this occupying—my bad, "liberating"—force was responsible for placing in power allowed for the horrific abuse of prisoners being held in detention.

And suppose the citizenry was more anxious about simply getting through the day without being blown up by their King's troops and/or the occupying—drat, "liberating"— power than accepting their ways.

And suppose because of all the rampant, withering violence, everyone pretty much agreed it would be impossible to go on living with this force in the country.

And suppose some of the more influential voices in the country—say, Rush Limbaugh, Billy Graham, Newt Gingrich—were encouraging their followers to boycott this new government.

And suppose entire communities—political parties, religious organizations, ethnic groups representing as much as 40 percent of the citizens—decided to resist this "liberating" force.

And suppose, despite the occupying—darn, "liberating"—force's pertinent desires to the contrary, it remained entirely possible that after all the bloodshed and chaos and anarchy, the country could wind up being sucked dry of its most precious commodity, oil.

And suppose it was altogether likely that, despite the people's wishes, the country would be occupied and, de facto, governed by all those liberators for years and years and years to come.

And suppose—from a purely hypothetical viewpoint, of course—that all those variables were in place in this country.

Would it make any rational sense not to revolt?

Just asking.

part 4
Tools and
Techniques

Success in integrating technology into instruction necessitates an expansion of knowledge and skills across several areas of pedagogy. Just as classroom management creates a critical foundation for teaching and learning, accommodations for a technology-infused environment may require some adaptations in the physical structure of the classroom as well as the learning context. Sensitivity to Internet safety and the selection of quality digital resources, including software, audio, and images, can best be facilitated by ongoing dialogue about evidence-informed decision-making and promising practices. The following sections provide an overview to these topics and may create the building blocks for the successful infusion of technology into social studies education.

Classroom Management

Monica Beglau

Introduction

Discussions of classroom management tend to conjure up images of techniques for controlling student behaviors. Managing a classroom actually requires attention to multiple factors: behavior management, instructional management, time management and the management of resources and materials. In technology-rich classrooms another category is added: equipment management. Classrooms in which teachers develop a sense of community and design student-centered instructional experiences tend to include students in many management tasks. This creates environments where students share in all aspects of classroom management rather than one in which teachers retain sole responsibility for all classroom management.

Implementation Strategies

Behavior Management Strategies

Linda Albert details highly effective methods of behavior management in her book, *Cooperative Discipline*.[1] Albert's methods, known as cooperative discipline, use building community as a lens for examining misbehavior. Rather than trying short-term solutions for a problem behavior, cooperative discipline advocates looking beyond the behavior and trying to determine what needs the student might be attempting to meet with a particular set of behavior choices. Teachers then use a logical process to define ways that support the student by finding positive ways to fulfill those same needs within the community of learners. Albert explains, "I try to encourage educators to see a broader meaning of the word discipline. The word really means to teach, not to punish. The goal of discipline is to teach students to choose appropriate behavior. Three sets of skills are needed: intervention strategies for the moment of misbehavior, encouragement techniques to reinforce positive behavior and prevent future misbehavior, and collaboration strategies that create a positive teacher-student relationship."[2]

In technology-rich classrooms, the goal of building a community of learners becomes even more important as an effective way to manage behavior. High-quality lessons that integrate technology require a classroom community where students feel comfortable taking risks, sharing ideas, working cooperatively and being responsible for learning. Students who experience the positive feelings associated with having their needs for attention, acceptance, and recognition met within their classroom community often display vastly improved behaviors and better attention to instruction when compared to students who have experienced more traditional forms of behavior control and discipline.[3]

Instructional Management Strategies

In technology-rich classrooms that are also student-centered, teachers and students share instructional management. Teachers guide students through the instructional experience rather than tell students what they need to do. Teachers provide the resources and tools students need to engage in inquiry and problem-solving. For older students who have the skills to engage in safe internet searching, teachers provide guidance to students and help them evaluate both the reliability and validity of their sources. Based on the needs of the students, teachers may choose to provide scaffolding (information-gathering guides, Venn diagrams, comparison charts, storyboards and so on). Visual examples guide students through the learning experiences. Instructional management is best achieved by identifying student learning needs and providing the tools to meet those needs as they appear.

Time Management Strategies

Helping students manage their time when engaging in long-term projects and technology-enriched activities, may require teachers to set up a project timeline with students. Teachers can guide students in examining the steps that are needed to help them arrive at a successful final product. Then, teachers can help students work backward from the product due date and set up a timeline for the project. When students work through the process of developing a timeline, they have a clearer understanding of the reasons they must finish certain parts of a project at certain times to meet a final deadline. After students have experience making timelines as a class, they can more confidently develop their own deadlines and action plans.

Management of Resources and Materials

Creating easy access to appropriate resources and materials as they are needed by students during the learning experience will assist teachers in overall classroom management. Teachers who facilitate student learning take into account the logistics of student access to resources and materials and the ways in which students will use the resources and materials, based on the context of the lesson as established in the planning phase of the learning experience. Examples of resource management include the following:

- Providing internet resources students need to access during a learning experience on a classroom website created by the teacher. Alternatively, teachers can create web resource lists that contain the initial internet resources students need to get started.
- Setting up a time when students have access to an outside expert through e-mail or video conferencing.
- Working with the district technology department to set up shared folders for the classroom.
- Teaching students about saving files, including file-naming conventions and file storage locations.

Equipment Management

Whether teachers have an array of technology resources in their classrooms, share a laptop cart with other classrooms, or use their school's computer lab, managing various pieces of equipment requires teachers to consider safety issues along with storage and physical movement issues. Some safety issues, such as wiring, cables, furniture and computer equipment, are the primary responsibility of computer lab personnel or technology coordinators; however, all teachers should be aware of the following:

- Securing wiring and cables away from areas where students and teachers walk.
- Periodically checking electrical connections to make sure they are firmly seated.
- Placing the keyboards at levels that facilitate healthy student posture for hand and wrist placement while working on the computers.
- Identifying locations in the classroom away from the computers where students may use resources that spill.

Teachers need to give the same consideration to the ways in which students will move through the classroom when all the students need to leave the classroom at the same time or move to a meeting area in the classroom. Looking for possible problem areas and developing a movement plan can avoid these problems.

Acceptable Use Policies (AUPs) include guidelines for using computer equipment and the internet. Many districts have AUPs that all teachers and students follow. In addition, some teachers who use high levels of technology in their classrooms, create their own AUPs. At the beginning of the year, teachers need to check the policies previously developed to determine if they require any changes. Insuring student safety online requires that AUPs include the following:

- Keep personal information private, including name, e-mail address, postal address, phone number, photo and school address.
- Do not share login names or passwords with anyone.
- If inappropriate material appears on the monitor, turn off the monitor and tell the teacher immediately.
- Notify a teacher or parent if any received e-mail creates uncomfortable feelings.

In classrooms where a strong sense of community has been developed, there is a pervasive shared sense of ownership of the equipment and responsibility for its care. The class as a whole can set guidelines and consequences for the misuse of equipment. This practice will greatly reduce undesirable student behaviors.

Classroom management in technology-rich classrooms or in classrooms where teachers integrate technology resources requires a perspective that includes a focus on the building of a classroom community so that teachers can attend to the facilitation of learning rather than controlling behaviors, monitoring equipment usage, and constantly checking what students may be viewing on the Internet. Building classroom community requires some work and planning initially but will pay large dividends in student productivity in the long run.

Resources
Cooperative Discipline or Building Community

Cooperative Discipline Overview, http://members.tripod.com/tkmoyer/CooperativeDiscipline/id17.htm

Teacher Modeling Group Redirection (Short video, requires QuickTime), http://www.coe.wayne.edu/wholeschooling/WS/Video/TalkRespect.html

Overview of Behavior-Management Strategy, http://www.disciplinehelp.com/teacher/instruction.cfm?section=step&sectiontitle=Introduction

Classroom-Management Strategies

IKE Project, http://www.k12science.org/ike/classmanagement.html

Managing Computer Use, http://www.intel.com/education/newtotech/managing.htm

Acceptable Use Policies

Revisiting the AUP: A Digital Double Take, http://www.educationworld.com/a_tech/tech018.shtml

Rice University's Permission Form WS, http://www.rice.edu/armadillo/aupenglish.html

Writing a Classroom AUP, http://www.teacheruniverse.com/profdev/features/hunt0301.htm

Electronic School, http://www.electronic-school.com/2000/01/0100sbot.html

Internet Safety

GetNetWise, http://www.getnetwise.org/

Kids' Rules for Online Safety, http://www.safekids.com/kidsrules.htm

eThemes Internet Safety: NetSmartz, http://www.netsmartz.org

Notes

1. Portions of the article are taken from eMINTS National Center professional development materials created by eMINTS staff. Jennifer Kuehnle, Roxanne Kerwood, and Michelle Kendrick, "Classroom Management in the Technology-Rich Classroom" (2005, University of Missouri: Columbia, MO)

2. Linda Albert, "Thirty Years of Making a Difference" (American Guidance Services, 2006), http://www.agsglobe.com/staffdev/albert.asp

3. Susan Tharp, "Classroom Climate, Instructional Practice and Mentorship Experience in the eMINTS Expansion Classrooms: A Two-Year Study" (eMINTS National Center, September 3, 2004), http://www.emints.org/evaluation/reports/expansionclassroom-climate.pdf

Internet Safety and Digital Literacy Strategies for the Social Studies Classroom

32

Carolyn E. Walpole

Integration of internet safety and digital literacy skills in the K–12 social studies classroom provides a meaningful platform and positive example on which students can build an understanding of the impact of technology on every facet of today's society. There is no better way to provide youth with the means to connect their online actions and experiences with the realities of social consequence in the physical world. "As cyberspace facilitates more global interactions, the necessity of competent skills for social involvement online will intensify."[1] You don't have to be a technology expert to successfully promote safe and responsible digital literacy to your students, but you do have to become an informed, prepared participant and recognize the relevance of the issues of cyber community citizenship, online privacy, online predation, cyber security, and intellectual property use to actual internet behaviors. This is a lot easier than you may think. Basic strategies to promote the development of safe, responsible, literate users of technology are age-appropriately applicable to all grade levels, and enable the educator to integrate concepts in ways that best fit existing curriculum.

Be informed. "Only by fostering their own understanding of the literacy needed for critical inquiry in the 21st century will educators be able to instruct students on the appropriate use of emerging resources and prepare them for civic involvement."[2] Begin by learning about the safety/responsible use issues and potential liabilities facing schools with internet access, the vocabulary and nuances of online behavior, and the risks youth are exposed to anytime they access the internet. This type of information is available through no-cost online internet safety professional-development programs, live workshops, or educational conference sessions. Once you have developed an understanding of the relevant issues, access standards-based cyber safety lesson plans, such as those from iSAFE.org, and look for ways to integrate them into your existing curriculum. Become familiar with the ways your students are using digital technologies, and recognize the potentials for empowering them with their existing expertise. The real goal of internet safety education is for students to develop the awareness, knowledge, and skills/responses they need to recognize and avoid danger-

ous, destructive, inappropriate, or unlawful online behaviors, situations, and places. One basic way to reinforce cyber safety awareness and skill is through meaningful classroom technology policy. If you aren't familiar with it already, get to know your school's Acceptable Use Policy (AUP). Use it to engage your students in creating and maintaining usable, age-appropriate guidelines for responsible computer use in the classroom that include descriptions of acceptable use, consequences for unacceptable use, and procedures for responding to unsafe or inappropriate online situations.

Plan ahead. Planning is key to successful integration of safe digital literacy strategies. Think about ways internet safety and digital literacy can be integrated into your existing lessons, and adjust your plan before you begin. Almost every real-world issue has a cyberspace counterpart through which to capture students' interest. Just as children and teens learn about citizenship and their roles and responsibilities in the physical community, they should be given opportunities to relate this knowledge to their experiences in the cyber community. For example, depending on age level, the online methods your students use to communicate, such as e-mail, instant messaging, chatting, or blogging, provide a basis to discuss and explore a variety of social and ethical topics, from the basics on modes of communication today to netiquette, cyber bullying, and online social networking. Let students examine how they are treated online, how they treat others, and why. Sometimes planning needs to be part of the students' learning experience; before turning older students loose on the internet to research a topic, discuss how a search engine helps with research, and engage in an example search. Have students make predictions about how key words or phrases can lead to more successful hits. Seize the teachable moment if your search turns up broken links or undesirable resources!

Above all, as you and your students explore the wonders of cyberspace don't be afraid to be adventurous. The use of digital technology is second nature to most youth; they've never known life without it. Use that to your advantage, and allow your students to show you a thing or two! Application engages student interest and provides the most meaningful means to promote appropriate, safe, and educational usage of technologies. Understand that sharing is an integral part of life in cyberspace. Use that concept to enable constructive learning by immersing students in peer-to-peer activities and by facilitating activities in which older youth mentor younger children in safe and responsible technology practice.

"We can celebrate students' opportunities to make connections with people around the world, but the concept of community necessitates a foundation in values, empathy, and human interrelationships."[3] Cyberspace is not a separate entity from the physical world; it is a real aspect of our community and social existence, requiring all of us to integrate safe and responsible digital literacy into every aspect of our learning and living. ▧

Notes

1. Michael J. Berson, "The Computer Can't See You Blush," *Kappa Delta Pi Record* 36, no.4 (Summer 2000): 158-62.

2. Ilene R. Berson and Michael J. Berson, "Digital Literacy for Cybersafety, Digital Awareness, and Media Literacy," *Social Education* 67, no.3 (2003): 164-168.

3. Cheryl Mason, Michael Berson, Richard Diem, David Hicks, John Lee, and Tony Dralle, "Guidelines for Using Technology to Prepare Social Studies Teachers," *Contemporary Issues in Technology and Teacher Education* 1, no.1 (2000), http://www.citejournal.org/voh/iss1/currentissues/socialstudies/article1.htm.

Software Selection: Finding a Needle in the Haystack

33

Linda C. Unger

If you're looking for high-quality software for your students, a search of CD-ROMs on the Social Studies School Service website will return more than 500 titles! The proliferation of technology for the social studies is impressive, but what a problem this presents for teachers looking for the best programs for their students. Chances are the technology dollars available in your school's budget are scarce. Worse yet, you may even be paying for software out of your own pocket, so you simply can't afford to choose the wrong title.

Then how do you decide which software to buy? Technology should serve the curriculum, so start by thinking about your reasons for choosing a software program in the first place. My personal rule of thumb is: Will this enable teaching or learning that is more effective, more efficient or more engaging? You should be able to answer yes to at least one of these three criteria. Otherwise, save your money and use a traditional method or material instead.

Next, think about whether the software will enable you to do something you couldn't do at all or couldn't do as easily without it. For example, you can teach students about the stock market by creating an in-class simulation using real data from the daily newspaper, calculators, and graphs to chart students' hypothetical "purchases." A stock market simulation software program, however, requires a lot less preparation, can save class time, and will likely be more fun for students.

If you're convinced that software is the right way to go, you'll have to do some homework to locate the best titles. Fortunately, the internet provides shortcuts for finding software. Online catalogs are one place to start, but there are also software ratings sites, such as the highly-recommended Educational Software Preview Guide (ESPG), which is maintained by a non-profit consortium of colleges and educator associations. Volunteer educators preview titles using a stringent evaluation instrument, which you can download from their website. In order for a software title to appear in the ESPG's online database, it must be favorably reviewed by multiple evaluators. "There is nothing in there that has not passed that litmus… That's why we think our [site] is so valuable," says Evye Woldman, long-time software evaluator and tech coordinator for the Massachusetts Elementary School Principals' Association.

Many technology journals also carry regular columns of software reviews, which are available by searching their online archives. Examples include:

+ *Learning & Leading with Technology*—http://www.iste. org/. Select "Publications," then "L&L," then "Past Issues" (right frame) then "Search Past Issues."
+ *Technology and Learning*—http://www.techlearning.com/. Use the pull-down menu on the right side of the banner to select "Reviews," then complete the search form.
+ *T.H.E. Journal*—http://www.thejournal.com

While reviews and ratings may make your selection task easier, until you actually see a program, you won't know whether it meets your own instructional goals. The next step should be to preview the software yourself. Many publishers provide for a 30-day preview of their products, and many dealers have liberal return policies. Take advantage of these opportunities to get a first-hand look.

Sure, this seems time consuming, but previewing a software title is a critical step for making sure it meets your students' needs, while saving you money. Letting a handful of students "test" the program can also indicate how engaging it is and whether there are any obstacles to its usability. Here are several critical factors to consider when previewing a program:

Does the program address state or national learning standards? The current emphasis on benchmarks that define student proficiency and performance, both in terms of knowledge and thinking skills, means that learning standards need to be at the heart of the selection process. Since publishers are well aware of this, most claim that their programs are "standards-based," but you'll need to look beyond the marketing materials to be certain. Often, information this detailed can only be found in the accompanying teacher guide.

Do the learning activities require higher-level thinking skills, such as application, analysis, synthesis, and evaluation? This may be one of the most important considerations. Look for programs that are more complex than a workbook or game delivered via computer. You can provide fun practice exercises without spending precious technology dollars, so look for programs that enable you to take learning to a higher level. *Time Engineers: Engineering the Past* from Software Kids is a good example. It enables students to explore ancient Egyptian pyramids, medieval drawbridges, World War II submarines and more from an engineering point of view. Students must apply problem-solving skills as they engage in open-ended activities.

Does the program address your specific performance objectives for the lesson(s) in which it will be used? Is it grade appropriate and matched to your local/state curricular frameworks? Again, it's best not to accept what the publisher claims about a product. It's not that these companies aren't reputable—in fact, most have experienced editors and instructional designers who are trained as educators. However, the editors don't know your students and their particular instructional needs, so it's wise to rely on your own good judgment. Look carefully at the learning objectives listed in the teacher guide. Check out the readability of the vocabulary used on screen. Run through the learning activities to see if the content is just what you need and whether students would meet your learning objectives by using this program.

Is the content up-to-date, accurate, and free of stereotypes? This may seem obvious at first, but you'd be surprised to discover that errors do occasionally slip through the editorial process. Thankfully, publishers are quite conscientious about representing diversity and avoiding bias. Still, a specific program may simply be inappropriate in your particular setting—a judgment that only you can make.

Does the software include an assessment activity or other means of measuring student progress? While teaching, you are continually monitoring the effectiveness of your instruction, as well as assessing student progress. A high-quality software program should assist you by including some way for you to determine student outcomes. Look for an evaluation activity and/or some record keeping mechanism that indicates what individual students accomplished while using the program.

While it may seem that there's a great deal to consider when selecting software, teachers who focus on learning standards, performance indicators, and higher-order thinking rather than entertainment value shouldn't have too much trouble finding pedagogically sound software. 🖾

Using Digital Images in the Social Studies Classroom

34

Lynn Bell

With the recent advent of reasonably priced digital cameras on the market, many teachers have added cameras to their arsenal of classroom equipment in order to document student learning activities for newsletters, Web sites, and electronic slideshows. Digital images can be used to engage students and help them learn social studies content, as well. Depending on the learning objectives (and your technology budget), you may have students create their own digital images of geographic features, historical scenes, interviewees for a local history project, or countless other subjects of interest to the social studies classroom. You may also take advantage of collections of existing digital images on the World Wide Web. The Web has become an almost limitless source of images and digitized primary sources to enhance the learning of history, geography, multicultural perspectives, responsible citizenship, and other social studies topics.

Implementation Strategies

As with every learning tool, digital images can be more or less effective in the classroom depending on the way they are used. After deciding your purpose for using images, the next step is for you or your students to acquire them. The following are some tips for obtaining and working with digital images.

Students Using Cameras

If you are fortunate enough to have a classroom set of digital cameras (or if several students have personal cameras available for classroom use), students can capture their own digital images. Before beginning a project of this kind, you will need to provide some basic instruction on how to operate the cameras and how to take useful photos. Most digital cameras have the following controls students need to know about (Figure 1):

+ On/off switch
+ Shutter button ("Hold the button down until you hear the shutter click.")
+ View finder vs. LCD photo display
+ Zoom lens control
+ Flash on/off control ("The flash uses extra battery power, and as the batteries run down, the camera may require a longer delay between photos.")
+ Shooting mode ("The automatic setting is the easiest to use.")

Give students an opportunity to practice taking some photos after reminding them that (a) the subject of the photo should fill most of the frame, (b) they should avoid pointing the camera toward the sun or placing the subject in front of bright light, and (c) they should try to eliminate distracting

Figure 1

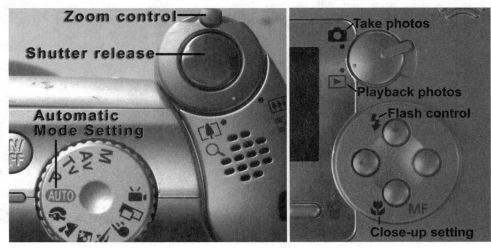

These photos show the locations of important camera controls on one brand and make of digital camera. Although the location of camera controls may vary according to camera brand, most use a common set of icons for designating the controls.

objects from the background of their photos (often, changing their point of view helps).

Several Web sites have more extensive photography tips your students may find helpful, such as the following:

- Kodak — www.Kodak.com (go to "Consumer Products," then "Taking Great Pictures")
- Ranger Rick: Six Tips for Better Pix — http://www.nwf.org/kidZone/. Click on "Ranger Rick" and select "PhotoZone."
- Short Courses on Photography — www.shortcourses.com

Before beginning any photography project, make sure you have extra batteries for each camera and a memory card large enough to hold the digital images your students will capture (at least one 64 MB card per camera or multiple cards with 16 MB or 32 MB).

Finding Images on the Web

According to research on the educational use of pictures, the most effective images relate directly to the content being learned. Images used only for aesthetic purposes have little instructional value and may even detract from learning. Whether you or your students are looking for digital images from the Web, the teacher needs to make the purpose of the images clear. What is the target concept you want students to learn from the images? Are you trying to engage them in a historical event or period? Are you illustrating cultural charac-teristics (dress, architecture, landscape, etc.)? Are you helping them understand the concept of chronology (old vs. new)? Are you trying to develop critical thinking or empathy? Are you illustrating geographic features?

There are many good uses for digital images and many good places to find them. If students are searching for images, provide the URLs for some safe Web sites to choose from. Remember that a Google search for images is not filtered and may turn up inappropriate photos. (See the sidebar for some safe sites where students can find digital images.)

Resolution and Format for Digital Images

With digital cameras, photographers no longer have to worry about film speeds and photo developing. However, working with digital images does require some basic knowledge of image resolution and file format.

RESOLUTION. Although good quality printed images require dedicated photo printers and high resolution images, most digital images in schools will be viewed from Web sites and electronic slideshows (like PowerPoint). For viewing digital images electronically, the resolution of the final picture (after cropping) needs to be around 72 pixels per inch (ppi). If you want the picture to fill the screen, it should be around 800-1,000 pixels wide at 72 ppi.

Higher resolution means the digital image will take up more file space than necessary. A Web site with high resolution images will take too long to load, and a slide presentation

---

Figure 2 *The photo on the left has a resolution of 300 ppi (pixels per inch). As the photo is cropped and enlarged, the resolution decreases, along with the quality of the image.*

300 ppi   72 ppi   38 ppi

Resources for Acquiring Digital Images from the Web

National Geographic
www.nationalgeographic.com/onestop

U.S. Library of Congress Prints and Photographs Reading Room
www.loc.gov/rr/print/catalog.html

U.S. National Archives and Records Administration
www.archives.gov

Virginia Center for Digital History
www.vcdh.virginia.edu/research.html
Includes images related to the following American history topics among others:

+ Civil War (http://valley.vcdh.virginia.edu)
+ Jamestown, Virginia (www.virtualjamestown.org/gallery.html)
+ Dolley Madison (www.vcdh.virginia.edu/madison/exhibit)
+ Television News of the Civil Rights Era 1950-1970 (www.vcdh.virginia.edu/civilrightstv)

Powerful Days in Black and White (Photos of Charles Moore)
www.kodak.com/US/en/corp/features/moore/mooreIndex.shtml

Open Photo
openphoto.net

Pics4Learning
www.pics4learning.com
Pics4Learning is a copyright-friendly image library for teachers and students. The Pics4Learning collection consists of thousands of images that have been donated by students, teachers, and amateur photographers.

Landscape Architecture Image Resource
www.lair.umd.edu

The Manzanita Project, Special Collections, California Academy of Sciences Library
www.calacademy.org/research/library/manzanita/html/images.html

file full of high resolution photos may become so large that it is difficult to transport to other computers. On the other hand, an image with resolution lower than 72 ppi will look blurred, with jagged edges (see Figure 2).

Images can be resized with image editing programs, like Adobe Photoshop Elements or the GIMP (a free download from the Web). Before enlarging a picture (or a cropped portion of a picture) make sure that the beginning resolution is higher than 72 ppi, because as you enlarge the picture, the resolution will decrease.

FORMATS. You will notice that the filename extensions vary for images you download from a digital camera or from the Web (e.g., gif, jpg, tif, bmp, png). These different extensions indicate different image file formats, and the format does matter, depending on your use of the image. Figure 3 is a highly simplified overview of image formats.

Figure 3: Digital Photo File Formats

Format	General characteristics	Appropriate uses
.tif/.tiff	High quality images; largest file sizes.	Printed photos and master copies of important photos. Web browsers are not well suited for viewing large .tif files.
.png	Relatively new format; high quality images; smaller file sizes than .tif but larger than .jpg	Web or printed photos.
.jpg	Good quality images; smaller file sizes.	Fine for smaller printed photos; great for onscreen display, e.g., the Web, email, and slide presentations.
.gif	Limited range of color	Best for line art and graphics.
.bmp	Older format; large file size.	Not usually supported by Web browsers. Suitable for wallpaper on a Windows desktop.

Image Editing

Teachers or students taking their own digital photos will need to transfer those images to a computer and may want to edit them. Many less-than-perfect photos can be improved with some basic editing features available on most photo editing software, such as cropping, resizing, and adjusting brightness and contrast.

Fair Use

Remember that images on the Web may be copyrighted just as text is. Although some educational uses fall under so-called "fair use" guidelines, this can be a murky area, so know your school district policies on this issue. Some districts have adopted the Educational Multimedia Fair Use Guidelines developed in 1996 by the Consortium of College and University Media Centers (see http://www.utsystem.edu/OGC/Intellectual Property/ccmcguid.htm). Although these guidelines were never adopted into law, they still provide a useful framework.

Conclusion

Even though this chapter has focused on digital photos, a number of other digital images on the Web are available for classroom use, such as maps, drawings, artworks, timelines, and digitized documents like letters and newspaper articles. More than ever before students have access to visual imagery and primary sources that can engage them in learning about the world—its history, geography, and people. Many students are already using these resources in their lives outside the classroom, and schools should grab every opportunity to encourage the use of these same resources whenever they are appropriate in social studies learning. 🌐

GLEN BULL, TOM HAMMOND, AND PATRICE GRIMES

The word *podcast* combines the words *iPod* and *broadcast*. A podcast is an audio file (typically in MP3 format), with the added convenience of automatic delivery via a free subscription service. When you subscribe to a podcast, the audio files are automatically downloaded to a computer or a handheld device such as an MP3 player. Subscribing to and listening to podcasts requires no special equipment: a free newsreader such as Bloglines (bloglines.com) or free software such as iTunes can be used to subscribe to a podcast's feed, and you can listen to the podcasts on your computer.

Like ham radio, podcasting originated with enthusiasts. However, podcasting has since entered the mainstream. National Public Radio (NPR) stations, for example, are making a variety of programs available as podcasts. If you wish to use an interview from an NPR program such as "On the Media," you can easily locate that audio and even cue up the exact point in the segment that you wish to play for the class.

The revolutionary aspect of podcasting is the ease with which podcasts can be created and distributed by teachers and students. For example, Eric Langhorst, a history teacher at Liberty Junior High in Liberty, MO, has an extensive set of podcasts he has created for his students and others. The podcasts, including "StudyCasts" for students to listen to as they prepare for Mr. Langhorst's tests, are available at SpeakingOfHistory.blogspot.com. Examples of student-generated content can be found on mpsomaha.org/willow/radio. This site features podcasts created by K-5 students at Willow Elementary, in Omaha.

Subscribing to a Podcast

A podcatcher is an application that can be used to subscribe to podcasts and automatically downloads them. iTunes is one of the most widely-used podcatchers, but other popular tools include Juice (formerly iPodder), jPodder, and Doppler. All of these applications are free to download and install.

We anticipate that future generations of mail managing software, such as Outlook or Thunderbird, will incorporate podcatching as an integrated function.

Podcasts for the Social Studies Classroom

One rich source of podcasts is the news media. The *Washington Post*, the *New York Times*, the BBC, and NPR all provide podcasts on current events. Many of these involve the latest news stories in text format, but these sites also provide background information and interviews in audio form as well (i.e., as podcasts). As might be expected, the NPR podcast directory (npr. org/rss/podcast/podcast_directory.php) is especially far-ranging, since audio is the primary focus of that organization. NPR has added a new feature that even makes it possible to subscribe to podcasts via cell phone.

The legislative and executive branches of the federal government have embraced podcasting. Members of Congress use them for personal radio addresses, and caucuses use them to stump for their issues. Even agencies provide podcast feeds, many of which can be browsed at firstgov.gov/Topics/Reference_Shelf/Libraries/Podcasts.shtml.

Other podcasts are specific to history or history educators.

Figure 1: Subscribing to Radio WillowWeb through iTunes (left) and Juice (right).

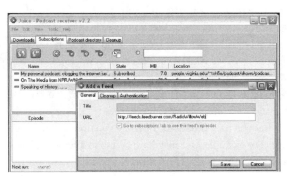

Historical sites

+ Colonial Williamsburg (history.org/media/podcasts.cfm) offers podcasts on topics ranging from colonial cooking to the research underlying the interpretation of historic figures such as Thomas Jefferson.

Historians

+ The Teaching American History website (teaching americanhistory.org) features more authors, such as James McPherson and Victor Davis Hanson.
+ Michael Farquhar, Steven Watts, and many other authors discuss their research in podcasts available at talkinghistory.oah.org.

K-16 instructors

+ The Education Podcast Network (epnweb.org) provides a directory of podcasts both by and for students, teachers, and support staff. The podcasts originate all over the world, and can be searched by age level or topic.

The historic conversations of the 20th and 21st centuries are increasingly being made available to history classes. At sites such as WhiteHouseTapes.org it is possible to listen to historic tapes of presidential conversations. A class discussing the Cuban Missile Crisis, for example, can listen to President Kennedy discussing the U.S. interpretation of these events as they are occurring. This provides the opportunity for a ringside seat at historic events.

Creating and Distributing a Podcast

Creating and broadcasting podcasts is more complicated than merely subscribing, but it does not require advanced equipment or expensive software. As long as you have access to a web server, you can use free software to record audio, post it to the internet, and set up the subscription service.

The process begins with creating an audio recording. An excellent free audio editor is Audacity, available for download at audacity.sourceforge.net. Once you download and install the program, you can use it to record audio (through a plug-in microphone or via your computer's built-in microphone), edit, and produce MP3 files.

Audacity is free and fairly easy to learn, but you can use other audio editors, such as GarageBand.

After you have produced the MP3, you upload it to a web server. For example, you may have access to a folder on your school's website. If you do not have accessible space on the

Figure 2: Editing captured audio and producing an MP3 using Audacity

school web server, you can transfer media files to services such as OurMedia (ourmedia.org) without charge.

At this point, you now have a decision to make: the simplest way to make the podcast available is to simply link from a web page (for example, a web page on your school's website) to your audio file. In the example below, Eric Langhorst's blog features a direct link (highlighted in the lower left corner) from the blog to his school's server, where the audio file is stored. A visitor can click on the direct link to manually download and store the podcast.

The more advanced step is to add automation. For example, in the upper right corner of Eric Langhorst's blog is a link to Feedburner (highlighted). Feedburner (feedburner.com) is a free service that handles the XML files that podcatchers such as iTunes read when adding a subscription.

Figure 3: Eric Langhorst's "Speaking of history…" blog and podcasts.
Adapted from http://speakingofhistory.blogspot.com/2006/02/podcast-15-example-of-studycast-for.html

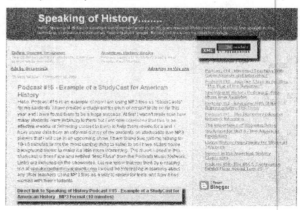

You don't need to be a web wizard to set up a subscription-ready XML file. ListGarden (softwaregarden.com/products/list-garden) is a free program that you can download and install. The application walks you through the process of setting up the feed, adding individual podcasts to your list, and placing the XML and HTML files on your webserver so others can see and subscribe to your series.

The originator of the Willow Elementary podcasts has developed a useful guide to creating podcasts, available at learninginhand.com/podcasting. Apple users will find a comprehensive description for using Mac software to subscribe, create, and publish podcasts (including video podcasts) at apple.com/education/solutions/podcasting.

Creating Podcasts as Social Studies Projects

There are a range of potential opportunities for creating podcasts in social studies classrooms. Any writing-based assignment, such as an essay or a fictional diary, can provide the foundation for a podcast. This offers the opportunity to incorporate live voices. This may be particularly appealing to students who enjoy working in an auditory medium.

The development of oral histories has been a long-standing tradition in many classrooms. In the past, these histories have typically been confined to transcripts of recordings, since there was no convenient way to disseminate them. The mechanism for podcasts offers a ready way to make these collections available to the community, inviting comment and further collaboration.

Podcasting also offers an opportunity for capturing and recording community events. The students in the Albemarle County Schools, for example, record school board meetings and make them available as podcasts. In the past many of these events could be heard as snippets or sound bites on local radio broadcasts, but now it is possible to make an entire event available in this way.

Voice-over-internet tools such as Skype (free at skype.com) create possibilities for arranging conversations that can then be captured and produced as podcasts. Use Skype to call your congressperson or a community historian and record the call (with the other party's consent!) on Audacity or another audio editor. You can edit the conversation and save it as an MP3. A particularly interesting option might be to have a studycast that incorporates students as part of a conversation with the teacher, or to record a reading circle of students as they discuss an assigned text.

Subscribing to a podcast feed makes it easy to follow an ongoing topic. Creating your own podcasts allows you and your students to enter a global conversation. Blogs provide authors of the written word with access to an audience. Podcasts provide the same opportunity in another medium.

Appendices

The Ten Themes of Social Studies
(Excerpt from the National Curriculum Standards for Social Studies)

The ten themes that form the framework of the social studies standards are:

❶ CULTURE

The study of culture prepares students to answer questions such as: What are the common characteristics of different cultures? How do belief systems, such as religion or political ideals, influence other parts of the culture? How does the culture change to accommodate different ideas and beliefs? What does language tell us about the culture? In schools, this theme typically appears in units and courses dealing with geography, history, sociology, and anthropology, as well as multicultural topics across the curriculum.

❷ TIME, CONTINUITY, AND CHANGE

Human beings seek to understand their historical roots and to locate themselves in time. Knowing how to read and reconstruct the past allows one to develop a historical perspective and to answer questions such as: Who am I? What happened in the past? How am I connected to those in the past? How has the world changed and how might it change in the future? Why does our personal sense of relatedness to the past change? This theme typically appears in courses in history and others that draw upon historical knowledge and habits.

❸ PEOPLE, PLACES, AND ENVIRONMENTS

The study of people, places, and human-environment interactions assists students as they create their spatial views and geographic perspectives of the world beyond their personal locations. Students need the knowledge, skills, and understanding to answer questions such as: Where are things located? Why are they located where they are? What do we mean by "region"? How do landforms change? What implications do these changes have for people? In schools, this theme typically appears in units and courses dealing with area studies and geography.

❹ INDIVIDUAL DEVELOPMENT AND IDENTITY

Personal identity is shaped by one's culture, by groups, and by institutional influences. Students should consider such questions as: How do people learn? Why do people behave as they do? What influences how people learn, perceive, and grow? How do people meet their basic needs in a variety of contexts? How do individuals develop from youth to adulthood? In schools, this theme typically appears in units and courses dealing with psychology and anthropology.

❺ INDIVIDUALS, GROUPS, AND INSTITUTIONS

Institutions such as schools, churches, families, government agencies, and the courts play an integral role in people's lives. It is important that students learn how institutions are formed, what controls and influences them, how they influence individuals and culture, and how they are maintained or changed. Students may address questions such as: What is the role of institutions in this and other societies? How am I influenced by institutions? How do institutions change? What is my role in institutional change? In schools this theme typically appears in units and courses dealing with sociology, anthropology, psychology, political science, and history.

❻ POWER, AUTHORITY, AND GOVERNANCE

Understanding the historical development of structures of power, authority, and governance and their evolving functions in contemporary U.S. society and other parts of the world is essential for developing civic competence. In exploring this theme, students confront questions such as: What is power? What forms does it take? Who holds it? How is it gained, used, and justified? What is legitimate authority? How are governments created, structured, maintained, and changed? How can individual rights be protected within the context of majority rule? In schools, this theme typically appears in units and courses dealing with government, politics, political science, history, law, and other social sciences.

VII PRODUCTION, DISTRIBUTION, AND CONSUMPTION

Because people have wants that often exceed the resources available to them, a variety of ways have evolved to answer such questions as: What is to be produced? How is production to be organized? How are goods and services to be distributed? What is the most effective allocation of the factors of production (land, labor, capital, and management)? In schools, this theme typically appears in units and courses dealing with economic concepts and issues.

VIII SCIENCE, TECHNOLOGY, AND SOCIETY

Modern life as we know it would be impossible without technology and the science that supports it. But technology brings with it many questions: Is new technology always better than old? What can we learn from the past about how new technologies result in broader social change, some of which is unanticipated? How can we cope with the ever-increasing pace of change? How can we manage technology so that the greatest number of people benefit from it? How can we preserve our fundamental values and beliefs in the midst of technological change? This theme draws upon the natural and physical sciences, social sciences, and the humanities, and appears in a variety of social studies courses, including history, geography, economics, civics, and government.

IX GLOBAL CONNECTIONS

The realities of global interdependence require understanding the increasingly important and diverse global connections among world societies and the frequent tension between national interests and global priorities. Students will need to be able to address such international issues as health care, the environment, human rights, economic competition and interdependence, age-old ethnic enmities, and political and military alliances. This theme typically appears in units or courses dealing with geography, culture, and economics, but may also draw upon the natural and physical sciences and the humanities.

X CIVIC IDEALS AND PRACTICES

An understanding of civic ideals and practices of citizenship is critical to full participation in society and is a central purpose of the social studies. Students confront such questions as: What is civic participation and how can I be involved? How has the meaning of citizenship evolved? What is the balance between rights and responsibilities? What is the role of the citizen in the community and the nation, and as a member of the world community? How can I make a positive difference? In schools, this theme typically appears in units or courses dealing with history, political science, cultural anthropology, and fields such as global studies, law-related education, and the humanities.

Excerpted from the Executive Summary of the Curriculum Standards. See National Council for the Social Studies, *Expectations of Excellence: Curriculum Standards for Social Studies* (Washington, D.C.: National Council for the Social Studies, 1994), pp. x-xii. The Executive Summary is also available on the internet at www.socialstudies.org/standards/execsummary/

National Educational Technology Standards for Students (NETS-S)

Technology Foundation Standards for All Students

The technology foundation standards for students are divided into six broad categories. Standards within each category are to be introduced, reinforced, and mastered by students. These categories provide a framework for linking performance indicators within the Profiles for Technology Literate Students to the standards. Teachers can use these standards and profiles as guidelines for planning technology-based activities in which students achieve success in learning, communication, and life skills.

Technology Foundation Standards for Students

1. Basic Operations and Concepts

+ Students demonstrate a sound understanding of the nature and operation of technology systems.
+ Students are proficient in the use of technology.

2. Social, Ethical, and Human Issues

+ Students understand the ethical, cultural, and societal issues related to technology.
+ Students practice responsible use of technology systems, information, and software.
+ Students develop positive attitudes toward technology uses that support lifelong learning, collaboration, personal pursuits, and productivity.

3. Technology Productivity Tools

+ Students use technology tools to enhance learning, increase productivity, and promote creativity.
+ Students use productivity tools to collaborate in constructing technology-enhanced models, prepare publications, and produce other creative works.

4. Technology Communications Tools

+ Students use telecommunications to collaborate, publish, and interact with peers, experts, and other audiences.
+ Students use a variety of media and formats to communicate information and ideas effectively to multiple audiences.

5. Technology Research Tools

+ Students use technology to locate, evaluate, and collect information from a variety of sources.
+ Students use technology tools to process data and report results.
+ Students evaluate and select new information resources and technological innovations based on the appropriateness for specific tasks.

6. Technology Problem-solving and Decision-making Tools

+ Students use technology resources for solving problems and making informed decisions.
+ Students employ technology in the development of strategies for solving problems in the real world.

The National Educational Technology Standards for Students are part of the National Educational Technology Standards published by the International Society for Technology in Education (ISTE), Washington, D.C. The standards were developed by the National Educational Technology Standards Project organized by ISTE. The standards can be accessed at http://cnets.iste.org/

Technology Position Statement and Guidelines

NATIONAL COUNCIL FOR THE SOCIAL STUDIES (NCSS)

This position statement was prepared by the NCSS Technology Select Subcommittee, and approved by the NCSS Board of Directors in 2006.

Electronic portfolios and digital projects are old ideas in technological clothing. Handhelds, virtual reality, and the merging of wireless forms of communication are examples of technologies that are changing life in and outside of the classroom, and are raising questions about what and how our students learn social studies. In turn, emerging information and communication technologies have the potential to reshape how National Council for the Social Studies and its members seek to fulfill the mission to prepare young people "to fulfill the duties of citizenship in a participatory democracy." As Fairey, Lee, and Bennett concluded:

> Technology and the social studies has the power to become a 'dynamic and forceful agent for change in the social studies curriculum' (Martorella, 1997), but only if the academic subject matter is enriched by a clear and comprehensive rationale for integrating technology with social studies.[1]

Articulating such a rationale, though, is a two-edged sword, which is why this statement is designed both to provide guidance to social studies educators and to raise questions about the relation between technology and social studies.

A rationale for integrating technology with social studies arises from the purpose of social studies, the role of technology in the lives of our students, and the nature of technology in the social studies curriculum. As concluded in the report, *Toward A New Golden Age In American Education: How the Internet, the Law and Today's Students are Revolutionizing Expectations:*

> There is no dispute over the need for America's students to have the knowledge and competence to compete in an increasingly technology-driven world economy. This need demands new models of education facilitated by educational technology.[2]

A similar argument holds true for students as they gain an understanding of democratic principles and values, as well as acquire the skills necessary for life in our civic society. As we as a democracy move into the electronic age, what might this mean for how we prepare our youth as citizens? One concern is how technological advances are changing how we politically and socially interact with one another. Will the arrival of on-line campaigning, for example, change significantly the process we now use to elect our political leaders? Will instantaneous access to news worldwide affect our ability both to digest and to reflect upon national and global policy matters? In turn, how might these technological changes influence how we conceive of citizenship? Will citizenship take on both national and global dimensions? Will it be connected to one's ability to have access to the newest forms of technology? Obviously, there are no ready answers to such questions; but by considering such questions, NCSS seeks to better enable social studies educators to prepare their students for life in a technologically-oriented civic society.

While such preparation is a long-term goal, students often are unable to see that far into the future. This is why we need to consider the role of technology in students' daily lives and its implication for classroom practice. How closely, for example, should students' worlds outside of the classroom match what occurs in the classroom? The ability of a student to send a friend a text message as opposed to a paper note represents the simplest example of cell phone capability. In turn, access to newer and newer forms of technology adds a new dimension to the idea of the digital divide as affluent students, for example, can surround themselves with technology that enables them to communicate instantly with friends nation-wide by sending them, [for example] digitized videos of last weekend's social highlights. Now, imagine moving from this digitally connected environment to what for many seems like the lifeless and adult-centered world known as a classroom, where learning means spending time gathering information by reading a book! In an age of standards and accountability, teachers need to include the realities of students' lives, technology use in students' everyday lives, and the role and use of technology when planning for instruction. How well do standards, which tend to focus on a static body of knowledge, align with students' growing abilities to access information in a way that enables them to manipulate and generate their own knowledge? As Mason, et, al., noted, "[T]echnology opens the door to learning social studies skills and content in ways impossible in the traditional classroom."[3] We need to capitalize on many students' ubiquitous, yet social, use of such technology and demonstrate the technology's power as a tool for learning.

We can accomplish this end by seamlessly weaving technology into the social studies curriculum. As Berson and Balyta observed:

[T]he discipline of social studies has had a precarious relationship with technology, simultaneously touting its potential benefits and critiquing its limitations in facilitating social studies practice.[4]

As an organization, we continually need to demonstrate and research how effective use of technology enhances social studies teaching and learning. The new technologies, for example, enable users to access, organize, and communicate information in ways unfathomable until recently. Imagine the impact that the digitizing of U.S. history, as exemplified by the National Archives and the Library of Congress, has had on social studies instruction. How do we measure learning when we send students online to the National Archives "Powers of Persuasion" exhibit of World War II posters, where they can investigate the use of propaganda techniques to secure support for America's war effort? How do we define student leaning when teachers make use of the Geographic Information Systems software to build inquiry-oriented lessons about voting patterns that draw upon data provided by the U.S. Census Bureau? An emerging body of research over the past five years is beginning to address such questions and the next step is to more explicitly link such research to best practice.

In turn, we need to consider the relation between the standards movement and the use of such technology, since the acquisition of knowledge cannot occur devoid of the learning and assessment of related skills. How well do the standards enable teachers to capitalize upon the growing bodies of online databases and enable students to demonstrate learning based on these data? How should we conceive of research and interpersonal skills in the classroom? In the past, students conducted research in the school library, where experts had chosen the books to stock on the shelves. Often, the media specialist undertook a second culling by selecting and placing on a cart those most appropriate for the students and their topics. Today, many students begin online searches without these benefits. What skills are basic as students conduct research on the internet? Discussion boards, online chat rooms, and e-pals are

examples of new tools available for students to interact with one another and with people worldwide. Previously, teacher discussions with students on how to interact with a person from another culture took place in the abstract; today, those discussions should be the prelude to initiating an online discussion. What skills do students need to engage in extended social and academic online discussions with culturally different individuals?

Finally, in relation to the curriculum, unlike most other disciplines, those of us in social studies also have an obligation to help students learn the relation of science, technology, and society. As Mason, et al., noted:

Science and technology have a complex interrelationship with society. While technology is the impetus to advancements in human development, technologies also contribute to the perpetuation of existing imbalances and inequities in power and diffusion of knowledge.

This harks back to the prior point about connecting the use of technology to the students' daily lives. As adults, we are aware of how technological advances are influencing society and how who we are as a society affects, in part, the direction that such advances take. How obvious, though, are such relations to young people? Just as we as an organization continually stress the need to connect knowledge and skills, so too we need to emphasize the links between the use of technology as a teaching and learning tool and the effects of the relation between technology and society.

As an organization we are not only obligated to assist social studies educators today, but also to realize that our mission obligates us to prepare young people for tomorrow. This requires us to consider how best to position NCSS for schooling in the twenty-first century. While we cannot predict the future, we can anticipate where the emerging communication and information technologies might take us and start discussing how best to prepare ourselves and our students for what might occur.

Guidelines

While Mason et. al., offered the following principles as "guides for the appropriate infusion of technology in social studies teacher preparation programs," they also serve as an excellent foundation on which to base K-12 social studies teaching and learning and have thus shaped the formation of the guidelines that follow. The guidelines are divided into five distinct areas, and are intended to serve as an overview of how technology may be integrated into the social studies in a variety of means and methods.

1. "Extend learning beyond what could be done without technology." One way to extend learning in a meaningful way is to use digital archives of primary sources to engage students in historical inquiry.

2. "Introduce technology in context." Students should use technology as a tool for learning social studies content and skills, rather than using technology for its own sake.

3. "Include opportunities for students to study relationships among science, technology, and society." Science and technology cannot be separated from their impact on society. Teachers and students should examine the benefits and risks of new technologies including the digital divide, the opportunity for global understanding, and concerns about inappropriate information and online behavior.

4. "Foster the development of the skills, knowledge, and participation as good citizens in a democratic society." Research suggests that many social studies teachers do not use technology's potential to revitalize citizenship education. In particular the internet's capacity to provide multiple current perspectives on controversial issues can promote the development of personal civic beliefs. Moreover, sites that provide opportunities for social and political action can help students develop the capacity for civic action both locally and globally.

5. "Contribute to the research and evaluation of social studies and technology." Educators should take advantage of the ways in which technologies advance the purposes of social studies education.

As a final thought, this position paper and guidelines are grounded in the theory that content must come before technology. In other words, technology should be thought of in terms of its effect on the teaching and learning of social studies, and should be considered for use only if it will provide an improvement in one (or both) of these areas. NCSS offers the following guidelines to technology use, and these are intended as a way both to guide social studies educators when making instructional and curricular decisions related to the use and study of technology, and to help frame the discussion over the questions raised above.[5]

Effective Use of Instructional Technology: Guidelines for K-16 Social Studies Educators

OVERVIEW: These guidelines, drawn from the National Educational Technology Standards, are to provide guidance on how to integrate the use of instructional technology into one's practice. A rationale for the guidelines is provided in a complementary position statement. National Council for the Social Studies is identifying resources to aid social studies educators in implementing the guidelines.

Technology Operations and Concepts: Social Studies Educators

1. demonstrate a sound understanding of technology operations and concepts as they relate to social studies education;

2. demonstrate introductory knowledge, skills, and understanding of concepts related to technology;

3. demonstrate continual growth in technology knowledge and skills to stay abreast of current and emerging technologies.

Planning and Designing Learning Environments and Experiences: Social Studies Educators

1. plan and design effective social studies learning environments and experiences supported by technology;

2. design developmentally appropriate learning opportunities that apply technology-enhanced instructional strategies to support the diverse needs of learners;

3. apply current research on teaching and learning with technology when planning learning environments and experiences;

4. identify and locate technology resources and evaluate them for accuracy and suitability;

5. plan for the management of technology resources within the context of learning activities;

6. plan strategies to manage student learning in a technology-enhanced environment.

Teaching, Learning, and the Curriculum: Social Studies Educators

1. implement curriculum plans that include methods and strategies for applying technology to maximize student learning in social studies;

2. facilitate technology-enhanced experiences that address content standards and student technology standards;

3. use technology to support learner-centered strategies

that address the diverse needs of students;

4. apply technology to develop students' higher order skills and creativity;

5. manage student-learning activities in a technology-enhanced environment.

Assessment and Evaluation: Social Studies Educators

1. apply technology through a variety of strategies to assess and evaluate student learning in social studies;

2. apply technology in assessing student learning of subject matter using a variety of assessment techniques;

3. use technology resources to collect and analyze data, interpret results, and communicate findings to improve instructional practice and maximize student learning;

4. apply multiple methods of evaluation to determine students' appropriate use of technology resources.

Social, Ethical, Legal, and Human Issues:
Social Studies Educators

1. model and teach legal and ethical practice related to technology use.

2. apply technology resources to enable and empower learners with diverse backgrounds, characteristics, and abilities.

3. identify and use technology resources that affirm diversity

4. promote safe and healthy use of technology resources.

5. facilitate equitable access to technology resources for all students.

Notes

1. Chad Fairey, John K. Lee, and Clifford Bennett, "Technology and Social Studies: A Conceptual Model for Integration," *Journal of Social Studies Research* 24, no. 2 (2000): 3–9; P. Martorella, *Interactive Technologies on the Social Studies: Emerging Issues and Applications* (Albany: State University of New York Press, 1997).

2. U.S. Department of Education, *Toward a New Golden Age in American Education: How the Internet, the Law and Today's Students are Revolutionizing Expectations* (Washington, D.C., 2004), 45.

3. Cheryl Mason, Michael Berson, Richard Diem, David Hicks, John Lee, and Tony Dralle, (2000). "Guidelines for Using Technology to Prepare Social Studies Teachers," *Contemporary Issues in Technology and Teacher Education* [Online serial], 1, (1). Available: http://www.citejournal.org/vol1/iss1/currentissues/socialstudies/article1.htm.

4. Michael Berson and Peter Balyta, "Technological Thinking and Practice in the Social Studies: Transcending the Tumultuous Adolescence of Reform," *Journal of Computing in Education* 20, no. 4 (2004): 141.

5. Retrieved from cnets.iste.org/currstands/cstands-netst.html on March 8, 2005.

This position statement, which was prepared by the Technology Select Subcommittee, was approved by the NCSS board of directors.

Technology Select Subcommittee: Linda Bennett, Joe Braun, Cheryl Franklin, Adam Friedman, Cheryl Mason Bolick, Joe O'Brien, Pamela Roach, Linda Unger, Zora Warren

The NCSS Technology Position Statement and Guidelines can be accessed at http://www.socialstudies.org/positions/technology

Contributors
and Index

About the Authors

EDITORS

LINDA BENNETT is an associate professor of social studies education at the University of Missouri-Columbia. She is editor of *Social Studies and the Young Learner* and has served on the editorial board for *Theory and Research in Social Education*. The subjects of Dr. Bennett's publications range from integration of technology in elementary social studies to teacher preparation of social studies educators. She can be contacted at lb@missouri.edu.

MICHAEL J. BERSON is a professor of social science education at the University of South Florida. He served as the Chair of the College and University Faculty Assembly of the National Council for the Social Studies and was vice president of the Society for Information Technology and Teacher Education. Dr. Berson has extensively published books, chapters, and journal articles. He can be contacted at berson@tempest.coedu.usf.edu.

CONTRIBUTORS

KADEE ANSTADT is a fifth grade teacher in Perrysburg, Ohio, who has used handhelds in her classroom for more than 5 years.

SAVILLA BANISTER is a multimedia/curricular specialist at Bowling Green State University, Ohio, where she partners with K-12 educators to integrate technologies into the classroom.

MONICA BEGLAU is Director of the eMINTS National Center, a collaborative program sponsored by the Missouri Department of Elementary and Secondary Education and the University of Missouri, that provides professional development to educators in support of high quality teaching powered by technology.

LYNN BELL works with the Center for Technology and Teacher Education of the University of Virginia, Charlottesville, and is co-editor of the online journal *Contemporary Issues in Technology and Teacher Education*.

CHERYL MASON BOLICK is an assistant professor in the School of Education at the University of North Carolina at Chapel Hill.

GLEN BULL is a professor of instructional technology in the Curry School of Education at the University of Virginia in Charlottesville.

DAVID CALHOUN teaches social studies at Liberty Middle School, Tampa, Florida.

BRIAN P. COLLINS teaches instructional technology at the New York Institute of Technology and is responsible for the content and editing of EASE History, a website that supports historical learning and teaching (www.easehistory.org).

ROBERT COVEN is a history teacher at Cary Academy, Cary, North Carolina, and is also a published author who has presented at a number of conferences.

TOM DARROW teaches world history and U.S. history at Stonewall Jackson High School in Prince William County, Virginia.

SHARON A. EDWARDS, who retired last year after a 35-year career as a first and second grade teacher in the Amherst (Massachusetts) Public Schools, is a clinical faculty member in the School of Education at the University of Massachusetts Amherst.

MARILYN EISENWINE is associate professor in the Department of Teacher Education at Angelo State University, San Angelo, Texas.

JASON ENDACOTT is an eighth grade social studies teacher at New Mark Middle School in the North Kansas City School District and a doctoral candidate in social studies education at the University of Kansas.

Kyle Evans teaches eighth grade social studies at Hosford Middle School in Portland, Oregon with a view to providing students with the skills to respect their history and challenge the future.

E. Thomas Ewing, an associate professor in the Department of History at Virginia Tech, is the author of books and articles on Soviet teachers in the Stalinist era, and project director of the Digital History Reader.

John Fischer is an associate professor at Bowling Green State University, Ohio, where he teaches and researches in the field of social studies.

Nancy P. Gallavan is a professor and associate dean in the College of Education at the University of Central Arkansas.

Eddie Gray is a social studies teacher and coach at Garner Senior High School, Garner, North Carolina.

Aaron Grill teaches computer skills and applications at the Browning School in New York City.

Patrice Grimes is an assistant professor of social studies education in the teacher education program at the Curry School of Education in the University of Virginia, Charlottesville.

Judith A. Hakes has been a professor in the Department of Teacher Education at Angelo State University in San Angelo, Texas for over 20 years.

Thomas Hammond is a podcaster and graduate fellow at the Center for Technology and Teacher Education at the Curry School of Education in the University of Virginia, Charlottesville.

David Hicks is an associate professor in the Department of Teaching and Learning in the School of Education at Virginia Tech, where his principal research focus is on how technology can support the teaching of social studies.

Erica Jacobs teaches at Oakton High School, Vienna, Virginia, and George Mason University, and writes an education column for The Examiner Newspapers.

Anne Jeschke serves Chillicothe R-II school district, Missouri, as a technology curriculum specialist after having taught grades pre-K-4 herself.

Casey Juliano is a kindergarten teacher and technology integration specialist in the Clark County School District, Nevada, and an adjunct instructor at the University of Nevada, Las Vegas.

Timothy Keiper is an associate professor in the Secondary Education and Instructional Technology Departments at Western Washington University in Bellingham, Washington.

Lynne Kirby teaches social studies at Hillcrest Middle School in Simpsonville, South Carolina.

Fred Koehl, who taught social studies and geographic information systems (GIS) in middle school for several years, now works for Greystone Valuation Services in Atlanta, GA.

Hilary Landorf teaches and actively researches in the fields of social studies education and international education at Florida International University in Miami, Florida.

Elaine M. Lawrence is an assistant professor in the Department of Secondary Education of the State University of New York at Oneonta.

Jane Lehr is a visiting assistant professor in the Department of Science and Technology in Society at Virginia Tech, whose research interests focus on social justice pedagogies, scientific knowledge, and constructions of scientifically literate citizenship.

Andrea S. Libresco is an assistant professor of curriculum and teaching at Hofstra University in Hempstead, New York.

Kati Linn teaches social studies at Riverside Middle School in Greer, South Carolina.

George Lipscomb is an assistant professor in the Education Department at Furman University in Greenville, South Carolina, specializing in social studies education.

MELISSA LISANTI is a National Board-certified social studies teacher and a doctoral student in Curriculum and Instruction at Virginia Tech.

DIANE LUKE is a former social studies teacher who is currently completing her M.A.T. at the University of South Florida.

ROBERT W. MALOY is coordinator of teacher education in history and political science in the School of Education at the University of Massachusetts Amherst.

PAULA S. MARRON, who holds a doctorate in education, is the assistant principal at Chatsworth Avenue School in Mamaroneck School District, Mamaroneck, New York.

LORI MATHYS teaches fourth grade at Chesterfield Elementary School in Rockwood School District, St. Louis, Missouri.

PERRY MCLEOD teaches U.S. history and oral history at Richland Northeast High School, Richland School District Two, in Columbia, South Carolina.

SIMON MESHBESHER teaches social studies at Liberty Middle School, Tampa, Florida.

DARCI MITCHELL teaches world geography and sociology at C.D. Hylton High School in Woodbridge, Virginia.

SPENCER MORRISON teaches social studies at Beaver Middle School, and previously taught social studies at Beaver High School, in the Beaver Area School District, Beaver County, Pennsylvania.

JOSEPH O'BRIEN is an associate professor in the School of Education at the University of Kansas.

CAROLYN O'MAHONY is an assistant professor of social studies in the Department of Teacher Development and Educational Studies at Oakland University, Rochester, MI.

PATRICIA A. PALMER is director of Operation Outreach at the Center for Economic Education in the University of Missouri-Kansas City.

SANDRA PEDERSEN teaches fourth grade at Santa Rita Elementary, a gifted magnet school in San Angelo, Texas.

ANN-MARIE PEIRANO teaches social studies at Hillcrest High School in Tuscaloosa, Alabama.

KAREN PHUA teaches sixth grade at Oaks School in Oceanside, New York.

DIANE PROVVIDO is a fourth grade teacher in the Oceanside School District, Oceanside, New York, who previously taught in schools in New York City.

APARNA R. RAMCHANDRAN, who works in the telecommunications industry, is the Flash/Multimedia developer of the EASE History interface (www.easehistory.org).

ANTHONY REID teaches social studies at Paul W. Bell Middle School in Miami, Florida.

KEVIN RICHINS teaches U.S. and world history at Lynden High School in Lynden, Washington.

DONNA SHABA teaches in the Troy and Birmingham school districts in Michigan.

RAND J. SPIRO is a professor of educational psychology and educational technology at Michigan State University, and has participated in the development of EASE History (www.easehistory.org).

MELINDA ODOM STAUBS is a sixth grade social studies teacher at Walter Wellborn Elementary in Anniston, Alabama, who is currently working on her doctoral dissertation at the University of Alabama.

BARBARA SLATER STERN is an associate professor at James Madison University who teaches middle and secondary social studies methods courses and researches the integration of technology into social studies classrooms.

ANDREW STOTZ teaches social studies at Park Street Intermediate School in the Southwestern City School District, Ohio.

JEFF STRICKLAND teaches U.S. government and history at Mill Valley High School in Shawnee, Kansas.

CYNTHIA SZYMANSKI SUNAL, who is professor of social studies education at the University of Alabama, is the editor of two online journals, and conducts research on the effects of technology on social studies education.

DENNIS W. SUNAL, who is professor of curriculum and instruction at the University of Alabama, has conducted extensive research on science-related social issues and the intersection of science and social studies.

GAYLE THIEMAN is an assistant professor in the Graduate School of Education at Portland State University (Oregon), where her fields of specialization include social studies methods; educational technology and instructional design; and teacher preparation.

MEGAN TWEEDIE teaches seventh and eighth grade social studies at Stamford Central School in Stamford, New York.

LINDA UNGER is associate director of the graduate online programs in the School of Professional Development at Stony Brook University in New York, and is a curriculum designer with almost twenty years of experience in educational technology and middle school teaching.

MARK VAN 'T HOOFT is a technology specialist and researcher at the Research Center for Educational Technology at Kent State University, where he specializes in ubiquitous and mobile computing research.

CHARLES VAUGHAN teaches global studies and AP human geography at Richland Northeast High School, Richland School District Two, Columbia, South Carolina.

BILL VELTO is an upper school history teacher at Cary Academy in Cary, North Carolina, where he teaches world history and contemporary issues, and is also a teaching fellow for the Choices Education Program of the Watson Institute for International Studies.

CAROLYN E. WALPOLE is the director of education and curriculum development for i-SAFE Inc., a leading non-profit internet safety organization providing professional development for teachers, K-12 curriculum, and community outreach programs for youth, parents, law enforcement and community leaders nationwide.

ELIOT WAXMAN teaches AP U.S. government and politics, as well as comparative religions, at Oakton High School in Vienna, VA.

ELIZABETH K. WILSON is a professor of social studies and reading education in the Department of Curriculum and Instruction at the University of Alabama in Tuscaloosa, where her research interests include technology integration in social studies education.

ANN WINKLER is director of education at Beach Park School in Tampa, Florida.

VIVIAN H. WRIGHT is an assistant professor of instructional technology in the College of Education at the University of Alabama in Tuscaloosa, where she works with teachers on innovative ways to infuse technology in the curriculum.

Index

V

W

Y